Southend

District Historical Notes

John William Burrows

Alpha Editions

This edition published in 2019

ISBN : 9789353605933

Design and Setting By
Alpha Editions
email - alphaedis@gmail.com

SOUTHEND-ON-SEA
AND DISTRICT:
HISTORICAL NOTES.

BY

JOHN WILLIAM BURROWS

(Editor of the " Southend Standard.")

Southend=on=Sea :

JOHN H. BURROWS & SONS, LTD.,

"STANDARD" PRINTING WORKS.

1909.

—

5s. NET.

ARMS OF THE BOROUGH OF SOUTHEND-ON-SEA.

PREFACE.

Errata.

On page 135 read "Josias" for "William" Unthank.

On page 6 the old boundaries of Milton included land lying to the west of High Street, and Milton Road was not the eastern boundary, as stated. See Benton, page 642, vol. 2.

On page 144 (lease of Technical School to County Committee) read "1910," and not "1911."

After the book went to press, Councillor W. R. King was elected Mayor of the Borough for the year 1909-10.

In presenting a history of this town and Hundred, no matter how short, there are two authorities whom it is essential to consult — Mr. P. Benton's "History of the Rochford Hundred" and Mr. H. W. King's MS. Volumes and other contributions, now in the custody of the Essex Archæological Society. Mr. King has rarely before been laid under contribution, and then only scantily. It has been the Author's privilege to have unrestricted access to these papers. Valuable information has

PREFACE.

These Historical Notes have been gradually collected and written over a period of years. The primary intention in presenting them to the public in book form is to counter the too prevalent and erroneous impression that Southend and district possess little or nothing of interest relating to the past. This impression is probably due to the absence of any book which gives in readable form, at a popular price, a sketch of the history of the Borough and neighbourhood. The Author hopes in this volume that need will, to some extent, be met, and result in a growing appreciation of the unique and valuable tradition of service which comes down to us from byegone days. Many of the episodes have not been treated as exhaustively as they deserved, the aim in this respect having been to indicate the lines upon which historical research should be undertaken. Particularly is this so in connection with the water traffic of the Estuary, which has nowhere been discussed as fully as its importance demands.

In presenting a history of this town and Hundred, no matter how short, there are two authorities whom it is essential to consult — Mr. P. Benton's " History of the Rochford Hundred" and Mr. H. W. King's MS. Volumes and other contributions, now in the custody of the Essex Archæological Society. Mr. King has rarely before been laid under contribution, and then only scantily. It has been the Author's privilege to have unrestricted access to these papers. Valuable information has *also been afforded in the two volumes which have been published of the "Victoria History of Essex."*

Thanks are expressed to Mr. J. H. Burrows, J.P., C.A., whose extensive knowledge of local government has been placed ungrudgingly at disposal; Mr. Roland Burrows, LL.D., Barrister-at-Law, by whose assistance much new and important matter relating to this district is published for the first time; Mr. H. H. Burrows for his advice in printing and producing the book; the Essex Archæological Society; Mr. A. G. Wright, Curator of Colchester Museum; the late Mr. E. M. Borrajo, of the Guildhall Library; Mr. R. Philipson, Secretary of the Port of London Authority; Mr. A. D. Cary, Librarian at the War Office; Mr. A. Allan, Secretary of the Royal Numismatic Society; the Director of Greenwich Hospital; the Manager of the "Globe" newspaper; the Manager of the "Illustrated London News;" Messrs. Spink and Son; the late and present Town Clerks of Southend; the Borough Accountant (Mr. C. E. Tweedale); the Clerk to the Justices (Mr. A. J. Arthy); the Principal of the Secondary Day School (Mr. J. Hitchcock); the Manager of Southend Waterworks Company (Mr. C. S. Bilham); the Secretary of Southend Gas Company (Mr. J. T. Randall); Councillor N. J. Osborne, Mr. Val. Mason, Mr. W. T. Pook, and Mr. E. H. Cole; and, lastly, to the Author's wife, but for whose kindly interest and unwearying readiness to assist, this work could not have been published.

SOUTHEND-ON-SEA,

November, 1909.

SOUTHEND-ON-SEA

AND DISTRICT.

❧ ❧

INTRODUCTORY.

SOUTHEND-ON-SEA is in the Rochford Hundred of
Essex and is situated on the north bank of the estuary
of the Thames. Although its development as a watering
place has largely occurred during the last thirty years, writers
for a century past have sounded its praises as a resort for those
needing restoration to health or a change of air. An early
Nineteenth Century author thus describes Southend's rise to
importance : " On the establishment of the recent prevailing
custom of sea bathing, its convenient distance from the Metropolis, the excellent state of the roads to it, the salubrity of its
air, and the favourable advantage of the tides flowing immediately to it from the open channel of the sea, numerous visitors
for health and pleasure were induced to this inviting spot, commodious inns and lodging houses were quickly raised, the passages
of the shore became convenient, bathing machines were provided, and many of the first families successively used its baths."
In 1794, with odd pomposity of style, " T. C." wrote in the

A

"Gentlemen's Magazine" that at Southend "Grandeur,
accompanied by Convenience, had chosen their seats, silently
inviting the summer loungers to hilarity and contentment."
He predicted that "South End" in a few summers would be
the rage, since, "even in its infancy, nobility had deigned there
to join in the mystic dance, and the loveliest of England's pride
to grace the promenade on the terrace." The fashion column
of the London "Globe" used regularly to contain a list of
the principal visitors. In a "Guide to Southend," published
in 1824, high medical testimony was given as to its recupera-
tive powers; eminent medical men of the day regularly
visiting the town with their families. Dr. Granville, writing
of the "Spas of England" in 1841, asserted that the "Cockney,
who, during the summer, stops short at Gravesend in his
excursion down the Thames, and is in ecstacies over that
commonplace sort of retreat, can form no idea of the beauties
he would enjoy were he to extend his steaming trip down the
river as far as Southend and stop on the north instead of the
south bank of the Thames."

The Extent of the Borough.

The area which modern Southend covers embraces at
least two parishes and there is evidence that possibly there
were three—viz., Prittlewell, the mother parish; Southchurch,
incorporated into the Borough in 1898; and Milton. The
latter at one time was a not unimportant maritime station.
Milton included roughly all the land lying west of Milton
Road and south of Leigh Road to the Leigh boundary; the
old name being preserved in Milton Road. The controversy
as to whether or not Milton formed part of the parish was a
very old one. In 1678, a vestry meeting at Prittlewell supported Josias Unthank in obtaining an order to compel the
inhabitants of Milton to pay for the building of a new bridge
over the brook in North Street. Milton Hamlet had a separate
overseer in 1707, surveyors from 1697, and a constable from
1720. As a result of further dispute, counsel was consulted in

1813 as to whether or no the Hamlet and Prittlewell were one. The struggle between the two parties evidently continued with vigour, for in 1815 surveyors for the former were appointed by the Justices under an order of the High Court. On the passing of the Poor Law Act they were amalgamated for relief purposes and subsequently the two places were bound together for local government under a Local Board, the predecessor of the present- Municipal Corporation. Tradition points to Milton having once had its own church, which was engulfed by the encroaching sea, but we have found no documentary evidence to support it. Holman, writing early in the Eighteenth Century, reported that "ancient men" of that day could remember seeing the foundations at low water.

The Origin of Southend.

Southend, as the word implies, was originally used to denote the south end of Prittlewell parish. In ancient maps no indication is given of its existence and in later charts it is always spelt with two words, South-End. The name "Southende" was first mentioned in an official document in the reign of Henry VIII (1509-47), and the records of Prittlewell Priory show that about the same time land was let adjacent "Southend." An officer of customs, of Leigh, reported to the Navy Commissioners in 1666 that a topmast and three small boats had come ashore at Southend from a wrecked warship. Southend was mentioned in the parish minute book in 1668 and it was rated as such in 1698. In 1758, what was known as Southend comprised Thames Farm and Arthur's Land, so named after its owner. The latter property was rated in one assessment and is said to have included the site now occupied by the Ship Hotel, Old Brewery, Pleasant Row and Marine Parade. Old Southend was thus bounded by Southchurch on the east, Porter's Estate on the north, and the high ridge of land on the west subsequently to be crowned by Royal Terrace and Hotel. Its development and subsequent absorption of the mother village of Prittlewell, of Milton, and of Southchurch is recent history.

Favoured by Royalty.

Princess Charlotte of Wales, when five years of age, was in 1801 ordered to Southend for sea bathing, and stayed at Southchurch Lawn. Two years later, Princess Caroline of Wales, the unfortunate wife of the Prince Regent, occupied a couple of houses in Royal Terrace. In 1874 Prince Imperial of France (who met his death in Zululand shortly after) stayed at the Royal Hotel whilst on an artillery course at Shoeburyness, and ran with a pack of foot beagles, being in at the death at Shopland, where he was presented with the "pad." Princess Louise, Duchess of Argyll, twice visited the Borough. In earlier days (1834) the Earl of Beaconsfield (then Mr. Benjamin Disraeli) sojourned at Porter's Grange, and is generally credited with having described Southend as the Riviera of Essex.

Notable Events.

At the close of the Eighteenth Century, the Ship Hotel was one of the headquarters of the leaders of the great Mutiny at the Nore; the line of revolted ships stretching across the river from the Kent to the Essex side. It was at the naval port of Sheerness immediately opposite that the battleship touched which conveyed the remains of Nelson to England after his victory of Trafalgar. From off Southend, in 1863, the flag captain to the Commander-in-chief at the Nore had the honour in the "Formidable" of firing a salute to Princess Alexandra on the occasion of her first arrival in English waters on board the Danish royal yacht. In 1904 the cruiser "Essex" lay off Southend to receive the service of plate, presented by the Countess of Warwick on behalf of a large body of subscribers, in honour of the County name being given to one of the vessels of the Royal Navy. The constitution of the Nore Division of the Home Fleet in 1906 again drew attention to the importance of the Thames Estuary as a naval base. The Dreadnought was the first flagship.

Some Residents and Visitors of Note.

These incidents and others to be mentioned in the sketch of events which follows are sufficient to remind visitors that this neighbourhood is possessed of real historic interest beside being a modern health resort. The town has appealed kindly to literary men. Sir Edwin Arnold, author of the "Light of Asia," resided for a time at Hamlet Court, Hamlet Court Road; Robert Buchanan, the poet, also stayed there, and lived, at a later period of his life, in a house upon the Cliffs; at last, in 1901, finding a resting place beside his wife in St. John Baptist Churchyard. There a monument, erected by friends and admirers, marks his grave. Thackeray's wife for long years resided in retirement at Leigh-on-Sea. There have also stayed with us a host of minor writers whose work has gained the recognition of publishers and the eulogy of critics. Douglas Jerrold, most noted of early Victorian humorists, was connected with a theatre at Southend in the first years of the 19th Century. In the crypt of the church attached to Nazareth House, London Road, rest the remains of Clement Scott, dramatic critic and author of "The Garden of Sleep," and Bishop Bellord, a Catholic Army chaplain, who had seen service in many parts of the Empire. It was in Southend that Rosina Brandram died, one of the best known Savoy artistes of the closing years of the Nineteenth Century. The Rev. Benjamin Waugh, founder of the N.S.P.C.C., also died here, after a lingering illness, and he was buried in the Borough Cemetery, Sutton Road. Whymper, one of the greatest of mountain climbers, has constantly stayed here, and George R. Sims' love for the place is known throughout London. Constable has painted two well-known pictures of Hadleigh Castle. Wyllie, the marine painter, has tried his luminous brush upon a sketch of the beach at Westcliff, and that eminent master of colour, Turner, was attracted to the town by reason of its brilliant sunsets. It is said that a stranger criticized one of these local canvases and observed "One never sees a sunset like that," to which the painter snapped out in reply, "Don't you wish you could?"

SOUTHEND-ON-SEA

AND DISTRICT.

❧ ❧

SOME POINTS OF HISTORICAL INTEREST.

IN order to give a complete glimpse of the history of this locality, it is necessary to take the reader farther than the borders of Prittlewell parish, for in years past the village of Prittlewell played only a subordinate part in the life of the Hundred, which comprises twenty-six parishes; bordered on the south by the estuary of the Thames, on the east by the North Sea, and on the north by the River Crouch. Two of the parishes on the western border (Thundersley and South Benfleet) formed part of the Barstable Hundred, but now being included in Rochford Poor Law Union, they are popularly reckoned as part of Rochford Hundred. Canvey Island became a separate parish comparatively recently. The centres of government were, at different periods, either at Rayleigh, where, in the days of the Norman Conquest, Sweyn, the greatest landowner for miles around, established a castle; at Hadleigh, where in the reign of King Henry III, Hubert de Burgh built a fortress, frequently the dower of

Queens; or at Rochford, where from Tudor times until well into the Eighteenth Century the great family of Rich, Earls of Warwick, possessed a residence (Rochford Hall) rivalling in size and magnificence the greatest houses in the land; the remains now existing giving but a feeble idea of its extent.

In Prehistoric Days.

Ages ago, Kent joined the Continent of Europe. Most of the southern part of the North Sea was low, flat, dry land, through which a great river ran straight to the North, draining mid-Europe. Near its point of discharge it received a western tributary, a kind of ancient Thames. At the spot now occupied by the estuary, the old river took a sharp N.E. bend and quite possibly formed a sort of delta amid the low-lying marshy ground of that period. As time rolled on there was a gradual subsidence of the North Sea land, the waters of the North Atlantic poured in, the North Sea came into being, and the modern Thames was born.

The district has proved rich in prehistoric remains, and numerous paleolithic implements, neolithic celts, bronze weapons, etc., have been discovered at Southend, Southchurch, Shoebury, Rochford, Great Wakering, Thundersley and Hullbridge; giving evidence that it has been peopled from remotest ages. At Southchurch, several examples of celtic pottery have been unearthed, and at Shoebury there was a discovery in 1891 of a hoard (now on exhibition at the British Museum) consisting of socketed celts, a palstave, part of a sword blade, etc. At the same place was also found part of the box of a chariot wheel, together with three bronze nails, probably used for holding the tyre. Quite recently Great Wakering was excited by the discovery, during trenching operations, of a portion of the limb of some prehistoric animal; the weight of the fragment being 26lbs.

Local Earthworks.

Tucked away from public observation on the northern boundary of Prittlewell parish lies a small field with a well-wooded fringe, forming part of Fossett's Farm. Coming upon it after traversing the field which separates it from the roadway, one notices what is apparently a rampart of earth covered with grass, and investigation discloses the fact that this is the outer edge of what was once an extensive system of entrenchments, capable of.affording protection to a considerable number of people. These earthworks cover an area of eight acres, and at the eastern end rises a mound, presumably the key to the system of defence. The probable date of this earthwork has not been determined, but it most likely had to do with the series of fortifications constructed during the Danish invasion, alluded to under the heading of "The Battle of Benfleet."

Benton, in 1886, referred to a mound on the Chalkwell Hall Estate, lying to the east of the house, and in the northwest corner of a field called Fishponds, which he was of opinion was Celtic in origin. It was first opened somewhere about 1860, when some bones, a few coins and a piece of chain were discovered. Eight feet of earth have since been removed from the summit and a quantity of bones unearthed. The mound was in 1881 still about four feet above the surrounding soil, and the author of the History of the Rochford Hundred thought it would repay further research.

There are many other traces of earthworks in the Hundred, notably at Benfleet, Shoebury and Canewdon, to which we shall refer later.

Roman Occupation.

At the time of the landing of Cæsar in Kent, the tract of land later on to be known as Essex was inhabited by the Celtic tribe of Trinobantes. One of their chieftains, Cassivelaunus, was in command of the East Anglian army assembled to oppose Cæsar's second expedition, which, like his first, did not result in permanent occupation. It was not until a century afterwards, about A.D. 43, that four legions—three of which had been serving in Germany and one in Hungary—under Aulus Plautius were ordered to invade

Britain. Plautius quickly made himself master of Kent, but
in the Thames marshes met with an obstinate resistance. The
Emperor Claudius travelled from Rome with reinforcements
(which included, it is said, a number of elephants), sailing
from Ostea to Marseilles. He then came chiefly by way of
the great rivers of Gaul to Britain, commanded the crossing
of the Thames and took Colchester (the key of the resistance
in south-eastern England), where he was saluted by his soldiers
as Imperator. For this exploit Claudius received the appellation of Britannicus from the Roman Senate. From this time
forward until their departure the Romans (save for Boadicea's
revolt) were in possession of the territory hereabouts. That
they actually had some settlements in Southend and the neighbourhood is proved by the discovery of Roman pottery during
building operations in Hastings Road and adjoining thoroughfares, and the unearthing of Roman remains at North and
South Shoebury and Great Wakering. At the latter places the
digging for brick earth revealed the existence of a peculiar
system of trenching, stated to be indications of the boundaries
of fields laid out according to a well-known Roman method.
Prittlewell Church contains a very early arch constructed with
Roman bricks, and there are traces of similar building material
in the walls of Hadleigh Castle. In those days, when no houses
hid the Thames from sight, the rising ground at Southend must
have afforded a commanding view of the entrance of the
Thames, an important artery of commerce to the Romans. It
may be that the district was occupied because of its strategic
value, or it may also be that even at that time, the invaders,
great lovers of oysters, had found the long, sandy foreshore
favourable to the cultivation of this dainty.

Anglo-Saxon Invasion.

The great struggle for possession which the Anglo-Saxons
waged with the Britons on the decay of Roman power—an
incessant warfare for three centuries—found the southern part of
Essex (the county inherits its name from having once been the

kingdom of the East Saxons) largely undisturbed. Green, in his "Making of England," remarks "that in the utter lack of any written record of the struggle in this quarter, we can only collect stray glimpses of its story from the geographical features of this district and from its local names. From both sets of facts we are drawn to the conclusion that it was not from the Thames that this district was mainly attacked. In that quarter there was little to tempt an invader. The clay-flats which stretch along the southern coast of Essex were then but a fringe of fever-smitten, desolate fens, while the meadows that extend from them to the west were part of a forest tract that extended to the marshes of the Lea. The whole region, indeed, beyond the coast was thick with woodland." To the northward, towards the Stour, the country became clearer and the enemy poured in its attacks from the estuary of that river. In 530, tradition says, the Saxons founded a city at Shoebury-ness called Scœbirig, which was afterwards destroyed by a great inundation of the sea. A place of interment has been discovered there, and also at Leigh, whilst other remains have been unearthed at Great Wakering.

A Centre of the Danish Attack.

When in turn the attacks of the Danes became a serious menace to Saxon dominion, this locality was much more developed ; the growth of the people, doubtless, driving them to establish new settlements. In Rochford Hundred was fought the deciding battle between the Saxons and their fierce rivals, and events enacted hereabouts had considerable influence upon national affairs.

The Battle of Benfleet.

In 894, after a time of comparative peace, there were two simultaneous Danish invasions, one in Kent (defeated by Alfred's son Edward) and the other under Hasting, a raider with a reputation for hard fighting. The latter landed first at Sheppey and then at South Benfleet. He established

earthworks in the neighbourhood of where the church now
stands, and forthwith commenced to harry the district.
Eadred, Earl of the Mercians, sailed or marched from London
with his army and a company of citizens to rout the invader.
The fight which followed, conducted in the absence of Hasting, culminated in a brilliant and thrilling feat of arms, for the
fort was carried by storm. Great spoil was taken, together
with a large number of women and children. The treasure
was conveyed to London. Some of the ships were also carried
to London or to Rochester, whilst others were burnt. Their
remains were uncovered during the construction of the railway
line in the Fifties. The chivalrous nature of Alfred bade him
return to Hasting his wife and children. The Danes were
chased across the country now covered by Leigh and Southend to Shoeburyness, where they threw up entrenchments
sufficiently strong to resist further attack. There they were
joined by the remnant of the army which had escaped from
Kent, and apparently made a formidable fort at the Ness. It
was situated near Rampart Street and was circular in form ;
one writer asserting that it was 1,600 feet long on the sea
front and ran 700 feet inland ; the boats being drawn up
inside the camp for repair or other necessary purposes. From
Shoebury the Danes made a daring raid right through the
centre of England, striking at Buttington-on-Severn. " For
many weeks the two armies sat watching each other, the river
flowing between them. At last, after the Danes had eaten
most of their horses, they sallied forth and crossed the river to
fight. The battle which followed was a bloody one, many of
the King's thegns falling ; but the slaughter on the Danish
side was greater, and victory remained with the English."
The defeated Danes, reinforced by fresh arrivals, made their
way to Chester. Here they were blockaded, but they
managed to escape into Essex, and took up quarters at Mersea
on the Blackwater. Alfred subsequently inflicted a terrible
defeat upon them on the river Lea. The reference to the

Danes eating their horses is very interesting, because Green has shown that in war the practice of these marauders was to seize all the horses they could when they landed, and by this means they secured a mobility which enabled them to strike terror by the suddenness and rapidity of their raids. Silver pennies of Alfred the Great's coinage and tokens of a like value of Archbishop Plegmund, of the same period, have been discovered at Leigh, and are now in Colchester Museum.

Canute's Triumph.

Gradually this quarter of the country fell almost exclusively into Danish hands, and one hundred years after the Battle of Benfleet, the decisive fight took place at Ashingdon, near Rochford. Canute was retreating through Essex to his ships lying off the Isle of Sheppey, when his opponent, Edmund Ironsides, jumped across his path at Ashingdon and forced the Danish leader to fight. The former drew up his forces in three divisions on the high ground, and as Canute moved forward to attack, Edmund hastened to grapple with him. Victory is alleged by early chroniclers to have been within the Englishman's grasp, when Edric Streona deserted with his force and wrought terrible confusion in the army. "The battle was a stubborn one ; the sun set on the still struggling hosts, but the day went against the English army," and Edmund and the remnant of his forces had to fly. The line of retreat probably lay over the Crouch at the ford now known as Battlesbridge. It was this battle which secured Danish ascendancy and ultimately led to Canute becoming King over all England. As a thanksgiving for his victory the Danish leader built a church at Ashingdon, on the hill now overlooking peaceful meadows which once witnessed the riot and wreck of war. It was consecrated with great pomp in the presence of Wolstan, Archbishop of York, assisted by many other bishops. The first priest was Stigand, afterwards to become a much-tried Archbishop of Canterbury in the reign of Edward the Confessor.

At the Conquest : Remarkable Extension of Wealth.

At the time of the Norman Conquest practically the whole of Prittlewell Parish (comprised in the Manor of Pritte Wella) was held by Sweyn, one of the few landholders who retained their property after William had assumed the crown. His estate covered nearly the whole of South-East Essex and was enlarged by doubtful means. Sweyn was the greatest sheepmaster in Essex, and it was reckoned his marshes would carry over 4,000 sheep. He built a castle at Rayleigh in the northern portion of the Hundred, in the centre of his estates, now remembered only by Castle Hill, a lofty mound in close proximity to the village. There is no trace left of the castle buildings, but this may be accounted for by the permit of Richard II, in 1394, to his tenants at Rayleigh to explore the foundations and take away stone for the purpose of repairing the chapel and erecting a belfry. The other manor was Mildentuna or Milton, owned by Holy Trinity, Canterbury, who also administered the Manor of Sudcerca, or Southchurch. Of the two smaller manors in Southchurch, Thorp was held by Inguar, and Torpeia, or North Thorpe, was in the possession of Godric, a thegn of Edward the Confessor, but it passed subsequently to Sweyn "by Odo." According to the Survey in 1066 there were serving on these manors thirty-four villeins, forty bordars and eleven serfs, with ten ploughs, twenty-three men's ploughs, eleven rounceys, twenty-five beasts, seventy-nine swine, and 269 sheep, but twenty years later there were thirty-two villeins, fifty-three bordars, and seven serfs, with eleven ploughs, twenty-five men's ploughs, eight rounceys, twenty-nine beasts, 144 swine, 730 sheep, 100 goats, fifteen hives of bees and three colts ; leading to the conclusion that the earlier return was either very imperfect or there had been a big increase in agricultural wealth. It must also be noted that the 1066 returns for Milton and Southchurch did not give the number of sheep, swine and goats. Apparently the advent of William did not greatly disturb this district, and increased security of life and property, coupled with enterprise, resulted in a remarkable growth of live stock, notably in respect of sheep, to the grazing of which the extensive marshes hereabouts were devoted. The annual value of the manors increased very considerably. Whereas they had been scheduled as worth £22 ; they were put down at £36 in the later returns. Most of the manors had pasture for sheep, whilst Milton, Southchurch and Thorp had woodland for swine ; the second named also being credited with two fisheries. Later on the number of manors increased, largely by the sub-division of Prittlewell manor, and so there came into being Priors Hall, Earls-fee, or Polsted Wic, Milton Hall and Chalkwell Hall, whilst the Thorpes became one, under the name of Thorpe Hall. In addition, the manor of Temple Sutton is partly in Prittlewell and partly in Sutton. For long years their owners were of high lineage, including the Dukes of Norfolk, the Earls of Nottingham, the De Veres, Earls of Oxford, the Riches, Earls of Warwick, the Knights Templars (their manor house was at Temple Sutton), and the Wellesleys, Earls of Mornington.

The Manor Houses

Of the Prittlewell manor houses little, if any, of the original structures remain. Priors had its centre, of course, in the group of monastic buildings, to be referred to later, situated at the north end of the parish on the Rochford road. These buildings were almost totally remodelled by Sir Thomas Audley, when he secured a grant of the estate from King Henry VIII. The present Earls Hall, on the opposite side of the road to the Priory, is a comparatively modern building, as is also Temple Sutton ; their use being now entirely devoted to the purposes of the tenant farmer. Milton Hall, now Nazareth House, has been practically re-built to afford the necessary accommodation for the work of the Catholic Sisters of Nazareth. Chalkwell Hall, a Georgian building, with the Park, belongs to the Southend Corporation ; the latter being

purchased for use as a public recreation ground and the former
serving as a shelter and refreshment room. Southchurch Hall
is in the centre of a building estate bordering on the Southchurch Road, and it will not be long before it is swallowed up
by the growth of modern Southend. Thorpe Hall has felt
the modern influence of sport, and is now the headquarters of
a golf club.

An Emphatic Curse.

Milton was at the time of the Great Survey in the
hands of the monks of Holy Trinity, Canterbury. It had
been granted to them by Edward the Confessor, and in the
grant appears the following emphatic curse : " If anyone shall
hereafter presume to deprive them of their lawful right or shall
consent to the same, let him be for ever anathematized and
damned with the traitor Judas."

Foundation of Prittlewell Priory.

Early in the Twelfth Century, Robert Sweyn, son of the
owner mentioned in Domesday, granted the Manor of Prittlewell, with other lands, to the famous Cluniac monastery of
Lewes, and upon this land was built the Priory of Prittlewell,
a remnant of which is contained to-day in the mansion subsequently erected upon the site. The Cluniac Order was a
branch of the Benedictines, and their name indicates their
place of origin, viz., Cluny, in the Dukedom of Burgundy. It
is easy to imagine the charm of the original spot. A woodland dell, through which ran a stream, hidden far away in a
corner of the country, at that time infrequently visited. An
idyllic situation, beautiful now, but infinitely more pleasing in
the old monastic days. Round about it were the hamlets of
Prittewella (Prittlewell), Sudcerca (Southchurch), Mildentuna
(Milton), Thorpe (Southchurch), Legra (Leigh), Berrewera
(Barrow Hall), Scopelanda (Shopland), Suttuna (Sutton),
Estwda (Eastwood), Essoberia (Shoebury), and Rocheforte
(Rochford). In 1291 the temporalities were valued at
£37 16s. 4½d. annually, collected from a large number

PHOTOGRAPH SHOWING PORTION OF EARTHWORK ON FOSSETT'S FARM, PRITTLEWELL.

See pages 12 and 13.

of parishes, but the greater part of the income was derived from the spiritualities. For its size, Prittlewell was unusually rich in church spoils, for it had appropriated at various times the churches of Canewdon, Clavering with Langley, Eastwood, Prittlewell, the two Shoeburies in Essex, and Stoke with the chapel of Nayland in Suffolk. It also owned the advowsons of the rectories of Great Horkesley, East Mersea, Rayleigh, Rawreth, Thundersley and Wickford, and portions in the churches of Hockley, North Benfleet, Bumpstead Helion, and Great Warley. Its influence was thus felt far wider than the boundaries of this Hundred.

In the reign of Henry IV the title of the monks was called into question and upon this was produced a grant by " Robert, son of Suen," showing that he had endowed the monastery "for the salvation of my soul and of my wife and my father and mother and of Beatrice my grandmother and of all those whose care it may be to maintain and increase that place." Too much reliance, however, is not to be placed upon the authenticity of the grant thus produced. Prittlewell Priory was a cell of Lewes Abbey and it was ordered that "the Priory of Prittlewell shall render to the Priory of Lewes yearly and in every year for ever on the feast of St. Pancras one mark of silver as a token." In 1518 Prittlewell challenged the right of Lewes to the tribute and there was great commotion at the time.

It was owing to the establishment of a monastery near by that we now possess the magnificent church of St. Mary the Virgin, Prittlewell. There was probably a church on the site from the earliest times. Certainly there are traces of a Norman building, but in the Fifteenth Century such alterations and extensions were made, probably by the design and under the superintendence of the monks, that the architectural character of the building was entirely altered. We deal more fully with the church in another article, at the end of the present volume.

B

Favoured by Thomas a Becket.

Thomas à Becket was much interested in the Priory, and Newcourt says "he became a great favourer thereof." Indeed, the Archbishop took the infant cause under his protection, for his charter runs : "The solicitude of the office we have taken upon us warns us to be watchful to carefully see to the peace and quietness of the servants of God. Therefore, we have under God and our care the monastery of the Blessed Mary of Pritewell with its chapels of Sutton and Eastwood and with all the tithings of the township of Middleton (Milton) and all the parochial rights over the said township." Archbishop Walter also issued a charter of protection, "following the not undeserving footsteps of our predecessor, that glorious martyr."

Fall of the Sweyn Family.

The Sweyn family did not long retain its almost princely fortune, for Henry de Essex, son of the grantee of the Priory endowment, Standard Bearer to the King by right of inheritance, was called upon by Henry II to serve with him in a campaign against the Welsh. In one of the skirmishes the courage of Henry of Essex failed him and he threw away his standard and fled. For this he was accused of high treason. As was the custom in those days he had to fight for his freedom in single combat. He was overcome by Robert de Montfort and exiled. The barony was forfeited to the Crown —a rich addition to Henry's impoverished exchequer.

Hubert de Burgh and Hadleigh Castle.

The fall of the Sweyns was responsible for the Hundred becoming connected with another historic family—the de Burghs. In 1217 a mandate was issued to knights and free-holders of the Honour of Rayleigh to hold under Hubert de Burgh, who had been granted the same by Henry III to hold during pleasure. The document was stated to be in similar terms to one executed by King John. There is also record of the grant in 1227 to De Burgh of several local manors, including the fairs and markets of Rayleigh and Hadleigh, and three years later permission was granted to Hubert and his wife to construct a castle at Hadleigh "without let or hindrance," though probably the licence was not obtained until its erection was nearly completed. The building of this well-known stronghold, guarding the estuary of the Thames, was naturally an event of immense importance locally. The castle, which was without a keep, was almost oval in form, and the entrance thereto was on the north-west side. It was defended on the north, east and west fronts by a moat, and on the south by the steepness of the hill. The building was of Kentish ragstone and a strong cement, largely composed of cockle shells brought from Canvey Island. De Burgh was later embroiled in a squabble with the Bigods, for interfering with their right that the men of the honour of Rayleigh should make suit to the Hundred of Barstable which they held. The King intervened and ordered restitution to the Bigods. There were also Royal orders respecting the keepership of Rayleigh Park and the right of holding courts of assize at Rayleigh, with which Henry de Burgh had some connection, and these were probably the consequence of this powerful minister's fall from favour. He was stripped of his possessions, but he subsequently placed himself at the King's mercy, and in 1235 the castle and other property were restored to him. In 1239 entry was made of the fact that De Burgh had submitted himself to "the King's liberality and grace," had been confirmed in his right to his former possessions, "with pardon for all offences up to the feast of St. Luke, 1238." It was not long, however, before the castle and estates were again at royal disposal.

Commercial Growth.

The Thirteenth Century saw a quickening of commercial intercourse in the Hundred. Hubert de Burgh established a market at Hadleigh. In 1257 sanction was given Guy of Rochford to hold a weekly market on Tuesdays at Rochford and a yearly fair on the Monday, Tuesday and Wednesday of Whitsun week. In the same year Hugh de Vere, Earl of Oxford, owner of the manor, was permitted to establish a weekly market on Fridays at Prittlewell, and also a fair on the Vigil Feast and morrow of the Nativity of St. Mary. There is record of the grant of market and annual fair rights at the same place twenty years before, but the entry is obliterated in essential details. The market did not exist long. Norden, in 1594, referred to Prittlewell as "sometyme a market town." A tradition exists that in exchange for the market rights Prittlewell received from Rochford a peal of bells, because Anne Boleyn disliked the sound of them, but there is probably little foundation for the story. An annual fair and another for toys were held until quite recent date. In 1345 there was litigation between Hugh de Neville and one Tybetot, on the ground that the latter had erected a market at Shopland, to the injury of the former's free market in Great Wakering. The result was a compromise, somewhat favourable to de Neville. In addition to the establishment of markets, extracts from the Patent and other Rolls show that maritime commerce was also an important factor in the industrial life of the Hundred. The earlier entries all relate to the transhipment of corn. In 1225, the bailiffs of Rochford and two other Hundreds were ordered to assist Thomas of Blumville, Constable of the Tower of London, to arrest those who loaded grain in the Thames for export without royal licence. The same year another writ was issued which shows that the land in these parts belonging to monasteries was largely devoted to the cultivation of corn ; the grain being shipped to afford sustenance to the monks. Thus the bailiffs of Rochford and Dengie Hundreds were instructed that the ships belonging to the Priory of Holy Trinity of Canterbury (who also owned the manors of Milton and Southchurch) should be allowed free transit for their grain, on security being given that it was intended for nowhere else than Canterbury. This licence was repeated in the following year. In 1317, a parson of Northreppes, Norfolk, William de Cusancia, relative of the Prior of Prittlewell, obtained permission, until the Feast of St. Margaret the Virgin, to take by water 200 grains of barley and 100 grains of oats from his church to the Priory for the sustenance of the inmates ; three citizens of London standing security for it not being taken elsewhere. The servants of the Master of St. Bartholomew's Hospital, London, obtained protection in the year 1326 to carry crops, victuals and timber from their manor of Wakering.

Coming to 1339, we pass from the difficulties of provisioning religious houses, to troubles incident upon a strict inspection of ships by the Customs officers. John Sturmy, sometime keeper of Hadleigh Castle, was ordered to France, with his men, to assist in the wars, and in order to maintain and feed them, Lawrence Burrell laded his ship, the Nicholas, of Hadleigh, with wool, cheese and wheat. The goods were seized because they had not passed the collectors of customs of Port of London. An instruction was issued for the return of the cargo to Sturmy, and this was apparently done, with the exception of the sacks of wool, for which an order for payment was given, " as the King had used them." The practice of the people inhabiting the Thames-side with reference to wrecks may be gathered from a report made in 1344. A ship of 100 tons burden, laden with forty-four tuns of wine, was found derelict by one of the King's officers in the waterway near Leigh. He arrested it, but the Leighmen came and seized ship, wines and goods, doing what they pleased therewith. A statement was ordered to be furnished forthwith of the names of the people who had " eloigned " the property. In 1338, the " takers and purveyors " of wool in Essex were ordered not to take any from Queen Philippa's manors of Rayleigh and Eastwood. Peaceful traders to our shores were liable to forfeit their lives to thieves. In 1438, John Camp, of Hadleigh, a husbandman, was pardoned by the King of alleged piratical crimes of bloodthirsty ferocity ; his plea being that he was indicted through the conspiracy of those at enmity with him. The allegation was that he went on board a little ship, belonging to Haarlem, Holland, lying off Leigh, and cut the throats of five Dutchmen ; stealing also a barrel of tin, a barrel of woollen cloth and twenty marks in money. A day or two later it was urged against him that during the night he attacked another Dutch ship lying off the Isle of Sheppey and there slew five men and a boy and carried off £100. Whether Camp was implicated or not, a voyage up the Thames Estuary must have been something of an adventure in early times.

There is also much evidence that people had an equal capacity for getting into debt in those days as in these, and for some considerable sums. Henry le Wyse, of Prittlewell, in 1344, acknowledged that he owed a debt of £60 to a London cornmonger, named Gill. This was still owing two years later, for in 1346 Gill gave instructions for a claim to be prosecuted against Wyse for the full amount. Whether le Wyse died and his son Reginald succeeded we can only guess. It may have been the same man, a mistake having been made in entering the Christian name. Anyhow, in 1348, a Reginald le Wyse, also of Prittlewell, was in similar trouble with a London mercer, named Hugh of Upchurch. Le Wyse owed the latter £80 and had promised the " Mayor of London " he would pay the money by Michaelmas, 1347. Both parties made another arrangement, however, at Prittlewell, for it was agreed that Reginald should pay £40 by Michaelmas in settlement. On going to London, however, Le Wyse was arrested for non-payment of an instalment of £20 under his former promise. He was released whilst appeal was made to the King, who held that an indenture made without the City was not binding. He ordered the matter to go before the justices, who were to hear both parties. Hugh did not appear and

Reginald protested against his long and unjust detention.   He was, however, committed to prison until the Michaelmas in question, and John de Prittlewell, Adam Hurrell, John Sperling and John Baloun were appointed his sureties, either to produce Le Wyse or pay the £80 in question and damages. Later in the year the Deputy Warden of the Fleet reported to the Court of Chancery that Le Wyse had been delivered into his custody.

A Royal Hunting Forest.

Rochford Hundred was a favourite resort for the early Plantagenets and a study of the countryside will soon make the reason clear.   In his map of Essex of 1594, John Norden shows three great parks lying comparatively close together— Rayleigh, Rochford and Hadleigh.   In those days, when the forests had not yielded to the demands of increasing population, the parishes of Thundersley, Rayleigh, Hadleigh, East-wood, Sutton and the borderland of Leigh and Prittlewell consisted largely of forest.   This was kept as a Royal hunting ground and used by monarchs as late as the reign of Henry VIII.   Henry III hunted at Rayleigh in 1222 and the three Edwards were constantly there.   Edward I was at Eastwood three times and Rayleigh twice ; Edward II was either at Thundersley or Hadleigh at some period in almost every year of his reign, in one year being at Thundersley three times.   On one occasion at Hadleigh he granted a yeoman the right to every eighth foal of his stud at Hadleigh. Edward III was at Hadleigh in 1342 and Richard II also hunted hereabouts.   The wood of the forest also provided timber for certain public works and it was customary to recognize services by the gift of either trees or deer from the parks ; but breaches of the forest laws met with severe punishment.   In 1231 the Bishop of Winchester was given, by Henry III, twelve oaks from Rayleigh Park " to make timbers."   Three years later Henry de Berneval, the King's chaplain, was granted five oaks, " with all their branches," the keeper being ordered to deliver them at the place Berneval selected, for they were to be used in the construction of a house. Hadleigh Park was dispossessed of 120 oaks in 1275 for repairs to the Tower, and a year later twenty oaks from Rayleigh Park were used in like service. In 1285, John of London received "an oak fit for timber" from Hadleigh Park. Orders were given for ten leafless oaks in Hadleigh Park, to the value of ten marks, to be cut down and sold, the money to be expended in the repair of many defects in the manor, which Edward III had heard "needed reform." A later order in the same year was to the effect that houses and ditches in the manor were to be repaired where necessary and certain of the houses shifted to more suitable positions. Six years after £20 worth of timber in Thundersley Wood was bought by the King "to construct certain engines in the Tower." There were also many gifts of deer. In 1276, Robert de Tybetot, a Shopland landowner, was given twenty deer from Rayleigh Park. Three years afterwards, Richard of South-church was released of a fine of 100s. which had been imposed upon him for being present at the taking of a hart by John de Burgh without the King's sanction. William Fitzwarenne, in 1281, was given three does from Rayleigh Park. In 1301, Hugh de Vere, of Hadleigh Castle, obtained permission to take twelve does from Rayleigh Park, but he took in addition two bucks and four fawns and the fawn of a hind, for which trespass he had to buy pardon. In Edward the First's reign, three commissions were issued to enquire into breaches of the rigid hunting laws, and in 1314 energetic steps had to be taken to deal with trespassing on Queen Margaret's dower lands in Hadleigh and neighbourhood. In the time of Henry VIII., deer were constantly taken from Rayleigh to replenish the herds in Greenwich Park.

Knights Templars at Prittlewell.

Many acres of land in Prittlewell and adjoining parishes were held by the Knights Templars, one of the military orders which arose out of the passion for crusading. They established a hospital on the borders of Prittlewell. In 1280 the master and brethren bought or were given seventy-two acres of land in Prittlewell and Eastwood. Thirteen years later they acquired a house and four acres at Rochford, a house and four acres in Sutton, and five acres in Sutton and Prittlewell. In 1303 they made considerable additions to their holding, obtaining in all nearly 100 acres. The only means we have now of identifying their former possessions is in the name of a farm, situate partly in Prittlewell and partly in Sutton, called Sutton Temple. It is near by the Corporation Cemetery in Sutton Road. The Knights Templars were suppressed in 1312. Their property passed to the Knights Hospitallers, and later on to private ownership.

Priestly Faction Fight at Prittlewell.

The opening of the Fourteenth Century was attended with much disturbance; two chief centres of rioting being Prittlewell Priory and Rayleigh. At the former place, William de Auvernaz was the cause of the trouble. He had been appointed prior in 1311. For incontinency he was deprived by the Prior of Lewes and in 1315 another man was preferred to the office. Auvernaz retorted by obtaining the protection of the King, who, early in 1316, appointed an official to manage the monastery revenues on account of its poverty. In December of the same year, however, James de Cusancia, monk of Lewes, was appointed Prior and admitted by the King, but William would not be dispossessed so easily. Auvernaz was summoned to appear before the Council. Before the day of hearing, William entered the Priory with an armed mob, "wasting the goods, expelling the monks, breaking chests, appropriating the muniments and common seal and with the seal sealing divers obligations and blank letters." Ordered again to appear before the Court of Chancery, William renounced his right to his superior, the Prior of

Lewes, and the King commanded the temporalities to be delivered to James. Again William took forcible possession of the Priory, committing "the same or greater excesses," and then the King gave command for the Priory to be taken over and all persons meddling with it arrested. At the same time he issued a commission to try fifteen people, including such well-known names as Neville and Boteler, for being concerned in the disturbances. William took his claim before the Archbishop of Canterbury (who decided in his favour) and Cusancia then appealed to the Pope. Whilst the suit was pending some monks from Lewes, by order of the Prior, came with an armed force to Prittlewell. Auvernaz was celebrating mass, but this did not prevent them attacking him. A fight ensued in the church. Auvernaz was wounded in the head and dragged from the high altar. Three of his monks were also injured. Cusancia's party bound them hand and foot and conveyed them to Lewes, where they were imprisoned. Subsequently William died, probably from the effects of his wound, and Cusancia reigned in his stead; occupying the position for fourteen years, until he became Prior of Thetford.

Rayleigh Court and Gaol.

Rayleigh at this time was the headquarters of the administration of justice and as early as 1229 three Judges were mentioned by name as being sent to "hear all cases concerning lands and tenements and all pleas of the crown in the Hundred of Rochford;" their instructions also leading to the inference that the Court was accustomed considerably before that time to meet at Rayleigh. One of the three was named Stephen Segrave, a lawyer whose political principle has been described as "obedience to the powers that were in the ascendant." He was one of the intriguers who brought about the temporary disgrace of De Burgh and, in fact, Segrave succeeded him in the office of Justiciar. For many years criminals awaiting trial were lodged in the gaol there. In 1352, Rochford

Hundred claimed at the Assizes at Chelmsford that the Justices should transact their judicial business at Rayleigh, and supported their contention by precedents. They urged that Judges were "wont to send one of the Justices to hold the pleas of all writs and all pleas of tenement within the Hundred and all pleas of the Crown, on condition, however, that the bailiff of Rochford should come before the Justice and elect on oath two knights of the Hundred, who should elect twelve out of the Hundred, on the coming of the Justice there, and receive from him the heads from which they should draw out their verdict." The precedents quoted comprised the selecting of the jury at various times in the manner recorded above and the trial of certain cases. They included a complaint by the Great Wakering parson that a man and his wife had raised a dyke there, which prevented him having access to the common pasture, and an allegation that at Hockley a man and his two sisters were burnt to death by a fire at the house of their father. The mother was missing and suspected of the crime. An agent of Queen Phillipa, who had received the Castle of Hadleigh and lands adjoining as part of her dower, erected, in 1338, a courthouse at Rayleigh. For some reason or other, the inhabitants resented this and turned out and destroyed it. The ringleaders, to the number of twenty, were arrested and tried. What became of them is not disclosed, but a few of the names of the prisoners are suggestive of their occupations, for they included Thomas the parker; Ralph the woodward, Roger the wright, Martin the tyler, John Brown the butcher, etc. We know that the chief of the culprits, Giles Brianzon, was released with permission to serve in the French wars, and having fought faithfully for a year, he obtained full pardon for his unruly conduct, with the proviso that he should serve the King for another year on wages. Whether this riot was the culmination of a long period of unrest is not certain, but many commissions had been issued in 1314 for the purpose of enquiring into charges of trespass, felling trees, destroying

houses and walls, and hunting and fishing on the dower lands;
Eastwood, Hadleigh and Rayleigh being particularly mentioned.
Trouble broke out again in 1352 and a commission was
appointed to enquire into the matter.

A Curious Right.

Reference to the administration of justice recalls that the
Dean and Chapter of St. Paul's, owners of the Manor of
Barling Magna, could exercise the prerogative of justice over
the people resident on their holding, even to the extent of life
and death ; also, to judge by the wording of the grant reproduced below, they were free of taxation.   They possessed the
power of "Infangenethef and Utfangenethef"—the right to
erect a gallows and execute robbers ; the men by hanging and
the women by drowning.   In 1235, the approval by the
Crown of this privilege was made in the following terms :
"Grant to the Dean and Chapter of St. Paul's, London, that
their manor of Barlings and their men thereof shall be quit of
counties and hundreds and amercements of them and of aid of
sheriffs and their ministers of carriage, of works, of castles and
bridges, of fines for murder, larceny and escape, of view of
frank pledge, so that the Dean and Chapter shall make the
view of frank pledge, where it was wont to be made in their
said manor of their men of the said manor before the bailiff of
the Hundred if he will come, and if he will not, it shall still
be held and all amercements arising therefrom shall go to the
Dean and Chapter, and their men of the said manor shall be
quit of ward penny, hundred penny and tithing penny, and
the said Dean and Chapter shall have in the said manor, soc
and sac, thol and team, infangenethef and utfangenethef."   In
1865, Mr. "Antiquary" King visited "a small ancient building of ragstone, about the date of the latter part of the
Fifteenth Century, with a flat-pointed doorway and mullioned
windows," situated upon Gaol Farm, Barling, and which he
presumed to have been the manorial courthouse.   He doubted

whether another example of such a building existed in the country. The gallows were said to have stood in a field on Mucking Hall, near the footpath from Barling to Rochford, leading to the wood in Shopland, and the spot afforded the victim a last look at the countryside ere he was suspended in mid-air. An old man who lived well in the Nineteenth Century asserted that he had seen the posts which used to support the gallows. The grant of the Hadleigh manor to De Burgh was somewhat similar to that of Barling.

A Monastic Episode.

In 1343 an incident occurred which illustrates one of the minor troubles with which monastic authorities had to deal. Among those who entered the holy life at Prittlewell was Henry de Suthecherche, illegitimate son of Sir Peter de Suthecherche. For eight years he served as a monk, but " afterwards the said brother Henry, seduced by the Devil, departed out of our said house and spurned religion and the monastic garb by a damnable apostacy, and for the space of twenty-six years and more wandered about as a secular vagrant." This Henry must have been a precious scamp. He forged a letter of instruction to a lawyer in the name of Sir Peter and by means of a forged will caused a mill, 530 acres of arable land, ten of meadow, thirty of pasture, twenty of wood and forty of marsh, and £12 13s. rent in Prittlewell, Thorpe, Southchurch, Leigh and Bowers Gifford, formerly the property of Sir Peter, to be handed to him. These possessions came into the King's hands through Henry being outlawed and he died unconvicted. John, son of Alice of Newington, the latter of whom was the beneficiary under the real will, took proceedings to recover the property and the King, in 1345, ordered the Justices to complete the matter without delay.

The Peasants' Revolt.

This famous Revolt in 1381, which had its beginning in an adjoining Hundred, had necessarily a close connection with

our locality. The Black Death had swept away half the
population, and the scarcity of labour gave the workmen an
independent position which they had not dreamt of before.
The feudal customs under which the villeins were bound to
their respective manors were disregarded. The aid of Parliament was invoked in favour of the landowners and acts
were passed, among other things establishing a fixed scale of
remuneration. The irritation aroused by these restrictions
was increased by the imposition of fresh taxes to meet the cost
of war expenditure in France, and with the levying of a poll
tax, which worked hardly on the poorer districts, the signal for
revolt was raised. Some sixteen miles to the west of Southend
are situated the villages of Fobbing, Corringham and Stanford-
le-Hope, bordering the Thames and overlooking Canvey
Island, and it was the inhabitants of these marshland parishes
who began the trouble. Mr. G. M. Trevelyan, in his
"England in the Age of Wycliffe," thus graphically describes
the outbreak of hostilities : "It was about the last week of
May, 1381, that Thomas Bampton, one of the poll tax commissioners, came down to Brentwood, a small town eighteen
miles north-east of London. Sitting there at the receipt of
custom, he summoned before him the inhabitants of Fobbing,
Corringham and Stanford-le-Hope, a group of villages lying
ten miles further south, on the lower Thames, not far from
Tilbury. It was in vain that the men of Fobbing pleaded a
quittance received from the commissioners who had levied the
tax during the winter. Bampton was inexorable. He insisted
on a second enquiry into their population and taxable
resources. He threatened them with penalties for their con-
tumacy, and seemed to dispose to rely on the support of the
two soldiers who had attended him from London. On this
provocation a small but angry crowd from the three villages
was soon collected. They told the commissioner flatly that he
would not get a penny out of them, and that the conference
must end. Bampton ordered his men-at-arms to make an

arrest. But the blood of the villagers was now up, and they chased soldiers and commissioner together out of Brentwood. Bampton galloped off to London to complain to his masters. The men of Fobbing, Corringham and Stanford, fearing the speedy vengeance of the government (for they were within half a day's ride of London), took to the woods, and passed from village, inciting the people of Essex to revolt. Other bands of outlaws were afoot. The obnoxious statutes regulating wages had driven many free labourers to take to the woods, and the runaway villeins preferred a roving life to the servitude from which they had fled. Meanwhile Bampton had arrived at Westminster with his story. The Chief Justice of the King's Bench was at once sent down into Essex with a commission of 'trailbaston' to restore order. He was treated with as little ceremony as the tax collector and driven back no less speedily to London. The inhabitants of the revolted fishing villages had roused the country. The rebellion was well afoot, and its ugliest aspect—massacre—was not wanting. The judge was spared, but the jurors were beheaded. Three unfortunate clerks who had been serving Bampton on his late commission were also caught and decapitated. Their heads were placed on pikes and accompanied the march of the rebels from day to day."

The Battle of Billericay.

From half the counties in the kingdom, but particularly from Essex and Kent, the peasantry poured along the main roads and with very little trouble secured possession of London. Lord Chief Justice Cavendish was murdered in Suffolk, John of Gaunt's beautiful palace of Savoy was destroyed, Archbishop Sudbury was executed, Treasurer Hales was beheaded and the Flemish Colony robbed and massacred. The Tower of London was the only refuge for the Royal family in so terrible a storm. But lack of discipline and hunger were soon to end the trouble, serious though it was. At a meeting between the

King and Wat Tyler, organizer of the rebellion, at Smithfield, the latter was killed by the Lord Mayor. Without a leader the rebels quickly began to disperse homeward and the Government assumed control. A large section of the Essex men, however, would not submit until they had fought a pitched battle with the Royal troops. The leaders sent out a summons for a mobilization at Great Baddow and Rettendon, villages on the main road from Southend to Chelmsford. The utmost pressure having been exercised a great host was got together. Oman thus describes the actual course of the fighting : "The rebels stockaded themselves in a strong position upon the edge of a wood near Billericay (a village some miles to the north of Southend), covering their flanks and rear with ditches, and rows of carts chained together, after the fashion that the English had been wont to employ in the French wars. Hearing of this muster, the King dispatched against it the vanguard of his army, under his uncle, Thomas of Woodstock, and Sir Thomas Percy, the brother of the Earl of Northumberland. There was a sharp fight, but the entrenchments of the rebels were carried at the first charge, and a great number of them—as many as 500, if the chronicles can be trusted—were cut down. The rest escaped under the cover of the forest in their rear, but the victors captured the camp, in which were found no less than 800 horses." One of the surviving bands was finally dispersed in Suffolk and the other in Huntingdon.

Hadleigh Castle Entrenched.

There was much activity at Hadleigh Castle in these troublous years. In 1377, four years before the outbreak, we find that Walter Whitehose, the Constable of the Castle, was empowered to garrison the place with sufficient men-at-arms and archers of the County of Essex against hostile invasion, though this had probably to do with a daring raid up the Thames as far as Gravesend by the French, who had at that

A REMARKABLE HEAD OF
A ROMAN FIGURE, FOUND AT
SHLEBURY, ESSEX, JAN. 1909.

See pages 13 and 14.

time command of the sea. In 1378, John Nief, whose name suggests an Anglo-Saxon of servile origin, obtained confirmation of the life office of porter at the Castle, but on March 8th, 1381, he was removed from that post, being paid 3d. a day instead on condition that he remained in the Castle under the keeper's orders. This latter proviso suggests that the authorities had doubts as to his loyalty, and his suspension may have been a precautionary measure in view of the unrest which was to culminate in the active revolt two months later. In 1379, Peter Coat, the local representative of John Blake, surveyor to the King's palaces, was granted a writ of aid, empowering him to take what was wanted for the repair of the Castle at what price he liked, and it is, perhaps, significant that in this same year the King promised to repay the "good men" of Hadleigh £50 which he had borrowed from them. Thomas Walsingham and William Hemery, both of Rayleigh, were in 1380 commissioned to take labourers to entrench Hadleigh Castle ; this being followed in 1381 by a writ of aid authorising Nicholas Raunche and John Goldman to cut and sell underwood at Hadleigh Castle and Thundersley Park to the value of £20 by survey of William de Paglesham (the King's steward), the proceeds to go to the repair of the Castle. In the same year summary powers to take "workmen, stone, etc.," were again given to Cook, deputy clerk of works, for the repair of the Castle, which was then in the keepership of Aubrey de Vere, a leading member of the family of the Earl of Oxford. The work of repairing and entrenching the Castle was largely done by forced labour and this would add fuel to the fire of discontent in Hadleigh and its neighbourhood. We have an interesting glimpse of the social condition of the working people of Hadleigh at this time. Upon the manor were twenty-seven free tenants and three villeins. These latter each held a messuage of five acres. They had to do one work per week for the lord of the manor from Michaelmas to the beginning of August, except during

c

one week at Christmas, Easter and Whitsuntide, and two
works per week from the beginning of August to Michaelmas.
Wages had a distinct tendency to rise at the time of the
Revolt. A thatcher at the end of the Thirteenth and beginning of the Fourteenth Centuries was usually paid 2½d. per
day. Before the end of the latter century he received 4d.,
and in the early part of the century following, 4½d. and 5d.,
whilst his assistant received 4d. and in some cases 3d. A
master carpenter was paid 3½d. per day and in the latter part
of the Fourteenth Century he received 5d. (the unskilled man
being awarded 4d). Wages continued to rise until they
reached 8d., though in the early Fifteenth Century 5d. and
6d. were the more usual rates.

The Rising in Prittlewell Town and a Raid on a Manor.

Certain of the inhabitants of Prittlewell suffered the
seizure of their goods for their participation in the rebellion
and the spirit of insurrection was rife all over the Hundred.
This may be conclusively proved by a review of the records of
the trials of local people which took place before Judge
Tresilian, who earned as unenviable a notoriety for his punishment of the rebels as did Judge Jeffreys some three hundred
years later in the West of England. A man from this district
was concerned in the actual outbreak. Associated with the
men of Fobbing, Mucking, Stanford and Horndon was a
"certain weaver" belonging to Billericay and John Newman,
of Rawreth, "a common thief." They were charged with
pursuing Bampton and other Justices, at Brentwood, with
bows and arrows with intent to kill them, and afterwards
breaking into Cressing Temple and the residence of the
Sheriff of Essex at Coggeshall. They were subsequently
joined by a considerable following from this Hundred. These
men included Thomas Spragge, of South Benfleet ("and
others of the same place"); Thomas Treche, of Leigh;

William Bocher, of Hadleigh ; John Mersh, of Hadleigh ;
Henry Fleccher, of Rayleigh ; John Sawyer, of Rawreth ; and
on their way to the main assembly they broke into the manor
Geoffrey Dersham, in Downham, near Wickford. Led by the
servant of the lord of the manor, they stole five oxen, three
bulls, twenty capons—obviously to serve as provisions—with
brass pots and pans, beside destroying the houses and outbuild-
ings. The case relating to Prittlewell shows without doubt there
was organization among the disaffected. When the news of
the rising at Brentwood was brought to this locality, John
Hurt, of Shoebury, and John Glasure, of Rochford, "messengers of the King's enemies," met Ralph Spicer, William
Croume, a chandler, and others, at Prittlewell, and the
labourers were called upon to revolt by Thomas Hilleston.
When the case came before the Courts it was pleaded that the
men acted under the orders of John Syrat, of Shoebury, who
commanded Hurt to go to Prittlewell. Croume also urged in
his defence that the King had, by letters patent, pardoned
him for his share in the revolt, "provided he be not one of
the principals concerned in the said insurrection, or in the
death of the venerable Father Simon, Archbishop of Canterbury, Brother Robert Hales, late Prior of the Hospital of St.
John of Jerusalem in England, the King's Treasurer, or John
de Cavendish, late Chief Justice, or the burning of the manor
of Savoy, or Clerkenwell, or in the death of the Prior of
Bury." As in many other cases, Croume was not allowed to
escape by this means, and certain persons were bound over to
present him before the King in the octaves of St. Hilary, after
which we do not know what became of him.

Suppression in this Hundred.

When the backbone of the rebellion was broken, steps
were quickly taken to restore peace. On August 8th, 1381,
William of Paglesham—a noted public servant of the time, and
for some years member for Maldon—and four others were

appointed to enquire into the complaint of John de Bampton that insurgents had entered his holding in Essex and taken his goods "to his utter ruin." In December Sir William Berland —a local landowner—and Sir Aubrey de Vere—keeper of Hadleigh Castle—were placed on an Essex commission to keep the peace, with power "to arrest those who congregate in unlawful assemblies or incite insurrection, to put down rebels and with armed force, if necessary, to suppress those assemblies." Three months later even these powers were made more severe, obviously with a view to the suppression of Lollardry, then rising into prominence. Sir William Berland, Sir Aubrey de Vere, Sir Richard de Sutton and others were members of the commission which was appointed to deal with " the treasonable hostile rising of divers evil doers in congregations and conventicles throughout the realm, and the perpetration of treasons, homicides, arsons, and so on." These gentlemen were ordered "to keep the peace in Essex, with power to arrest, imprison and punish rebels and inciters to rebellion, to suppress their meetings, arrest their goods or to take security. If suspicious meetings are held or are too numerously attended they are to raise the posse comitatus and to lead them against the rebels and seize any found committing the above offences and to do justice to them at once." They were also empowered to deal promptly with those who refused to assist them. On December 21st, 1382, over eighteen months after the Rebellion had broken out, another commission in the same strain was issued, showing that the restoration of order was a long and difficult process.

Preparations to Resist Invasion: The Minster and Beacon.

Three years later, 1385, saw the appointment of a strong commission in this Hundred to deal with a threatened invasion by the French of these coasts. The conquests in France by Edward III had been gradually lost. The junction of the

French and Spanish fleets made them masters of the Channel and the mouth of the Thames, where they preyed upon the commerce of England and the Low Countries, whilst a French force reduced the great trading city of Ghent. To add to this serious menance Scotland allied herself with France. It was in these circumstances that Sir Aubrey de Vere (Keeper of Hadleigh Castle), the Prior of Prittlewell, Sir John Chanceaux, John FitzSymon, Ralph Danyell, John Baryngton, William of Paglesham, John Wodeham, John of Prittlewell, and the Sheriff were appointed to array all men-at-arms, armed men and archers who lived in Rochford Hundred, and arm all able-bodied men each according to his estate and distrain upon all those able in estate, but not in body, to fight, to supply armour and contribute to the expenses. These men they were to keep arrayed and to lead to the sea coast where danger threatened. To add emphasis to the fear of invasion which the Government had, it was ordered that the beacons were to be placed in the accustomed spots to warn people of the coming of the enemy. Benton mentions that there is a minute of Prittlewell Vestry, dated March 23rd, 1667, respecting the sum of £5 15s. for the beacon watch, consisting of firing, pitch and tar, which was put before the Vestry, who refused payment, and a resolution passed that it should be referred to the treasurer of the County. Where that particular beacon was raised is not clear, but early maps show a beacon existing near by Cliff Town Parade, and at other times there has been a fire suspended from Prittlewell Church Tower.

Of the gentlemen charged with this important work of defence, Sir John Chanceaux was a landowner of Canewdon, whose ancestors are said to have come over with the Conqueror from Chauncy, near Amiens, Picardy, and the name is found in the roll of Battle Abbey. Thirteen years before this time he had married Margery, widow of Thomas de Staple, owner of Hamstalls, Prittlewell. John Wodeham and John Fitz-Symon were both landowners in North Shoebury, and John

Baryngton was keeper of the King's Park at Rayleigh. He was the last of the male line of Barringtons who traced their descent from Adam of Barrington, said to be a convert to Christianity through the preaching of St. Augustine. John of Pritwell or Prittlewell was, as his name implies, a landowner of the ancient village, and it was in his house, say some chroniclers, that fifteen years later, the Duke of Exeter was arrested when fleeing from justice.

Troublous Days.

The lawless condition of the populace at this time is best illustrated by the large number of murders which occurred between 1388 and 1392. In the former year a man named Robert Reynolds, of Prittlewell, was pardoned for killing his wife ; John Foot, of Little Wakering, was similarly reprieved for the murder of William Grimston, of Great Wakering, in a field ; Robert Weld, tailor, for the death of John Taillour, of Rochford, and John Symond, of Hadleigh, for the death of a chaplain, named Robert Windle.

A Sad Home-coming.

It was in the reign of Richard II that Thomas of Wood-stock, Duke of Gloucester, one of his uncles, was murdered by his orders. It was a case of plot and counter-plot, in which Richard suddenly struck home. He caused the Duke to be seized at Stratford by a band of men under the Earl of Huntingdon (afterwards Duke of Exeter), conveyed to Calais and there strangled. This tragic event is mentioned by Froissart, who refers to this locality whilst relating the manner of the Duke's burial. He says : " His body was embalmed and cased in lead and covered, and so sent by sea into England, and the ship that carried him arrived at the Castle of Hadley, upon Thames' side, and from thence he was carried by chariot simply to his own church at Pleshy (Essex) and there buried in the church."

Retribution came shortly after the accession of Henry IV. In 1400, the Duke of Exeter, who was a half brother of Richard II, tried to escape from the country in consequence of an unsuccessful plot against the new King. He fled into Essex and there took ship for the Continent, but driven back by contrary winds he was taken at the Hamlet Mill in Prittle-well (some say whilst he was dining with John of Prittlewell) by the villagers and carried to Pleshy. Here the late Duke of Gloucester's mother-in-law had his head cut off, fearing that the King might be induced to spare him. Before the execution, with barbarous cruelty, the servants tortured and tore his body.

Henry the Fourth Chased by the French.

In 1406, Henry IV was nearly captured by French pirates—at that time the scourge of English commerce. The King was crossing from Sheppey to Leigh on his way to Pleshy ; his intention being to avoid London on account of the plague raging there. Four vessels of his squadron were captured and among the prisoners of rank was his Vice-Chamberlain. Henry, himself, was only just saved by ignominious flight to the Essex shore. Hollingshed, in his Chronicle, stated : "They followed the King so near that if his ship had not been swift, he had landed sooner in France than in Essex, but such was his good hap that he escaped and arrived at his appointed port."

A Lucrative Superstition.

The church at Ashingdon became a centre of much devotional activity in the early years of the Fifteenth Century. A rector, named David, who had been presented to the living by Sir William de Coggeshall, son-in-law of Sir John Hawkwood, the greatest leader of free lances of his day, reported that he had discovered an image of a certain saint to be possessed of certain miraculous powers. The church quickly attracted crowds of pilgrims, who daily crawled

up the hill to the shrine upon their hands and knees to offer
their petitions. The virtues of the image were supposed to be
particularly beneficial to barren women desiring children. The
offerings of the faithful were quickly making the rector a
wealthy man and his brethren in the neighbouring parishes,
either moved by jealousy or by a diminution in their own
incomes, petitioned the Bishop of London to stop the practice.
He granted a commission " to the official of the Archdeacon
of Essex, and to the Vicar of Prittlewell, to go to this church
and search into the form and quality of this image, and to
make a report after due search about the imposition of miracles
and into the cause of such a sudden confluence of people
thither, and threatening excommunication against any man
circumventing the people by any false inventions, sequestering
in the meantime whatever oblations had been made to it."
The result of the enquiry is not known, but at the time of
the Reformation, memorials of " feigned miracles, pilgrimages,
etc.," were taken away.

The Guild of Jesus at Prittlewell.

The great revival of religious feeling in the Fifteenth
Century found expression in the re-building and enlargement
of churches and the foundation of guilds. Prittlewell Church
was affected by both these movements. The fabric was not
only restored, but enlarged—an incident in our history which
is dealt with under another heading—and a guild instituted
known as the Jesus Guild. In this chapter it is proposed to
describe the Guild, because, although it was a religious institution, its objects also closely touched the social habits and needs
of the people. These Guilds were common in Catholic
Europe ; some of them being of ancient foundation. Their
objects may be summarised as being, in addition to the proper
performance of religious devotions, the mutual assistance of the
Guild brethren, in old age, in sickness, in impoverishment, in
losses by fire, water or shipwreck, by loans, provision of work

and burial of the dead. Assistance and visitation were also afforded those not belonging to the Guild and what was of importance in the Middle Ages, regard was had to the education of poor scholars, the maintenance of schools and the payment of schoolmasters. The scope of the Prittlewell Guild is set out in the royal licence dated the 7th May, 1478, in the reign of Edward IV, which ran :

"The King, to all whom, etc., greeting. Know ye that "we have lately understood that certain of our faithful "lieges of the parish of Pritwell in the county of Essex, "being led and excited by the spread of devotion to the "love of the name of Jesus, have devotedly commenced a "certain Fraternity or Guild among themselves both of "themselves and of others desiring to be of that Fraternity "or Guild and with the aid above all of God and our Lord "Jesus Christ and our licence in this behalf having been "requested, obtained and had, have proposed to continue "the same Fraternity, and on behalf of our same lieges it "has been most humbly supplicated to us that for the due "foundation and establishment of the same Fraternity or "Guild we would deign to grant our licence in this behalf. "We, assenting to the same application, of our said grace "and especially that we may subsequently become partici- "pators in so pious a work, have granted and give licence "and by these presents do give and grant for us and our "heirs as much as in us is to our beloved Thomas Mont- "gomery, Kt., and to John Lucas, clerk, Thomas Bayen, "Robert Plomer, Thomas Cok, of Pritwell, Thomas Eston, "John Hacche, Robert Sweete, John Broke, John Frye, "Robert Thomson, Richard Kyrkeby, William Shethe, "Thomas Wedde, Thomas Castelyn, Stephen Spotyll, "Richard Tylewerth and John Sterlyng, that they or any of "them who shall survive shall be able to make, found, erect, "ordain and establish, to the honour, glory and exaltation "of the most sweet name of Jesus, to whom is duly bowed

"every knee of celestial, terrestial and infernal (beings), a
"certain perpetual Fraternity or Guild of one master and
"two wardens, persons ecclesiastical or secular, and other
"persons of either sex whomsoever desiring to be of that
"Fraternity or Guild at present admitted or henceforth for
"ever to be admitted brethren and sisters of the same
"Fraternity or Guild in the parish church of the Blessed
"Mary of Pritwell in the County of Essex, to endure for
"all future times ; and that the same master and wardens
"and brothers and sisters shall be able to augment the same
"Fraternity or Guild as often and whenever it shall here-
"after seem to them necessary and opportune ; and every
"year on the Feast of Corpus Christi or within the Octaves
"of the same they shall be able to elect and to make from
"themselves one master and two wardens to support the
"burden of the affairs touching or concerning the said
"Fraternity or Guild and to rule and govern the same Fra-
"ternity or Guild."

The charter also empowered the brethren to acquire land,
to make statutes and ordinances, to use a common seal, to hold
a meeting "to eat and drink in a convenient place in the
town of Pritwell every year," and to acquire property of the
yearly value of ten marks for the support of a chaplain to
perform divine service daily in the parish church and for such
other purposes as the members should approve.   Mr. King
believed that the Guild was formed some ten years before the
date mentioned.   Probably it was at first dependent upon the
voluntary contributions of the members and the royal licence
was not required until it began to acquire land, and this could
not be held without the King's consent.   Of the names mentioned in the licence reproduced above, Sir Thomas Montgomery, so far as is known, had no connection by property or
othewise with Prittlewell.   He lived at Faulkbourn Hall and
was one of the most eminent men of his day.   John Lucas was
vicar of Prittlewell in 1475 and died in 1477-8, some months

before the date of the document. Robert Swete was the occupant of Chalkwell Hall, and his curious will is mentioned in another chapter. John Fry was a property holder in Prittlewell, as was also William Shethe. Stephen Spotyll belonged to a very well-known Essex family of that day, whose name was variously spelt Spotell, Spotyll, Spottell, Spodell, Spuddill, Spudall, Sputelle, Sputtle and Spuddle.

The Prittlewell Guild had a chapel in the parish church, known as the Jesus Chapel, and also a guild house, where the members met for the transaction of business and for feasting. The chapel, where service was said daily, was in the south aisle of the chancel of St. Mary's Church and measured 24ft. 10ins. by 19ft. 3ins. Its chief glory in the present day is the east window with a beautiful series of Biblical scenes in stained glass, which was taken in the Fifteenth Century from the church of St. Ouen, Rouen, and which was erected in the Nineteenth Century. The furnishing of the interior at that time is best given in a description by Roger Martin of a similar chapel in Melford Church, Suffolk : "There was a table with crucifix on it, with the two thieves hanging, on either side one. There were also two fair gilt tabernacles from the ground up to the roof, with a fair image of Jesus, in the tabernacle at the north end of the aisle, holding a round ball in his hand, signifying, I think, 'that he containeth the whole round world' ; in the tabernacle of the south end there is a fair image of our Blessed Lady, having the afflicted body of her dear son in her lap, the tears, as it were, running down pitifully upon her beautiful cheeks, as it seemed bedewing the sweet body of her son ; therefore, named 'the image of our Lady of Pity.'" The will of Agnes Fry, of Putney, proved in 1501, shows that a statue of our Lady of Pity existed in Prittlewell Church, and William Fuller, in 1524, left a sum of money for the purpose of gilding the tabernacle of our Lady in the Jesus aisle. The Guild maintained a chaplain to celebrate the service and he had also

charge of the education of the poor boys of the parish. There
are architectural evidences that there was a room situated near
the south porch of the church, and it is surmised that this was
the lodging or schoolroom of the priest of the Guild, as was
the constant custom in those days. A house, formerly known
as the church lodge, now existing and situate at the entrance
gates to the church, might, however, have served as the priest's
apartment. The position of the Guild house has been located
with tolerable certainty. On the south side of the street,
opposite the church, there existed until recently a house
formerly called Jesus house. It was used as a beer house until
its licence was transferred and then it was pulled down. The
building presented no marks of antiquity, but it probably
replaced the older Guild house, for a deed relating to the
same property in 1799 described it as " Jesus Hall."

It was the custom of members to remember the Guild in
their wills. For instance, Agnes Fry, of Putney, who had
considerable property in Prittlewell, left, among other things,
to the Brotherhood of Jesus, her second brass pot and half a
dozen pewter vessels. A will also referring to the Guild was
that of Thomas Cocke, of Prittlewell, which was proved in
1545. It was dated at Calais and the testator described
himself as a yeoman of the King's Guard. His witnesses were
John Smith and Thomas Byrch, also of the Guard, and
Thomas Salmon, of Leigh, and William Salmon, of Prittlewell. The Cocke family attained considerable wealth and
position in the time of the Tudors, and for many years a
member of the house lived at Little Stambridge Hall. Their
place of origin was probably either Leigh or Prittlewell ; but
however that may be, they were largely concerned in maritime adventure, and the family name occurs with some
frequency in the records of the time, either spelt as Cok, Cock,
or Cocke. One branch subsequently married into the Went-
worth family. Thomas Cocke owned land in Foulness Island
and Shopland, and houses, shops, woods and crofts in Prittle-

well. The latter included a house he bought of the Brotherhood of the Jesus Guild (probably their guild house). Cocke also referred to the fact that the same institution owed him £8 10s., and he ordered they should spend five marks in table cloths and other necessaries for the feast.

It was not long after this, however, before the Guild fell on evil days. The dissolution of the monasteries by Henry VIII was followed by the suppression and confiscation of the revenues of the chantries by Edward VI. At that time the Prittlewell Guild held sixty acres of arable land near Shopland, called Reynoldes, and twelve acres of land in North Shoebury, known as Palgraves, both legacies, and the latter of which had been left to them by John Quyk, of Prittlewell, in 1469. The report of the Commissioners of Edward VI, dated 14th February, 1548, consisted of a return of the "lands and tenements in Pritwell put in feoffment by two wardens, one master and one priest and certain bretherne and sisterne there, to divers persons, to find a priest called a Jesus Priest there for ever, by licence of King Edward IV. And one, Sir William Rowbothum, clerk, of the age of fifty-two years, of honest conversation and teacheth a school there, having none other living, is now incumbent thereof. The said town is a populous town, having in it 300 houseling people. The said priest singeth within the said church of Prittlewell." The yearly value of the property was returned at £7 14s. gross and £6 14s. 3d. net, together with 46½ozs. of plate, which included twenty-four silver spoons, and other implements valued at £4 5s. 2d. Rowbothum swore he had ten marks paid him annually by the wardens and, therefore, could declare nothing. The property was seized by the Crown, and in the same year Walter Farre and Ralph Standysshe, of London, bought a large quantity of chantry land in Essex for £821 11s. 9d. and this included the estate lately belonging to the Guild. The institution at Prittlewell did not last long. Licensed in 1478, it disappeared in 1540—after an existence of only sixty-eight years.

A Curious Will.

An instance of the manner in which property was disposed of in the Fifteenth Century is contained in the will of Swete (mentioned above) who was a tenant of Chalkwell Hall. He disposed of his property after "considering with becoming meditation the condition of weak human nature in this vale of misery," and went on : " I, therefore, wishing, as far as is allowed by the Supreme Maker of the world, to take precautions, and not wishing to leave my goods conferred upon me by God undevoted to the praise and honour of my Creator Himself, for the health of my soul, this xiiith day of the month of August, in the year of our Lord, 1443, concerning my goods bestowed upon me, make my last will in this manner. In the first place, I give and commend my soul to the Most High God, my Creator, who redeemed me on the cross by His precious blood, and to the Glorious Virgin Mary, His mother, and to all the saints that they will deign mercifully to receive my said soul when it has departed from this life into everlasting joy, by the merits and prayers of which saints I firmly believe on the day of judgment my merits and demerits will be effaced. My body to be buried in the churchyard aforesaid (St. Mary's, Prittlewell) near my parents. Also I leave to the high altar for my tithes, negligently forgotten, 6s. 8d. and three sheep to be driven before my body on the day of my burial." This latter provision was known as a mortuary offered in kind. Sheep were often utilized for this purpose in this part of Essex and became known as a "foredrove." The list of property devised shows Swete to have been a man of substantial means, probably largely derived from sheep farming, for he had over 300 on Foulness Island and others at Havengore and Templegore. Many other wills of this period were couched in similar phraseology.

Was there a Market Cross?

In the will of John Cocke, of Little Stambridge Hall,

dated 1574, he makes the following bequest : "To the building of the market cross of Pritwell, 100/-." No record or
trace of this structure exists, so that it is probable the testator's
beneficent donation was transferred to other channels.

The Field of the Cloth of Gold.

Henry VIII's celebrated meeting with the King of
France in 1520, since known in history as the Field of the
Cloth of Gold, is of particular interest to this locality because
the oak forests hereabouts furnished some of the wood with
which, at any rate, one of the ships of Henry's fleet was built.
Among the items of expense of making the "Katherine
Plesaunce," "for transporting the King to Calais," Peter
Coliar was paid 14s. for the carriage of fourteen loads of
timber for trenails from Benfleet to Deptford. William Cotyll
was also reimbursed 33s. 9d. for the wages of eleven carpenters
at 4d. and 6d. a day, who had been employed hewing timber
in Thundersley Park and the ground of the Prior of St. Mary,
Spitals. For the conveyance of the timber to Benfleet, from
which port, no doubt, it was floated to Deptford, thirty-one
carts were employed at a cost of 4d. a piece. It is interesting
to note that in a certificate of musters taken at Billericay in
1539, South Benfleet was reported to have fifty men capable
of bearing arms, so that, as the size of places went in those
times, this port must have been of some importance.

Duke of Norfolk and the Possibility of Invasion.

As a sidelight upon the fear of invasion by France, which
still existed, there is a letter extant from the Duke of Norfolk
to Mr. Secretary Paget, in 1545, in which the former stated
that he had, according to instructions, been along the sea coast
on the Essex side as far as Shoebury. He was accompanied by
the gentlemen of the locality, and, after inspection, came to
the conclusion that there was no great danger of the enemy
landing there ; the country being very strong in hedges and

ditches. " I think the most hurt they can do is to burn a
town of mine called Prittlewell and another small town called
Lee." The Duke was then owner of the manor of Earls-fee
with Polsted Wic.

Anne Boleyn and Rochford Hall.

Tradition of the most romantic colouring is existent in the
Hundred connecting Rochford Hall with Anne Boleyn and her
conquest of the affections of Henry VIII. There is little beyond
conjecture, based, however, upon good ground, to suggest for
her an intimate connection with this Hundred. Anne Boleyn
was the younger daughter of Thomas Boleyn, who inherited the
Rochford Hall estate from the Ormond family. Sir Thomas
was a man of much distinction in his day, being employed on
several important embassies and is said on one occasion to have
refused to kiss the Pope's toe upon being granted audience.
Boleyn rose successively in rank to Viscount Rochford, Earl of
Wiltshire and Earl of Ormond ; the viscountcy being assumed
as a courtesy title by his son. The family sprang originally
from Norfolk and, coming to London, amassed considerable
wealth in commerce. Anne Boleyn's birthplace has never been
incontrovertibly settled. Tradition hereabouts says that she
was born at Rochford Hall, but the family possessed two other
seats, Bickling Hall, in Norfolk, and Hever Castle, in Kent.
Most of the children came into the world at the latter place and
it is not improbable that Anne herself was born there. What
is most likely, however, is that Anne was a frequent visitor to
Rochford and the tradition as to her having a bower at the Hall
may have some foundation. Norden, in his map of Essex, prepared in 1594, shows that the royal park of Rayleigh was only
a short distance away from the park of the Boleyns. Henry
was passionately addicted to hunting, and for that purpose
came frequently into Essex. That he knew Rayleigh park
well may be gathered from the instructions which he gave
under his signet in 1525 for the creation of a great lawn there

ROCHFORD HALL (NORTH SIDE).

from " the west syde of the grete ponde," and in his privy expenses is an item of £74 12s. 4d. for presents to my lady Anne, " of Rochford." It is, therefore, a reasonable assumption that Rochford Hall provided an admirable retreat whereat Henry could avow his passion. After six years of ardent wooing and intrigue with the Pope for the dissolution of his marriage with Catherine of Aragon, Henry obtained judgment in 1533 from Archbishop Cranmer's Court, nullifying his previous marriage, and a declaration that his union with Anne, whom he had married five days earlier, was lawful. On June 1st she was crowned Queen and three months later gave birth to a daughter. " Chapuys, the Spanish Ambassador, scarcely considered the matter worth mention. The King's ' amie' had given birth to a bastard, a detail of little importance to anyone, and least of all to a monarch like Charles V. Yet the ' bastard' was Queen Elizabeth, and the child, thus ushered into a contemptuous world, lived to humble the pride of Spain, and to bear to a final triumph the banner which Henry had raised." As to the Queen's beauty, there were varying opinions. A Venetian wrote that " Madame Anne is not one of the handsomest women in the world. She is of middling stature, swarthy complexion, long neck, wide mouth, bosom not much raised, and in fact has nothing but the King's great appetite, and her eyes, which are black and beautiful." Her early friend and admirer, Sir Thomas Wyatt, addressed many sonnets in praise of her loveliness, and he described her eyes as " sunbeams to daze men's sight." She had, without doubt, a mole on her neck and a defect in a nail of one of her fingers.

Anne's Execution.

Anne was destined to only three years of regal union. Henry's lightsome love turned to others of the fair sex, and as the warmth of his affection waned, so he found in his wife reasons for his change of feeling. He objected to the flippancy

D

of her conduct with certain courtiers and the arrogance of her
demeanour. Many of the leading families of the day were
jealous of the growing power of the Boleyns, and it is not
unlikely that the Queen largely owed her fall to their machin-
ations. The blow fell upon her suddenly, for on 2nd May,
1536, she was arrested without warning and sent to the
Tower. She was accused of incest with her brother, Lord
Rochford, and of intercourse with four others, all of whom
were arrested. The men were tried, condemned to death,
and executed, though none confessed guilt, save Smeaton, who
was a musician. Lord Rochford was a sonneteer of much
skill and elegance and the night before his death composed
some verses, entitled "Farewell, my Lute." On the scaffold
he "made a very Catholic address to the people, saying he
had not come there to preach, but to serve as a mirror and an
example, acknowledging his sins against God and the King."
Three days later the Queen was put upon her trial before a
panel of twenty-six peers, presided over by her uncle, the
Duke of Norfolk. A unanimous verdict of guilty was returned
and she subsequently met her death bravely, proclaiming her
innocence. When she heard that an executioner had been
brought over from St. Omer to cut off her head she is said to
have laughed heartily and, putting her hands round her small
neck, to have observed how easy the executioner's task would
be. She was not permitted to bid farewell to her daughter
Elizabeth, then nearly three years old, and sent a farewell
message to the King that he had made her a Marchioness and
a Queen and now gave her innocency the Crown of martyrdom. On the day of execution, Anne gave Margaret Lee,
Sir Thomas Wyatt's sister, a book of devotions bound in gold,
as a farewell gift, and so overcome were her attendants that
they could not remove her neck attire and she had to perform
the task herself. She died bravely at the age of 36. It is not
known where her remains were buried. Two years later,
Anne's father died and Rochford Hall passed to Mary Boleyn.

She had previously married William Carey, who died in 1528, and was subsequently united to Sir William Stafford, with whom she lived in retirement at Rochford Hall until her death, when the estate came to the Carey family. Her son, Henry Carey, Lord Hunsdon, had a distinguished career under Elizabeth, and his youngest son, Sir Robert Carey, was the first to convey the news of the death of Elizabeth to James I.

Anne of Cleves and Katherine Howard.

This district also had connection with two others of Henry's wives. The ill-favoured and unfortunate Anne of Cleves, so soon married and so soon divorced, was granted, as part of her allowance, Hadleigh Castle, the fishery of Hadleigh Ray and the draggings for mussels in Tilbury Hope. A year later she received, among other property, the manors of Hockley and Paglesham and some marshes in Canewdon, "in consideration of her willingness to remain in England and that she accepts the law of the realm and is content to renounce her marriage with the King." Her Hadleigh possessions were bestowed upon Katherine Howard, Henry's fifth wife ; who quickly forfeited his favour and was executed in 1542, after two years of married life, on charges of immorality. These do not appear to have possessed the elements of doubt which so strongly favoured Anne Boleyn.

The Reformation.

Large portions of the agricultural land of the Hundred were held by clerical proprietors and, consequently, the organic ecclesiastical change of the Sixteenth Century had a profound effect. This district, as befitted its connection with Anne Boleyn, who was reputed to have been a supporter of the Reformers, was greatly in favour of the change, and right through the long years of religious unrest which followed the Reformation—the Rebellion, the Restoration, the Revolution —until the present day, the Hundred has been in the main

Protestant and Free Church. For many years prior to the reign of Henry VIII there had been a growing feeling in the nation that the monastic lands should be expropriated and used for the benefit of the laity. This agitation, fomented by the greed of the nobles, was aided by the abuses which existed in many of the foundations. Therefore, when Henry, piqued at the Pope's refusal to divorce him from his first wife, Katherine of Aragon, sundered the connection of the English Church with that of Rome and substituted a National Church, with the Sovereign as its head, he had largely the sentiment of the nation in his favour. Formal severance of relations with the Pope and the placing of the King of England under an interdict were quickly followed by the appointment of commissioners to enquire into the condition of the monasteries and nunneries, the formal step prior to their dissolution.

Dissolution of Prittlewell Priory.

Prittlewell Priory was among the first to go under. The report upon it showed that it contained only seven monks and was of the annual value of £155. When suppressed, the prior was pensioned off with £20 per year. The inventory of the goods of the Priory was made by the King's Commission on June 8th, 1536; the parties being Sir John Seyntclere, knight; Humfrey Browne, serjeant-at-law; Francis Jobson and Thomas Myldemaye, commissioners to the King, and Thomas Norwiche, the prior. The goods and chattels were to be safely kept to the use of the King. The debts due to the house were £6, there was £3 14s. 8d. in ready money and apparently a clear value in goods of £143 9s. 11d. From this inventory we gather there were seven chambers or bedrooms, each specially named; they were the Great Chamber, the Draught Chamber, New Chamber, Lumberdy (or Lombardy) Chamber, Italy Chamber, Pennys Chamber and the Butler's and Porter's Room. If we take the Great Chamber we have a typical instance of the way the bedroom of the comparatively well-to-do was fitted up in those days. The room was hung with green "saye," or serge (not many years later to become a distinctively Essex production, owing to the Flemish immigration, consequent upon Spanish persecution) with a painted border. There was a tester containing a feather bed, together with carpets, cushions of carpet work, a table standing in the window and another with leaves, half-a-dozen stools, a chair, a cupboard painted green, a candleholder and a set of fire irons. The bedding consisted of a coverlet of tapestry, bolster and pillow, pair of sheets and pair of woollen blankets. The other rooms also had feather beds, except two, which were furnished with flock beds. The ornamental colour schemes were not intricate, for the Draught Chamber was hung with old stained cloth and the New Chamber with yellow and red linen, having a painted border. The hall furniture was not of much value, the chief item being four tables with trestles and forms, probably used for the purposes of feeding the poor. In the pantry the table silver was not plentiful, a silver salts and one dozen silver spoons being the chief items, together with a stock of drapery and plain linen table cloths, towels and napkins. The kitchen, when the utensils were cleaned up and polished, presented a bright appearance with its array of burnished brass pots, pans and kettles, and its frying pans, dripping pans, chafing dishes, saucers, porringers and colanders, and last, but not least, "three greate spitts and a byrd spitt." In the napery store there were only four pairs of sheets. The list of farmyard stock showed that the monastery possessed five carts with a small stock of hay and barley. The brewhouse and bakehouse were well fitted up and there was a fair quantity of live stock. There were seventeen horses, sixteen head of cattle, 119 sheep, forty lambs at 7d. and thirty-six at 8d., together with a pack of wool and some odd pounds of the same material. Wool was an important article of export to Flanders, then under Spanish dominion, and one reason for hostilities not breaking

out between Spain and England over the celebrated divorce
suit was our intimate commercial relationship with the
Lowlanders, too valuable to be lightly disturbed either by
Henry VIII or Charles V.

The Ecclesiastical Fittings.

Attached to the monks' residence was the church, and
this contained a lady chapel and a rood chapel, whilst there
were also altars to St. John and St. Thomas, and a choir and
vestry.   In most of these there were tables of alabaster, and in
the Lady Chapel and Choir, a pair of "organes," valued at
46s. 8d.   There were several sacring bells.   The communion
silver was complete and they also possessed a cross of silver and
gilt.   The stock of vestments was extensive ; several of them
being made either of red satin with flowers of gold, silk or red
and green damask.   There was also a small chapel beside the
Prior's Chamber hung with red cloth.   The inventory, therefore, affords evidence that the monastery was well found for
the purposes of worship and also well provided with the things
of this life.

Priory Lands Under Other Owners.

The Priory was granted, on its dissolution, to a member
of the Audley family, on "the humble petition and request "
of Sir Thomas Audley, Lord Chancellor, one of King Henry
VIII's favourite ministers, the fortunate owner's younger
brother.   In consideration of the payment of £40 (say, £800
in modern value) Audley became possessed of the "house and
site lately the Priory of Prittlewell, otherwise Pritelwell, in
our County of Essex, suppressed and dissolved by authority of
Parliament, and also the whole church and the lead upon it
and the belfry and the cemetery of the former priory and all
its messuages, houses, buildings, stables, dovecots, yards,
orchards, gardens, waters, ponds, fish stews, lands and soil
beneath the surface and existing in round about and to the

said Priory and all our lordship and manor called Priours Manour with its appurtenances at Prytewell." Audley was also given the manorial rights and other privileges belonging formerly to the monks, including the right of presentation to Prittlewell Church. Beside this he secured Horsleigh Woode, South Bryge Wood, West Bryge Wood, Northbrigge Wood Sherberne Grove in Prittlewell, and also land in Eastwood, Hadleigh and Leigh. Audley did not retain his holding long, for a few years afterwards the property was acquired by the powerful Rich family, soon to assume the famous Warwick title. The Riches bought land in this Hundred by parishes and also secured large estates in Mid-Essex. Although their principal seat was Leighs Priory, the successive generations of the family were constantly at Rochford Hall, and they transformed the old residence into one of the finest mansions of that age.

It was probably soon after the dissolution of the Priory and the consequent changes in the ownership of the soil that Porter's Grange was built, a Tudor hall, lying near All Saints' Church. It is one of the few examples that remain locally of that unique age of house building. A London merchant, named Browne, built it and his family occupied it for many generations. The name Porters is believed to be derived from a former owner of the soil, for in the Thirteenth Century a Porter held land hereabouts. Porter's Grange has, of course, given its name to Porter's Town—one of the first districts to be built on when the town began to feel the beneficial effect of railway communication.

John Frith's Attempt to Escape from Milton Shore.

In 1534, there was apprehended at Milton Shore—a well-known place of departure for the Continent in the Sixteenth and Seventeenth Centuries, situate between Leigh and Southend—John Frith, one of the earliest martyrs of the Reformation. He was educated at Cambridge and subsequently joined the college founded by Cardinal Wolsey, now known as Christchurch, to study for the Roman Catholic priest- hood. The doctrines of Luther, then beginning to move the civilized world, took strong hold of the young man and his adherence to them led to the Dean of the College (Higden) imprisoning Frith and others in a deep cave underground, where the salt fish of the college was kept. Some died from the effects of their confinement, but the youthful Protestant escaped, only, however, to fall athwart ecclesiastical authority by reason of his heretical opinions concerning purgatory, tran- substantiation and consubstantiation. He further incensed the Government by his effective intervention in a controversy with which Sir Thomas More, the celebrated author of "Utopia," was concerned. More denounced Frith as an obstinate heretic. It was then that he made his unsuccessful attempt to escape to the Continent. He was arrested at Milton, accused before Cromwell and examined by Cranmer. He was condemned, with another, to be burned in a slow fire at Smithfield ; the execution taking place on July 22nd, 1534. Frith embraced the faggots and exhorted his companion to trust in God. They were in acute agony for two hours before their death, owing to the wind blowing the flames away from them and thus preventing their suffocation.

Notable Beneficiaries.

The immense amount of landed property placed at the disposal of the King by the suppression of the religious houses was the supreme opportunity for favoured courtiers. In this Hundred many acres changed hands. Lord Cromwell, suc- cessor to Cardinal Wolsey in the office of chief minister, the contriver of this ecclesiastical revolution, was appointed steward of the Honour of Rayleigh and bailiff of the Hundred of Rochford. It was whilst holding this office that Cromwell was approached by Cranmer, the celebrated Archbishop and martyr, on behalf of a Rayleigh rector, who sought exchange to the benefice of Sutton. Cromwell was granted land at Hockley, formerly belonging to Barking Abbey, and also land in North and South Benfleet and Bowers Gifford, which had been held by St. Osyth Priory. William Lord Parr succeeded to Cromwell's offices in this Hundred upon the latter's execution, Sir Thomas Seymour became possessed of monastery lands in Great and Little Wakering, and other ecclesiastical property passed to minor gentry in Rawreth, Foulness Island and Rochford, and land in different parts of the County belonging to Prittlewell Priory.

Church Property Seized and Sold.

An incident of note occurred in the short reign of Edward VI. Protestant feeling was overwhelmingly in the ascendant and there was consequently a considerable sale of church plate and other articles of value. There was hardly a parish in the Hundred in which the authorities did not realize comparatively large sums of money, which were variously stated to have been used either in church repairs, the repair of highways and bridges, the support of the poor, or the equipment of the King's soldiers. At Rayleigh the churchwardens sold two silver basins "parcelgilt" for £9 3s., and devoted the proceeds to church repair ; at Great Stambridge the parish authorized the sale of a salver for £2 and of certain deacon's garments for 6s. 8d., the money to be expended in repair of the church ; at Prittlewell the large sum of £37 16s. was received for a silver-gilt monstrance, three cruets, a censer and two boxes ; South Benfleet disposed of five marks' worth of plate and spent it in repairing the fabric and in equipping soldiers for the wars ; the latter task admirably suiting that busy seaport, which in Henry VIII's reign had fifty men capable of bearing arms. Other sales are also reported, and Leigh obtained £8 6s. 8d. by this means, Canewdon £26 15s. 8d., and Prittlewell £56 5s. 7d. In such a time of unrest robbery was also not infrequent. The most daring and impudent of these was by a landowner, named Sir William Stafford (husband of Mary Boleyn, previously mentioned), who seized the church bells of Rochford, Ashingdon, South Shoebury and Foulness Island, and only in the latter case is there record of the proceeds being devoted to the public benefit, viz., the repair of the sea walls there.   The Essex Commissioners who took inventories of the churches' possessions usually left for use a cope and vestment, and in this district " every church had its ' herse cloth ' or parish pall, and occasionally the ' care cloth,' which was the name for the bridal pall of fine linen held over the bride and bridegroom during their marriage mass."   In some parishes a cope and vestment were allowed and at Hockley a case for the holy oils was assigned for the use of the church.   At Rayleigh two chalices were left because the parish was great.

The Marian Persecution : Local Martyrs.

The persecution of Protestants by Mary in her vain attempt to coerce the people to Roman Catholicism was severely felt in the County, and one writer has asserted that " the religious annals of Essex prove the pre-eminence of that county in determined and earnest Protestant nonconformity." The south-eastern corner of the County did not suffer as did Colchester, seventy-eight of whose inhabitants were dragged from their homes and imprisoned in London, yet the persecution was very bitter.   Lord Riche, the chief landowner and a notorious character of those days, was the superintendent of the burning of heretics in Essex.   He was very active, yet when Elizabeth ascended the throne he was able to make his peace.   He died at Rochford Hall and was buried at Felsted, bequeathing a strongly Puritan succession, of which more will be heard later.   The first intimation of change was an order binding over John Hammond, of Prittlewell, Edward Berrye, of Eastwood, Francis Clopton, of Barling, and James Baker, of North Shoebury, in the sum of £100, to cause decent altars to be set up in the parish churches within a fortnight. The most important of these gentlemen, evidently Justices of the Peace, was Edward Berrye. His name constantly appears in the records of the time. First mention of him is found in the reign of Henry VIII, when he was granted the manor of Bulphan, formerly part of the estate of Barking Abbey. He evidently carried out the functions of his judicial office without regard to principle or sentiment, for he was thanked by the Privy Council, along with others of Rochford Hundred, "for coming so honestly and of themselves to Colchester and other places in the Shire and assisting the sheriff" at the executions, but this did not prevent him being just as active in the discharge of his duties in the reign of Elizabeth. Some idea of how widespread was the Protestant belief is to be gathered from the fact that of the eighty-nine Essex clergymen who were deprived of their benefices by Bishop Bonner during Queen Mary's reign, twelve held cure of souls hereabouts, viz., at Great Wakering, Eastwood, Ashingdon, Prittlewell, Foulness Island, Paglesham, Sutton, Shopland, Thundersley, Hockley, South Benfleet and North Shoebury. One of the most active of the Justices in apprehending heretics and forwarding them to Bishop Bonner for examination was Edward Tyrrell, sometime M.P. for Maldon. He was owner of a manor at Rawreth and was buried in Rawreth church, where a memorial brass records the fact. He was a fanatical adherent of the old faith, and he probably had a hand in the arrest of all the men mentioned below and others in different parts of Essex beside. The most touching story of persecution bravely endured was that of a curate of Hockley, named Tyms. He was deprived of his office by Mary, but subsequently returned and began preaching in the wood adjoining ; gathering to him a congregation of one hundred or more. He was betrayed to Tyrrell in 1555 and taken to London, in company with the rector of Thundersley, named Drake, and four others. At his examina-

tion by Bonner, he was charged with being a ringleader among
heretics. He refused to recant and was sentenced to death.
Whilst awaiting execution, he busied himself with correspondence with his former parishioners. To one of them,
named Glascock, after exhorting her to hold fast to the faith,
he wrote with his own blood these words : "Continue in
prayer, ask in faith, and obtain your desire. By me, W. Tyms,
in the King's Bench for the Gospel of Christ." In April,
1556, with his five fellow sufferers, he bravely met his death
at Smithfield stake. There were two similar executions at
Rayleigh. The first was in the early part of 1555, when
Thomas Causton, of Thundersley, was executed. So great
was popular feeling that he was led to the place of death
bound in a cart for fear of rescue. The second martyr was
John Ardeley, of Great Wigborough, and he suffered for his
faith on June 10th, at the same time as his companion in misfortune. John Sanson, husbandman, of the same place, was
similarly dealt with at Rochford. The examination of these
men by Bonner created great public excitement. Ardeley
told the Bishop that if every hair of his head was a man he
would suffer death for the opinion and faith he professed.
Both men were willing to give the Queen all their goods and
lands provided they might be permitted to live with free con-
sciences. Suspected heretics were incarcerated on arrest at
Rayleigh gaol, and in 1557 the gaoler there had to clear himself before the Privy Council of a charge that he had permitted
one of these to evade his custody. In Elizabeth's reign the
rector of Little Stambridge (a living since amalgamated with
Great Stambridge) was deprived for refusing to subscribe
to the oath of supremacy. Recently a movement was successfully inaugurated to commemorate the local martyrs by a
granite obelisk, erected in the main street at Rayleigh. It was
unveiled on Wednesday, September 23rd, 1908, by Mr. Rowland Whitehead, M.P., in the presence of a crowd of over
2,000 people.

An Escape and a Prophecy.

In Queen Mary's reign, Milton Shore again came prominently before the authorities, for it was from there that Dr. Sandys, Vice-Chancellor of Cambridge University, sailed to Flanders. He was implicated in the unsuccessful and tragic rising of Lady Jane Grey, arrested, but escaped from the Tower. He made his way, probably by water, to Milton Shore and concealed himself in the house of a shipmaster, named Mower, evidently a prosperous man, for an immediate descendant of his was elevated to a baronetcy. His arrival, however, became noised abroad. The good doctor thought it expedient to make himself known, explain the facts to the maritime populace and rely upon their loyalty to enable him to escape. So successful was his advocacy that his cause was warmly espoused, but he only narrowly escaped recapture, for the vessel was just sailing away when the Queen's messengers came in sight. When Sandys left he said to the wife of his protector, who had been married eight years and was still childless, "Be of good comfort, ere one year be past, God will give you a son," and tradition has it that within the twelve months Mower was blessed with an heir. With the death of Mary, Sandys returned to England and subsequently became Archbishop of York.

A Poetical Refugee.

Milton Shore was connected with yet another incident in these restless days. In Elizabeth's reign, a Catholic, named Tyrrell, who had offended the Government of the time by an outspoken expression of his opinions, sought to escape to Dunkirk or Bruges from this coast. His secret was not well kept and he was taken back to London and there incarcerated in Fleet Prison. He made his peace with the authorities and was released, but they never trusted him and in 1587 he made his home in Amsterdam. The following lines were said to have been composed by him whilst impatiently wandering on the shore, fretting at the unpropitious state of the weather, which prevented his departure :

> Lyke as a marchawnt, wch on surginge seas
> In beaten barcke hathe fellt the grevous rage
> Of Aolus blasts, tyll Neptune for hys eas
> Bye princelye power thear cholars did asswage
>   Even soe my muse
>
> Doth seeme by fortunes cruell spyte
> To feel her cupp so myxt wth bytter galle,
> As noe conceapt coulld make her to delyght
> Untyll she chawnst in scholoshypp to fall
>   W^th you, my ffrend
>
> Whom myghtye Jove hathe sent me for relefe,
> When heavye cares woolld seek for to oppres
> My pensyff mynd and slylye as a theffe
> Holld me captyve styll in sore dystres.

The Rise of Leigh, Milton and Other Local Ports.

Constant references in the records of the past to local ports betoken the commercial importance of this Hundred. It is a branch of local historical study which has never been thoroughly followed, and no record of this country-side can be adequate or complete which does not linger awhile upon our connection with the busy maritime world lying beyond the Estuary of the Thames. The attention of the historian has been almost entirely attracted to the deeds of the men of the West Country in the great age of dauntless effort which was ushered in with the Sixteenth Century, but the men of the Thames shore were just as enterprising and as brave as the men of Devon. The Renaissance and the Reformation did much to free the intellect and give rein to the imagination. The discovery of America provided an outlet for the marvellous activity in warfare, commerce and colonization which subsequently developed. The discovery of gold in the new land conjured up visions of fair cities glowing in the burnished splendour of the precious metal. The Spaniard endeavoured to preserve for his own

uses this rich treasure and the profits of trading with the
natives. This led to innumerable conflicts on the high seas,
when the English privateers—manned by men animated by
inveterate hatred of their opponents, and also, it must be said,
by greed of gold—lay in wait for the galleons and more often
than not carried them as prizes into English ports. This war
upon the seas was the training ground for the seamen who
were later to overthrow the Armada. To other men the discovery of the new Continent gave opportunities for visionary
schemes for the foundation of states and cities rivalling those
of the old world, but better adapted to improved modes of
living and of government, with no restrictions upon learning and the free play of intellect. In those days of feverish
enthusiasm and fierce activity the port most frequently mentioned hereabouts was that of Leigh. It rapidly grew in
importance during the Fourteenth Century, became of national
consequence in the Fifteenth and flourished thereafter for two
hundred years. It was within easy distance of the Continent
and a large share of the trade with France and the Low
Countries was carried on in ships that gave Leigh as their port
of origin, though usually owned by London merchants.
Further, the mouth of the Thames grew increasingly valuable
strategically. During the long and bitter struggle with Spain,
the latter's possession of Holland rendered it an excellent
shelter for privateers keen to attack English commerce passing
to the North or up the Thames itself. When Spain's power
had been humbled, the rise of the Dutch to maritime empire
and the constant warfare which ensued with them for naval
pre-eminence made the protection of the Estuary of paramount
importance. Again, expeditions fitted out in London and
Gravesend required a port of call at the mouth of the River
prior to their final departure. The benefit of these consider-
ations was, as we shall see, largely reaped by Leigh. The town
must have been of considerable size and if it be asked, "Where
are the traces of its former houses?" an explanation may be

suggested in the fact that though two charters, dated 1579 and 1608, mentioned certain tenements abutting on the King's highway, to-day neither the houses nor the King's highway exist, so quickly may traces of former occupation disappear.

First, let us note its growth as a shipping centre. As early as the Fifteenth Century, Leigh possessed a guild of pilots intimately associated with a similar institution at Deptford ; the Leighmen taking charge of the inward bound ships, whilst Deptford provided pilots for the outward bound. Both guilds were incorporated by Henry VIII as the Fraternity of the Most Glorious and Indivisible Trinity and of St. Clement. An incentive to Leigh shipbuilding was provided by Henry VII, who commenced a bounty system under which an occasional tonnage allowance was made to builders of new ships suitable for use as war vessels. Under Elizabeth the practice settled into a grant of five shillings per ton on all vessels over 100 tons. In 1564-5, Leigh was returned as having thirty-one vessels, with thirty-two masters and owners, 230 mariners and fishermen. Barling came next with twenty-three vessels, fifteen masters and owners and forty-eight mariners and fishermen. Prittlewell had ten ships, fourteen masters and owners and thirty-six mariners and fishermen ; South Benfleet, five vessels, with a similar number of masters and fifteen seamen ; North Shoebury coming last with one vessel and master and a crew of four. This return showed to what an extent shipbuilding and commerce had thriven, for this district provided one-third of the vessels trading from Essex ports, and over one-half the crews. A register of coasting ships, made seven or eight years afterwards, gave Leigh a fleet of forty, of which twenty-seven were between fifty and 100 tons. Milton Shore (part of Prittlewell Parish) had three of the bigger ships, with five of twenty tons and under, whilst Barling, Hullbridge and Canewdon had two each of the smaller vessels. About the same time, Leigh was said to have built one ship of 140 ton and two of 130. In 1572 another return was drawn, probably of vessels and crews at home at that time, and Leigh was given fourteen ships and eighty men. In 1581 the Trinity House examiner reported no increase of vessels at Leigh ; but this cannot be reconciled with the fact that a year later the Spanish Ambassador gave Philip the information that Leigh had built two vessels of 100 tons and upwards ; two between eighty and 100 tons were owned there, together with twenty-seven under eighty tons. Moreover, a bounty was paid on the "Speedwell," of Leigh, of 105 tons, which was built in 1579. Prittlewell also had seven ; Little Wakering six, and Paglesham six. Leigh felt, too, the great expansion of oversea commerce which followed the destruction of the Armada, for in 1594 a bounty was paid on the "Vineyard" of 240 tons, "Merry Edward" of 190, "Ruby" of 280, the "Mary Ann" of 302, and the "Salamander" of 180 ; showing that the demand for ships was also accompanied by increased tonnage. These were not all the vessels launched in that year, for a warrant was issued to the Exchequer to strike a tally on the customs of the Port of London for 686 crowns for John Goodlad, John Bridecake and Richard Harris, of Leigh, towards the cost of building three ships, the money to be taken from the customs due for merchandise brought in by the ships. In the same year two more warrants were issued ; one for 640 crowns for Richard and William Goodlad and Lawrence Moore, of Leigh, for three ships, and the other for 620 crowns to William Hand, Robert Salmon and John Skinner, also of Leigh, for a further three. In 1597 the "Pleasaunce" and "Dainty," each of 310 tons, and in 1599, the "Globe," 340, also received the bounty.

From a mercantile as well as a shipbuilding point of view, Leigh and district also rose rapidly in importance. Several of the Admiralty Courts were held at Milton Shore. In 1543 a precept was issued summoning the jurors from South Benfleet to attend an Admiralty Court at Milton. The

E

bailiff and constable of the place were warned, under penalty of
a fine of £5, to "admonish six, four, or two at the least, honest
men of that parish to appear before the Lord High Admiral of
England, or his deputy, at the King's Court of the Admiralty,
to be holden at Milton, in the said County of Essex." This
notice was signed by Richard Reed, commissary, probably the
same man who acted as valuer in a case mentioned below.
In a presentment to the Court as to goods found derelict,
dated 1539, we note that on the 28th June of that year, John
Scott, of Milton Shore, mariner, found an ownerless ship's
boat of three tons burden at the South Deep, opposite Minster, in the Isle of Sheppey. He secured it and had it valued
at 30s. by Richard Reed, Richard Pulter, William Murdock
and Thomas Byam, all mariners, of Milton Shore, and William
Norman, mariner, of London. The boat was afterwards sold
to William Damyn, of Foulness Island, for 36s. 8d. According to the laws of the sea Scott paid one half of the purchase
money to the Lord High Admiral and gave security he would
pay over the other half to the Court should anyone prove
ownership within a year and a day, less his expenses. A
curious case of piracy was tried before an Admiralty Court in
1540. It arose on the petition of a London fisherman,
named Sharp, and was directed against one, Pope, of Leigh.
Sharp alleged that at Easter, 1539, he was in a peter boat
coming towards Leigh to buy victuals, when he was called by
Pope, who said, "Come on land." He came ashore, supposing the latter to require some fish, but as soon as he
arrived, Pope hauled the boat on to the land and then took
a peck of fish, giving Sharp the rest, "which were but few and
all the smallest and worst." The fisherman asked for some
recompense, but got for reply, "What! Knave! Shall I never
rid the country of you?" Sharp alleged that he and others
had been misused several times, but it was stated in defence
that the fish were taken from a creek in the manor of Leigh,
which belonged to William Stafford, and over which he had

rights of jurisdiction. A petition was filed in 1544 in the Admiralty Court by John Cocke, the elder, and John Cocke, the younger, mariners, of Leigh, against a ship named the "Olyvant," belonging to John Camp, of Hadleigh. In the early part of the year the "Olyvant," whilst lying at anchor off Prittlewell, damaged certain ropes, tackle and merchandise to the value of £4 17s., belonging to a ship owned by the Cockes, named the "Anthony," of London, laden with grain for Antwerp. Camp had neglected to pay the amount of damage and the ship was seized ; the petitioners praying for an order giving them possession.

Disputes respecting the seizure of Leigh vessels and their cargoes were of constant occurrence and occasionally assumed an international character. In 1542 John Wright, grocer, of London, owning the "Katharine," of Leigh, loaded it in Flanders with twenty-six lasts of herring for France. The customs officer at Rye seized her on suspicion of illicit trading. She was released on the owner giving security to produce the safe conduct for the journey from the Emperor (presumably Charles V), which he did. To aid in the unsuccessful succour of Calais, when besieged by the French in Queen Mary's reign, a general licence was issued to all subjects to trade with Calais, and Leigh was named immediately after Ipswich in the Essex and Suffolk list. A year later Sir H. Willoughby's squadron, which tried to find the North-East passage to Cathay, stopped in Leigh Road before finally sailing upon a quest from which they never returned, for they were afterwards found in Greenland frozen to death. Leigh, Foulness and Wakering were returned as seaports in 1565, and the examiner of customs at Harwich said of the first-named : "It is a very proper town, well furnished with good mariners, where commonly tall ships do ride, which town is a common and special landing place for butter, all manner of grain and other things." It was about this time that Leigh was granted a trade and customs officer. An interesting international

incident was the capture, in 1575, of the "Mayflower," of
Leigh, by the celebrated " Beggars of the Sea." She belonged
to a London merchant and the Privy Council made strong
remonstrances to the Prince of Orange for its return. An
amusing controversy arose between the citizens of London and
Leigh over the subject of beer. What the precise details of the
quarrel were is not clear, but the Privy Council were appealed
to and on December 8th, 1573, they solemnly decreed that
Leigh could have from London four tuns of beer a week ;
Edward Berry, of whom we have heard before, being appointed
to issue the necessary certificate that it had safely arrived.

The Armada : A Naval Base.

For military purposes Leigh and her shipping were constantly used. In 1514, when Henry VIII was waging war
with France, Captain Adrian Duncan, of the "Peter," of
Leigh, was allowed £22 12s. for transporting thirteen soldiers
and two guns. In the war with France and Scotland, in
1557, Leigh supplied victualling transports, and when Norreys
and Drake sailed with a fleet to harass Spain, the town provided some of the hired merchantmen which accompanied
them. The threat of Spain to send a naval expedition,
later to become famous as the Armada, was long held
over the country. Preparations began in 1572, but it was not
until sixteen years after that the fleet was ready to sail. The
mouth of the Thames saw little of the fighting. When the
Spanish fleet had been chased out of the Channel; despair seized
them and instead of boldly endeavouring to secure the Estuary
and threaten London, they decided to go round Scotland on
their way home. In the stormy seas of the North most of
the surviving galleons were sunk or shattered upon the
rocks and it was only a remnant that crept back to Spain.
Tilbury—a town some twenty miles up river from Southend
—was designed to be the centre of resistance should an
attack be made on London. A great camp was formed

on July 23rd, 1588, and by August 4th, 20,000 men had been concentrated there. The object was to defend the Metropolis from the Duke of Parma's troops in Holland, which it had been arranged should be convoyed over by the Armada. This plan never fructified and, therefore, the Tilbury troops were not tested. The Essex levies were ordered to mobilize at Brentwood to the number of 4,000, and from that point were sent to Tilbury. The celebrated review of the troops by Queen Elizabeth is one of the most romantic episodes of our history. An incident, however, concerning her visit is not so well known and throws considerable light upon what an experienced general thought of this hastily collected army. Dr. Plume, a Maldon worthy of the early Seventeenth Century, records that whilst at Tilbury the Queen sent for General Norris—reputed the best soldier in the world at that time, except the Duke of Parma—and asked him what he thought of the camp. Had he ever seen such a sight before? The wily old soldier replied, "Madam, I see here never a fearful man but myself." His men were all confident and full of hope, but he knew the King of Spain would send over veterans, whilst he had only raw soldiers to meet them. On the other hand, there were some who had no fears on that score. Lord Leicester was a decided optimist and he greatly praised the appearance of the Essex men. Lord Hunsdon, another of the chief commanders of the forces, was owner of Rochford Hall. It is said of him that he had ambition to become the Earl of Ormond, but the offer was not made until he lay dying and he then observed, "If I was unworthy of these honours when living, I am unworthy of them now I am dying." There is little record of the preparations made in this Hundred, but the glimpses we have are exceedingly interesting. As early as 1571, the Commissioners of Musters for Essex wrote to the Privy Council giving an account of their measures to put the shore in a state to resist invasion. The quota of men needed for the Tilbury army was raised without trouble and, in addition, Leigh was joined with London in an assessment of eight ships and two pinnaces. Leigh fishing boats were deputed to keep watch and signal the approach of the Armada. As the Spaniards were creeping near the south-eastern coast, Captain William Burrow reported to Walsingham, the Secretary of State, that he was cruising between Sheppey and Essex to convey warning to the camp at Tilbury if the enemy arrived. County historians have asserted that John Vassal, London merchant and an Eastwood landowner, fitted out at his own expense two ships of war, named the "Samuel" and the "Little Toby," which he commanded in action against the Spaniard. It has since been found that of these vessels, the first named was paid for by the Queen and the second does not appear on the list at all. A big ship, called the "Toby," 250 tons, was supplied at the cost of the City of London. Thus a picturesque local legend is discounted, and it is to be regretted that the facts of history prove so often destructive to the romance of tradition.

In a memorandum of Sir Robert Cecil's, Leigh was reported, in 1590, to have shipping capable of transporting 300 men and of carrying provisions for four days. Two years later the seaport was one of four appointed for the embarkation of troops to invade Normandy. There was, however, a complaint in 1595 that fifty men were wanting in Captain Harris's trained band, partly caused by the immunities enjoyed by the inhabitants of Leigh and partly by the decay of able men in that part of the county. This was a decline from the standard of previous years, when, in 1569, the township provided weapons and armour for soldiers, powder and shot for their training and victuals for their sustenance, whilst ten inhabitants patriotically defrayed the cost of "two haquebutts and two morians," and a sum of 45s. was subscribed by the town for recruiting soldiers who were not required. When the Earl of Essex went to Cadiz, in 1595-6, and wrought great damage, there were Leigh vessels present, but without permission, though they shared in the plunder. Outbreak of trouble with France saw 1,000 men, raised in Bedford, Suffolk, Norfolk and Essex, embark at Leigh in 1598, and a year later the Essex contingent of 400 men, to replace veterans serving in the Netherlands, was shipped there. With the advent of James an important period of local as well as national history was brought to a close. But only temporarily, for with the advent of the long, grim and deadly struggle with the Dutch, Leigh again became an important naval centre. In 1589 Fynes Moryson embarked at Leigh on the first of his travels on the Continent ; his experiences, published in book form as " Fynes Moryson's Travels," being read with appreciation in the present day.

A Great Journey.

There is a further incident connected with this period of which Leighmen may be for ever proud. In 1589, a year after the Armada, Andrew Battell, a native of Leigh, shipped in a little expedition of two vessels, the " May-Morning " and the " Dolphin," each of fifty tons, led by Abraham Cocke. Their destination was the River Plate ; obviously to prey upon Portuguese commerce from Brazil. Philip had, in 1580, become King of Portugal as well as of Spain, and the former country had also to suffer, for that reason, the persistent attacks of English seamen. Cocke was probably connected with the Cockes of Prittlewell and Leigh, a family which had then flourished for a century. He already possessed fame as an adventurer. In 1587 an expedition, organized by the Earl of Cumberland, fell in with a Portuguese vessel in the neigh- bourhood of the River Plate and in her found " Abraham Cock, of Leigh, near London." He was brought home and two years later he led the expedition now referred to, which Battell joined. The latter returned to Leigh about 1610, bringing with him a little negro boy, who claimed to have been the captive of a gorilla. The narrator of his story is the Rev. Samuel Parchas, vicar of Eastwood from 1604 to 1613, who

included it in "Purchas: His Pilgrimes," first published in
1625. The vessels spent some time cruising about St.
Thomas, in the West Indies, and then ran down to the River
Plate on the look-out for Portuguese vessels homeward bound
from Buenos Aires. They landed on the Isle of St. Sebastian,
near by, and whilst some engaged in fishing, others gathered
fruit. A party of Indians, landing on the other side of the
island, crept through the woods and captured five of the seamen, including Battell. They took them to Rio de Janeiro.
Cocke, after this disaster, put to sea and was never heard of
again. Battell and a companion were transported to the West
Coast of Africa, where the former began a series of adventures
and travels, the story of which "bears the stamp of truth and
has stood the test of time. It is unique, moreover, as being
the earliest of travels in the interior of this part of Africa, for
apart from a few letters of Jesuit missionaries, the references to
Kongo, or Angola, printed up to Battell's time, were either
confined to the coast or were purely historical or descriptive.
We are even able to claim on behalf of Battell that he travelled
by routes not since trodden by European explorers." On
arrival at the West Coast of Africa, he lay ill for eight months
at Luandu, situated between two and three hundred miles
south of the Congo. He attempted to escape on a Dutch
vessel, but was re-captured and then sent to the interior, where
he spent six miserable years. A second attempt to escape also
failed and was followed by three months' imprisonment in
irons in Luandu. A native rising in the interior enabled him
to exchange prison for service in the field. He was absent
from Luandu for three years and returned with a wound in
his right leg. When this injury had been cured, he was
employed by the Portuguese Governor for two years and a
half on trading trips up and down the coast. In the course of
one of these, well to the south of the Kongo, he joined a fighting tribe, named the Jagas, and he spent twenty-one months
with them. Battell was highly esteemed by the chief because

he killed many men with his musket, and in the numerous small wars in which the tribe engaged the Leighman was given important commands. In the course of one of these forays Battell came near to a Portuguese settlement, close by Luandu, and with the aid of negroes, who came to buy slaves, he escaped from the Jagas and once again entered the confines of civilization. He stayed with the Portuguese until the death of Queen Elizabeth was announced in 1606—three years after the event—and peace ensuing between England and Spain, he was promised his liberty. The Governor repented his assurance and Battell again escaped, this time making for the North. He suffered terrible privations. After living six months on dried flesh and fish in the forests near Luandu, he constructed a box, nailed with wooden pegs, and provided with a rail, so that the sea should not wash him out. With a blanket for a sail, in the company of two natives, he floated down the Bengo, a river a few miles to the north of Luandu. He safely journeyed to the sea and made efforts to reach Loango, a native kingdom some hundreds of miles up the coast. Happily, he came across a small trading vessel, the captain of which was a friend. At Battell's entreaty he took him to Loango, and there he remained three years, "well beloved of the King, because I killed him deer and fowls with my musket." It is not recorded by what means Battell came home, but he arrived at Leigh in 1610—twenty-one years after his departure. His subsequent movements are uncertain, but he probably lived in retirement until his death, which took place somewhere prior to 1625, because Purchas wrote the narrative from papers which came to him after Battell's death. Save for the information given by Purchas, nothing is known of Battell. There is no tombstone in the churchyard to his memory, neither is there anyone of the same name at present living in Leigh. Several old Leigh names have survived, but there are many that have shared the fate of Battell.

A Famous Cleric.

A word or two is necessary concerning the Rev. Samuel Purchas, the author referred to above, and whose contributions to the history of travel have earned him considerable post-humous fame. His works have recently been made accessible to an appreciative public by an ambitious scheme of republication, carried out by a Scottish firm. Purchas was the son of a yeoman and was born at Thaxted, in Essex, somewhere about the year 1576. He was educated at Cambridge, where he took the degree of M.A. in 1600 ; afterwards receiving the B.D. of Oxford. A year later he was the curate of Purleigh, and towards the end of 1601, he married a lady, named Lease, the daughter of a Suffolk yeoman. Three years later, on the presentation of the King, he became vicar of Eastwood. After ten years' residence there, he was appointed chaplain to Dr. Abbott, Archbishop of Canterbury, and Rector of St. Martin's, Ludgate ; his brother Thomas succeeding him in the living of Eastwood. Purchas spoke of this latter piece of preferment as having "delivered him from a sickly habitation," and joyfully declared it would give him "opportunities of bookes, conference and manifold intelligence, and as the benefice was not of the worst, so was it best suited in the world for his content." He only lived to enjoy his comfortable surroundings for a short space, for he died in 1626, twelve years after his removal from Eastwood and one year after the publication of "Purchas : His Pilgrimes."

Mr. H. W. King, in commenting upon Purchas's will, has written a short description of the position of Leigh of that day, which assists us to appreciate the more truly how Purchas became possessed of many narratives of the voyages which he chronicled : "Strange as it may appear, upon mere superficial investigation of Essex history, when Samuel Purchas took up his residence at Eastwood, it threw him into the society and into the very midst of a set of remarkable men, great voyagers and travellers such as I confidently believe he could have met with nowhere else in the Kingdom at that period. One such his friend and neighbour, John Vassall, who had visited Barbary, was then living at Coxethart, within a short walk of the parsonage. He is mentioned in the Pilgrimage. Careful examination of Purchas's folios and competent acquaintance with the family and documentary history of the district during the Sixteenth and Seventeenth Centuries will prove that this does not depend upon conjecture, but rests upon certain evidence. Leigh was in the Sixteenth and Seventeenth Centuries a place of considerable foreign trade. Its merchants were trading to, and its master mariners and seamen were visiting, France, Spain, Portugal and the Canaries, the Mediterranean, the Coast of Barbary, the River Plate, the East and West Indies and the Greenland Seas. Contemporary with Purchas and living there were the Moyers, the Salmons, the Goodlads, the Haddocks, the Bonners, the Harrises, the Hares, the Cockes, the Chesters and many others, some of whose names, as well as their letters and journals, are mentioned in the Pilgrimage." Many of these men are referred to in other parts of this book, but it is here interesting to note that of the Moyers, a grandson of Lawrence Moyer, of Leigh, was a merchant in the time of the Commonwealth and a Judge of the Court of Probate, whose eldest son, Samuel, was created a baronet. He died in 1716, when the title became extinct. Modern representatives of Lawrence Moyer's family were the late Simon, Earl Harcourt, and Dr. Vernon Harcourt, late Archbishop of York. In respect of the Hares, from John Hare, a Leigh mariner, who died in 1572, descended Francis Hare, successively Prebendary of St. Paul's, Dean of Worcester, Dean of St. Paul's, Bishop of St. Asaph, and finally Bishop of Chichester, who died in 1740.

Great Leigh Seamen.

Several Leigh families stand out prominently in the period which began with the Sixteenth Century and ended with the Eighteenth. They were all similar in origin and achieved prominence towards the close of the Fifteenth Century.

To take the Salmons first, Robert Salmon, who died in 1591, was, so far as we know, the first of his family to achieve more than local distinction. He was Master of Trinity House in 1588 and was much esteemed for his good qualities. His son, also named Robert, obtained an even greater reputation. Born in 1566, he married in 1598 a widow, who was sister of Andrews, Bishop of Winchester. Salmon was Master of Trinity House in 1617 and Sheriff of London in 1640. This would make it impossible for him to have been the Royalist who suffered so severely, financially, at the hands of Parliament. His eldest son, also named Robert, died in 1636, so he, too, was not the proscribed Royalist, unless a younger son was also named Robert. Robert Salmon, senior, died in 1641, and his memory was commemorated in Leigh Church by the following lines :

> Do (marble stone) preserve his name
> And be ye treasurer of his fame,
> But if thou fail his name will be,
> A lasting monument to thee.

He took a prominent part in the Greenland whale fishery and it is not unlikely that many of the whaling ships were fitted out and sailed by Leigh men. Salmon was in Greenland in 1618 and again in 1621. In the former year he wrote to "Master Sherwin," reporting the progress of whaling in Sir Thomas Smith's Bay, on behalf of the Greenland Company. He complained of the presence of 1,500 tons of Flemish shipping, which was competing with them, and although he admitted they were very kind to them, yet he requested that better ships should be sent out, so that "the knaves might be driven out of the country." He added, "We will let them rest this year and let who will take care the next year, for I hope not to trouble them." In 1619,

Robert Salmon, "Junior," wrote home, and the Flemish trouble was still unsettled. He understood there were eleven sail of Flemings and Danes in northern waters and doubted not that they would call them to account as to how many tons of oil they had made, as they, the Flemings, had done the previous year. " My love is such unto them that I protest I could wish with all my heart that we might go and see them and to spend my best blood in the righting of my former wrongs." Two years later he wrote from Sir Thomas Smith's " unfortunate " Bay, where fair weather was as scarce as whales, and referring to some previous quarrel with the Flemings, he added, " I do verily persuade myself that God is much displeased for the blood which is lost in this place and I feel a perpetual curse still to remain." In 1635, a Robert Salmon, as one of the two Trinity House officers, wrote complaining that John Browne, owner of a row of trees at Porter's Grange, which were used as a sea mark by the King's ships, had cut some of them down and intended to destroy the rest. An order was issued stopping the demolition under a statute of Elizabeth, commanding that no trees were to be cut down which were used as a sea mark. Another member of the Salmon family, named Nathaniel, was captain of one of two ships which set sail from Gravesend, in 1611, under the command of Thomas Best. The object of the expedition was to trade in the East. They came into collision with the Portuguese off Goa, and Salmon received much praise for the way in which he handled his ship. He sank one of the enemy's frigates ; eighty of her crew being drowned. Salmon also commanded one of five ships sent out by the East India Company in 1616, which encountered considerable opposition from the Dutch.

In 1623, the Greenland fleet above mentioned was captained by Captain William Goodlard, or Goodlad, of Leigh, and beside trouble with the Flemings he lost his brother Peter. He wrote that he was asleep and all the

boats were out fishing. His brother lay by the ship's side.
He spied a whale, followed him and struck him. The rope
being new, it ran out in kinks, which overthrew the boat ;
the man and a boy, named Bredrake, being drowned.
William mourned his brother's loss sincerely and termed it the
dearest whale to him that was ever struck in that harbour,
" Bell Sound."   Goodlad commanded the fleet of the Company for twenty years, and in 1634 escaped from imminent
peril at the hands of his own countrymen.   There was great
rivalry between the Thames men and a competing company
from Yarmouth.   They met in Greenland and from wrathful
argument proceeded to blows.   Goodlad had a musket presented at him five times, but it missed fire on every occasion.
He did not long survive this experience, for he died in 1639,
after having served as Master of Trinity House.   The Goodlad family continued to follow the sea, for there was an
epitaph narrating the virtues of a Captain Goodlad, who died
in 1693 :

> In this dark cell remains the silent dust
> Of one who was both merciful and just.
> True to his word and (what was seldom known)
> A Pious Seaman, who his God did own.
> A real friend and lover of good men,
> Ready to serve them with his purse and pen.
> A man of public spirit, too, concerned
> For weal of Church and State—one yet had learned
> That no man for himself is born, but must
> Serve God and country, too, or be unjust.
> Resigned to death and fled the other day
> To the celestial orb there to possess
> Eternal ease and perfect happiness.

The Haddock family won a more warlike fame than any
other in Leigh and rose high in the naval service. It is
said that the regularity with which the Haddocks served in
the Navy was only to be equalled by that with which they
named their children Richard, to the perpetual confusion of
their biographers.   Their connection with Leigh has been

traced back to 1327 and it was not until 1707 that the house, in which many generations of the family were born, was sold by the greatest seaman of them all, so that they flourished for quite four hundred years. Within a century (the Seventeenth) this family gave no fewer than two admirals and seven captains to the naval service ; nearly all of whom proved capable and zealous officers. There is a Fifteenth Century memorial in Leigh parish church, which refers to Richard and John Haddock, their wives, and their numerous progeny, comprising ten sons and eleven daughters. Although little trace of them has been found in the Sixteenth Century, the family must have grown in position and importance. On the south side of the church is a large tomb, which bears an illegible inscription. A copy of this has, however, been preserved and shows that the tomb was erected by Sir Richard Haddock, Kt., in memory of his grandfather, Captain Richard Haddock, who died 22nd May, 1660, aged seventy-nine ; also to his father, Captain William Haddock, who died in 1667, at the age of sixty years, and his mother, who died in 1688, in her seventy-eighth year. Sir Richard and Lady Haddock (his second wife) were also buried there ; the latter in 1709, aged fifty-nine, and her husband in 1715, having reached eighty-five. The Captain Haddock first mentioned was of considerable assistance to the Parliamentary cause and in 1652 was awarded £40 for his services. There was a still earlier Richard Haddock, for a gentleman of that name retired from the command of a ship at Portsmouth owing to failing eyesight. Captain William Haddock served with distinction in the fighting with the Dutch during the Commonwealth, and the Government granted him a gold medal for his services. The decoration was exhibited a year or two back at a meeting of the Royal Numismatic Society. A commission appointing Captain Haddock to the command of the "America," in 1650, was signed by Blake and Dean and was preserved for many years by the family. He was not long in charge of this vessel, for in 1653 he was gazetted captain of the "Hannibal." Captain Haddock, on retirement, lived at his native place, where he purchased property. Sir Richard Haddock, his son, was born at Leigh about the year 1629, and entered the naval service whilst he was very young, for at twenty-eight he was in command of the frigate "Abragon," part of the squadron patrolling the Channel, off Dunkirk, in connection with the operations carried on by the French and English against the Spaniards. It was whilst engaged upon this service that the young captain addressed several letters to his father, who was on a voyage to the Mediterranean. They are most dutiful in tone and betray a skill in correspondence which shows that an early apprenticeship to the sea had not prevented him acquiring an easy and not ungraceful command of the English language. These letters form part of a collection of manuscripts now in the British Museum. The latter was at one time much larger, but unfortunately, after the death of Sir Richard, his papers were placed in the hands of William Locker, lieutenant-governor of Greenwich Hospital, who contemplated an edition of naval biography. The project was never carried out, though later Charnock's " Biographica Navalis " was written from the same material. The whole of the manuscripts were not recovered and the loss is exceedingly unfortunate, for " as specimens of letter-writing of a seafaring family of the Seventeenth and Eighteenth Centuries, the letters have a value of their own apart from the interest which they inspire as the record of long and honourable service." In the letters to his father, Richard Haddock frequently mentioned his wife, named Lydia, supposed to have been a daughter of a Leigh family of the name of Steevens. This lady died some years later and he then married a lady whom he addressed as "Betty," but whose surname has not been discovered. Domestic concerns increase the charm of the correspondence. In one of them he says to his father, " My wife desires you, please, on your

GOLD MEDAL AWARDED TO CAPT. WILLIAM HADDOCK, FOR
DISTINGUISHED SERVICE, BY THE COMMONWEALTH
GOVERNMENT.

*The Medal was formerly in the collection of Mr. T. M. Whitehead
and was sold at Sotheby's in 1898 for £430 by Messrs. Spink and
Son, of Piccadilly. It is now in private ownership.*

arrival at Venice, to buy for her a foiled stone of a measure I conceive was given by her sisters to brother Andrew at Leigh ; also a pot kettle and two stew pans, one lesser than the other ; also a jar from Leghorne and other things necessary for the house to the value of £3 or £4, which shall be thankfully repaid." Later on Richard Haddock was appointed captain of the " Portland," and served in the first and second Dutch wars, but on the conclusion of the latter, from 1667 to 1671, he left the naval service and traded in the Mediterranean. Upon the outbreak of the third Dutch war, in 1672, he became captain of the " Royal James," the flagship of the Earl of Sandwich. At the drawn battle of Solebay or Southwold Bay, the vessel took fire and Haddock was almost the only surviving officer. The Earl refused to leave the ship and Richard, wounded in the foot, saved his own life by leaping overboard. Upon his return, Charles II, to mark his appreciation of his services, took his silken cap off his head and placed it upon that of Haddock. A week or two before this battle the captain wrote to his wife : " We do our utmost endeavour to get to them (the Dutch). If they have a mind to fight us to the westward of the Downs they may easily be with us, but we judge their design is to engage us among the sands, which possibly they may be deceived in expectation. God Almighty come along with us and give us the victory over our enemies. I know I shall not want the prayers and well wishes of my dear relations for my preservation. We have a brave fleet and in the main well-manned. For our part we don't complain, having over 900 men on board us ; the Duke (of York), 1,000, I believe, and upwards. It is probable before we engage them we may have ships in the river join with us, which are ten or eleven men of war and four fireships. I desire we may put our strength in God Almighty, but so noble and brave a fleet have not been seen together in our days." There are other letters which give minute accounts of the different operations which preceded the battle itself and of the

F

numberless little luxuries which the friends of Captain Haddock sent him to ease his lot at sea. A detailed account was furnished by him to the Duke of York of the severe handling which the " Royal James " received from the Dutch and her subsequent destruction by a fireship. Haddock took part in the battles which closed the war in 1673, first being in the " Royal Charles " and then in the " Royal Sovereign." After one of them the fleet came for re-fit into the Thames, and in his journal the old sea dog minutely described the weather (which was stormy and wet), the visit King Charles paid to the fleet, and the journey of Prince Rupert to both the Kent and the Essex shores. When peace had been concluded, Haddock was made a Commissioner of the Navy and in 1675 he was knighted. Five years later he was appointed to the command of the ships of war in the Thames and the Narrow Seas. In the next year he became First Commissioner of the Victualling Office. After the Revolution he was named Comptroller of the Navy, which office he continued to hold till death. For some years he received a pension of £500 a year and was one of the joint commanders-in-chief of the fleet in the expedition to Ireland in 1690. For a short time he represented the Borough of Shoreham in Parliament. It is possible that the Haddocks ceased in Sir Richard's time to reside at Leigh, though it is probable they still held property there and for another generation members of the family were buried in the old churchyard.

Sir Richard had at least six children : three sons and three daughters. Richard, the eldest son, served in the battle of La Hogue, in 1707, but had the misfortune to be surprised by the French whilst convoying the Archangel merchant fleet and lost fifteen ships. Despite this misfortune, he was gazetted to another vessel in the following year, but he did not see much more active service. He was appointed Comptroller of the Navy in 1734 and held the post for fifteen years, dying in 1751. Nicholas, the third son, obtained as much distinction as his father as a naval officer, and at the time of his death in 1746, aged sixty, he had attained the rank of Admiral of the Blue. At an early age he distinguished himself at the battle of Vigo, in 1702. At the battle of Cape Passero, in 1718, Haddock led the van and disabled four Spanish ships of heavy metal in succession. As Rear-Admiral, he hoisted his flag in the " Namur," a ninety-gun battleship. In 1738-41, he was protecting British commerce against the Spaniards, during which time he captured two prizes of the value of two million dollars. From this service he was invalided home. He was promoted Vice-Admiral of the Blue, and in recognition of his efforts to preserve trading ships from injury in the Mediterranean, the Italian merchants of London presented him with a magnificent gold cup. At the close of his career he became Admiral of the Blue and his portrait was included in the collection of celebrated naval officers at Greenwich Hospital. Nicholas, like his father, was for a short time in Parliament and he represented Rochester in 1731 and again in 1741. Some years before his death, which took place in 1746, he purchased Wrotham Place, Kent, but he was buried with his ancestors at Leigh. The high character of the man may be gathered from his last words to his son as he lay dying : " My son, considering my rank in life and public services for so many years, I have left you but a small fortune, but it is honestly got and will wear well ; there are no seamen's wages or provisions, nor a single penny of dirt money in it." It was this saying in which Nelson found consolation a year before he fought Trafalgar. He was watching the French fleet off Toulon and an appointment was made that deprived him of the prize money which would be due to the commanding officer as his share of the capture of the enemy's merchant ships. He comforted himself in his vexation, however, with the following : " But what I have I can say, as old Haddock said, ' It never cost a sailor a tear, nor the nation a farthing.' This thought

is far better than prize money—not that I despise prize
money—quite the contrary, I wish I had one hundred
thousand pounds this moment." Within a comparatively
few years the male line of the Haddock family failed and we
hear no more of them.

Connected with Leigh by family alliances and near
relationship to the Haddocks were Admiral Sir Edward
Whitaker and his brother, Captain Samuel Whitaker, both of
whom played distinguished parts in the siege and capture of
Gibraltar. Another naval hero who was buried in the churchyard was Captain John Rogers, upon whose memorial the
inscription ran : " Near this place lyeth Captain John Rogers,
who after several commands at sea, executed with great
courage and fidelity, was made captain of His Majesty's ship,
the 'Unicorn,' in which he behaved himself with incom-
parable valour and conduct in three bloody engagements with
the Dutch in the year 1672, for which remarkable services he
was advanced to be captain of the 'Royal Charles,' and then
of the 'Henry.' He was buried, to the great grief of all who
knew him, November 30th, 1683, after he had lived in this
town 36 years. He died aged 65."

How important a position Leighmen of the past occupied
in the maritime affairs of the nation is well expressed in a
memorial in Leigh Church, which runs :

"To the Glory of God and in memory of their Brethren
"of by-gone days, who, for a long period, carried on at the
"Port of Leigh the work of their Guild, this tablet has
"been placed by the Elder Brethren of the Corporation of
"Trinity House, London, in the year of our Lord, 1906.
"Living in this parish, they laboured worthily for the wel-
"fare of mariners, and dying were laid to rest in this church
"and this churchyard. Some of them were distinguished
"in the service of their country and the names of those
"whose tombs or monuments can be traced are here
"recorded.

"Their tombs and those of their kindred have been
"repaired, and the epitaphs, with the exception of that on
"the tomb of Admiral Nicholas Haddock, which has
"perished, have been transcribed into two books, of which
"one is deposited with the registers of this church and the
"other in the library of Trinity House, Tower Hill,
"London.

"The Elder Brethren desire also to honour the faithful
"services of others, their predecessors, who dwelt and
"laboured here, though their final resting places are not
"known, and to add their names, if these should come to
"light :—

"RICHARD HADDOCK, died 1453.

"JOHN HADDOCK, son of the above.

"CAPTAIN RICHARD HADDOCK, died 1660 ; a Brother of
"the Trinity House.

"SIR RICHARD HADDOCK, died 1714 ; son of the last
"named ; Comptroller of Her Majesty's Navy, and Master
"of the Trinity House, 1687.

"ADMIRAL NICHOLAS HADDOCK, died 1746 ; son of the
"last named, and buried with fifteen others of the family in
"the churchyard of this Church.

"ROBERT SALMON, died 1471.

"THOMAS SAMAN, died 1576.

"ROBERT SALMON, died 1591 ; Master of Trinity House,
"1588.

"ROBERT SALMON, died 1641 ; Master of Trinity House,
"1617.

"JOHN BUNDOCKE, died 1601.

"JOHN BUNDOCKE, died 1652 ; son of the last named ;
"a Brother of Trinity House.

"RICHARD CHESTER, died 1632 ; Master of Trinity
"House, 1615.

"CAPTAIN WILLIAM GOODLAD, died 1639; Chief Com-
"mander of the Greenland Fleet; Master of Trinity
"House, 1638.

"CAPTAIN RICHARD GOODLAD, died 1693; a Brother of
"Trinity House.

"JAMES MOYER, died 1661; a Brother of Trinity House,
"1630."

A sad story of the destruction of the memorials of these
old naval worthies in Leigh churchyard was told by Mr. H. W.
King, in the "Gentleman's Magazine" for 1865: "My
attention was first directed to the spoliation in 1842; and on
visiting the church I found that two monumental inscriptions
in brass had been abstracted—one in memory of the ancient
family of Salmon, dated 1472, and another for the family of
Bonner, dated 1580; that the marble tablet in memory of
Admiral Nicholas Haddock had been totally destroyed; that
three memorial tablets had been removed from the church,
and that other acts of vandalism had been committed. I have
no direct evidence, however, to prove that the brasses were
actually stolen during the repairs. An attempt was made to
excuse the destruction of Admiral Haddock's tablet on these
grounds: that it was replaced, but fell, and was broken in
two; again it was replaced, and again it fell, broken into fragments beyond the possibility of restoration. No masonic skill,
in short, was sufficient to refix with security a mural tablet
which had withstood the frosts of nearly a century! . . . . .
The history and fate of the other memorial tablets is instructive.
They were three framed oaken panels with inscriptions and
devices curiously illuminated in gold and colours, and richly
emblazoned with armorial bearings. That of most interest
was in memory of a distinguished naval officer, Captain John
Rogers. . . . . . The other tablets were commemorative
of some of a family named Hare. . . . . . From correspondence which has come into my possession, it appears
that these memorials were absent from the church three

or four years. Repeated application was made to the rector for their restoration, but all knowledge of their existence was denied. Further enquiries were made ; at length it was discovered that they were in a 'lumber room' at the rectory—or, as I am now, I believe, more correctly informed, 'concealed in a loft over the rector's stable.' Application for their restitution was at once renewed, and at last they were conveyed to the church, and placed upon the floor of the vestry, where they stood exposed to injury at least as late as 1848, and, I think, until 1858. All efforts to get them suspended either in the church or vestry were ineffectual, and every remonstrance was silently rejected. Their destruction seemed inevitable. When in the neighbourhood I once more sought for these tablets and was informed that nothing was known of them. On further investigation I found that a man who had been a servant to the rector was promoted to the office of sexton. From under the very eyes of the clergy and churchwardens, and without attracting observation, he conveyed these three large tablets to the vestry. From that of Captain Rogers he obliterated the inscription, defaced the arms, and then cut and adapted it to a cupboard door ! . . . . . The fate of the others I cannot learn. A few years ago I took a rubbing of the fifteenth century brass effigies of Admiral Haddock's ancestors, when I noticed that a part of the inscription plate (dated 1453) had been recently fractured and detached. I directed attention to it at the time. It has since been lost or stolen. The brass inscription-plate upon the gravestone of Robert Salmon, Esq., Master of the Trinity House in 1617, had also been wrenched from its matrix, and was then lying loose in the church. . . . . . In 1848 the churchwardens committed another flagrant act of vandalism in the destruction of the tomb of the Rev. John Sym, a seventeenth century theologian and rector of the parish, who is also believed to have been a native of the town. If in this instance, upon the demolition of the vault, they had permitted the slab, with its perfectly legible inscriptions in Latin and English, covering the entire surface of the stone, to have been replaced in situ, there would have been less to have complained of, but the slab was broken into three pieces and cast into a remote corner of the churchyard ! "

The Locality in the Sixteenth and Seventeenth Centuries.

The earliest and best known effort to map out the county and to describe the principal places of interest was made by John Norden in 1594 ; his " simple description " of Essex being dedicated to Lord Burleigh, the founder of the Cecil family. Norden was a well-known topographer of his day and surveyed several counties in addition to Essex. This county was stated to be " most fat, fruitful, and full of profitable things, exceeding (as far as I can find) any other shire for the general commodities and plenty. This shire seemeth to me to deserve the title of the English Goshen, the fattest of the land ; comparable to Palestina, that flowed with milk and honey. But I cannot commend the healthfulness of it, especially near the sea coasts, Rochford, Dengie and Tendring Hundreds and other low places about the creeks, which gave me a most cruel quarterne fever. But many and sweet commodities countervail the danger." The Rochford and Dengie Hundreds yielded milk, butter and cheese in abundance ; the huge cheeses which were manufactured being " wondered at for their massiveness and thickness." This locality had evidently lost some of its pre-eminence in sheep-rearing, for few places were mentioned as having many sheep. The county, as a whole, was without " great flocks," although six towns were specially mentioned for manufacture of clothing ; Coggeshall having the distinction of making the " best whites " in England. The shore lying between the Blackwater and the Crouch contained the best oyster layings ; producing a variety well known as the Walfleet, which was " a

little full oyster with a very green fin." Canvey Island was
described as being composed of low, marshy ground. The
passage to it over the creek was unfit for cattle and the land
was, therefore, used for the feeding of ewes, the milk of which
was made into cheese, "such as it is." Rochford Hundred
had few springs and the supply was chiefly derived from standing water. A map accompanied the descriptive matter,
and Norden made an industrious effort to include everything of note. All the parishes, as we now know them,
were mentioned. He drew, also, a few roads and all
these, save one—the lower road through Pitsea—passed
through Rayleigh to the outer world. They appear to be,
roughly, the main routes which are in use to-day. The
most northern thoroughfare was that running from Foulness
Church, right along the sands to South Shoebury, thence
going westward through Southchurch, Prittlewell, Leigh and
Hadleigh. Here it branched off; one section leading to
Grays and the other traversing Thundersley and Rayleigh,
where it formed the outlet to the London, Chelmsford and
Maldon roads. At Southend the main road branched off by
the corner now known as All Saints' Church, and passing
through Sutton, Rochford and Great Stambridge, ended at
Creeksea Ferry, the line of communication with the Dengie
Hundred. At Rochford this road sent a branch through
Hockley to Rayleigh. Further along the Hadleigh Road
another thoroughfare ran through Eastwood to Rayleigh.
From Rayleigh, also, the traveller could journey to South
Fambridge. Rayleigh was, therefore, the centre of the road
system and through it passed—except when merchandise and
produce were shipped along the banks of the Thames or the
Crouch—the bulk of the commerce of the Hundred. For
this reason Rayleigh was the market town and its great,
wide street was the scene of much animation on Satur-
days. Norden, himself, observed that Rayleigh was "an
honour of great privilege and had courts of strange preroga-

tives." The judicial business of the Hundred, which had centuries before been transacted at Rayleigh, was then heard at Chelmsford. Leigh was described as being well furnished with seafaring men and fishers. Prittlewell was "sometyme a market town," but beyond the three parishes thus mentioned, the Hundred contained no other place worthy of comment. Three parks were noted — Rochford Hall, Rayleigh and Hadleigh. The first named was in the possession of Lord Rich, together with many other manorial halls in the Hundred and elsewhere.

Camden, in his "Britannia," the first edition of which appeared in 1582, also dealt with this district. The map was not so complete as Norden's, but that published in the edition in 1622 showed a much more developed system of roads. From the Hadleigh Road there was a branch thoroughfare running up what is now North Road to Prittlewell, thence to Rochford ; the Sutton section not being given, though no doubt it existed. The road from Foulness was also not represented, but this was probably due to oversight and not because it had ceased to be used. Great Wakering, however, was shown to be on a circular road leading either via Shopland and Sutton to Rochford or by Shoebury to Southend. The probabilities are that this thoroughfare existed also at the time of Norden's survey, though its importance did not impress itself upon him. Camden's description of the district is well-known to every reader of historical works dealing with Rochford Hundred. He said the land at Canvey ("the Cannos" of Ptolemy) was so extremely low that it was very often quite drowned, except a few higher hillocks, which served as a retreat for sheep. Of these there were commonly fed 4,000, "the flesh of which is a very excellent taste. I have observed the young men with their little stools milking them like women in other places and making cheese of the ewe's milk in their little dairy houses or huts built for the purpose, which they call wicks." Leigh and Rayleigh were "pretty little towns;" the former being "well stocked with lusty seamen." Prittlewell was only worthy of mention as being the site of a cell of the Priory of Lewes.

At this period there disappeared an important means of communication with Maldon and Colchester by the destruction of Hull Bridge. It has been suggested that the River Crouch at Fambridge and Hullbridge was spanned, as their names denote, by bridges, over which the Romans used to pass rapidly from the mouth of the Thames to the settlements of Maldon and Colchester. Fambridge existed at the time of the Domesday Survey, and "less engineering skill than that of the Romans would hardly have succeeded in spanning the wider part of the river at Fambridge at the remote period at which it appears to have been bridged over, for it had given its name to the parishes north and south of it in the reign of William the Conqueror." There are documentary references to Hullbridge. In 1492 Sir John Montgomery (one of the founders of the Chantry at Prittlewell) bequeathed £20 to the making of Hullbridge if it were not made before his death, and in 1494, John Tyrrell, of Rawreth, disposed of 40s. in the same manner. In the reign of Elizabeth, John Creke, of Hockley, held a tenement lying near Hullbridge, and in 1588 a Prittlewell gentleman, named Lawson, left £100, payable in five years, for setting up again the stone structure, which had for some reason fallen into disrepair. It is probable the bridge was not re-placed, and from that time the vehicular traffic had to go round over Battlesbridge until the construction of the Great Eastern Railway in the Eighties of last Century enabled goods from this Hundred to enter the Dengie via Wickford. We have, therefore, in this respect to pursue a much more roundabout road than did the Romans. One of the best-known of county antiquarians has stated that the piers of the Roman structure at Hullbridge were visible until well into the Nineteenth Century, when a barge owner caused them to be destroyed to give better means of access to his vessels.

The Draining of Canvey Island.

Canvey has of late had a fascination for novelists, and several popular story-tellers have made the Island the chief scene of adventure. Grant Allen, Robert Buchanan and Coulson Kernahan have each used it, and the last named made reference to the sea wall which "so effectually protects the low-lying marshland that, standing inside the wall, one seems to be at a lower level than the water, and can see only the topmost spars and sails of the, apparently, bodiless barges and boats that glide ghost-like by." The Island's remoteness and inaccessibility, coupled with its quaint scenery and quiet, retired life, make it an admirable retreat for those needing rest. Ptolemy mentioned it in the Roman days and some evidence of its occupation at that time is afforded by the quantities of Roman tiles dug up at various times. It was used for several centuries for sheep-rearing purposes, though always liable to be flooded at times of exceptionally high tide. In Charles the First's reign a vigorous effort was made to place under cultivation thousands of acres of land in the country which had previously been marshland and only suitable for the feeding of cattle. In the Fen district great irritation was shown at the importation of Dutchmen to carry out the drainage works, and Cromwell took a prominent part in upholding the common rights of certain Huntingdonshire men which had been threatened by the landowner in his grants to the Dutch engineers. Portions of the Thames marshland were also dyked and drained by the new method; the chief effort at reclamation being at Canvey Island. In 1621 Sir Henry Appleton (afterwards a noted sufferer in the Royalist cause) and other owners contracted with a Dutchman, named Jooz Croppenburg, a London tradesman, for the draining of the Island, 4,000 acres in extent. As compensation for his work Croppenburg was to be given a third part of the land, and a year later his portion, known as "Third Acre Lands," was conveyed to him, though the work is supposed to have been actually designed and supervised by the celebrated Dutch engineer, Vermuyden. As a result of Croppenburg's contract, the Island was largely populated by Dutchmen, and in 1628 "Low Country strangers," to the number of 200, petitioned the King to allow them to worship in their own language. His Majesty granted their request and the Bishop of London was ordered to see it carried out ; the service and minister to conform to the Dutch Church in London. The cause flourished for some years and the ministers frequently attended the Synod meetings in the City. At the close of the century the church fell into decay, owing, probably, to the departure of some of the strangers and the absorption of others into the population of the country-side. The advent of the Dutchmen was unpopular locally. There were some disturbances, and a ballad was published concerning them, which found considerable favour. In 1712 a Church of England was established by an officer in the Victualling Office, and dedicated to St. Katharine. It was consecrated by the Bishop of London on June 11th and the first sermon was preached by the Rev. S. Hibbard, M.A., Prebendary of Lincoln and Rector of Stifford. His text was the familiar "I was glad when they said unto me, let us go into the House of the Lord." The reverend gentleman, in the course of his sermon, referred to the "generous disposition" that had given them the opportunity of meeting in that place. He added : "It is a pity the endowment is no larger, that there might have been sufficient maintenance for the minister, but what is wanting in an effectual provision of lands and tithes for this sacred use and purpose, it is to be hoped will be sufficiently made up by the generous and voluntary contributions of those of my brethren to whom the care of the inhabitants' souls of this Island is committed." The edifice fell down and another was erected about 1745, partly by contributions and partly by a benefaction of the Scratton family, of Prittlewell. From that time forward service was performed in the summer months and at such other times as the weather permitted. The church was nearly rebuilt in 1849, and is now in regular pastoral care.

. A curious system was in vogue on this Island until a few years ago. It was parcelled amongst several parishes and separately rated—relic of a period when certain manors had rights of pasture there. The parishes possessing these privileges included Prittlewell, Bowers Gifford, North and South Benfleet, Pitsea, Vange, Southchurch and Hadleigh ; Prittlewell and North Benfleet having no fewer than three pieces, in distinct portions of the Island. Canvey has now been made into a separate parish. This system of the division of islands suitable for grazing amongst neighbouring parishes also obtained at Foulness Island—lying to the northeast of the Hundred—until it also was constituted a parish. Wallasea Island to this day is divided among five parishes ; one of them (Eastwood) being seven miles away.

Canvey is rapidly losing the charm of solitude and picturesqueness. Several of the farms have been sold to land speculators and at the present time it is being developed as a summer resort ; wooden bungalows being built for the temporary convenience of the visitor at its eastern end. A series of engravings of typical Essex scenery was published in the Victoria History of Essex and first place was given to a view of Canvey Island, taken from the heights lying above South Benfleet.

Lady Arabella Stuart's Escape.

Leigh Roadstead links us with the sad romance of Lady Arabella Stuart. This young lady was a cousin of James I and by some was preferred as sovereign. She gave no sign of such ambition and, consequently, no restraint . was placed upon her movements. In 1610, however, she became betrothed to William Seymour, son of Lord Beauchamp, who, through the house of Suffolk, had some claim to the throne. When the betrothal became public, the Privy Council ordered the young couple not to marry and they promised not to do so. Despite their pledge they were later on privately united. Arabella was put under restraint at Lambeth and her husband was sent to the Tower. As they still contrived to exchange letters, the King ordered the lady's removal to Durham. On the journey thither she became unwell and made a stay at Barnet. Whilst there she arranged a plan of escape with her husband. Arabella arrived at Blackwall in man's clothing, but her husband did not appear in time. Her attendants insisted on her taking boat down the Thames to Leigh. John Bright, master of the "Thomas," of Lynn, stated subsequently that three men and two women in two wherries hailed him whilst he was at anchor in Leigh Road and offered him money to take them to Calais. He refused to do it and at their request directed them to a French ship, on board which they went. When nearing Calais Arabella had sail shortened in order that she might obtain news of her husband and whilst doing so was captured by a King's ship. She was lodged in the Tower, lost her reason, lingered four years and then died. The saddest aspect of it all was that her husband, arriving late, was lucky enough to find a collier, which carried him safely to Ostend.

A Wild Alarm.

War broke out with Spain in 1624 and gave the Dunkirk privateers an opportunity of preying upon commerce passing in and out of the Thames. Little was done to suppress them and consequently the whole of the seaboard population suffered serious alarm. The apprehensive state of the public was revealed by an occurrence at Wakering in 1628. On the morning of September 6th the rumour spread that the Dunkirkers had landed at Wakering, that the town had been fired and the people had fled from their houses. One woman with a child on her back tramped sixteen miles in her terror and she reported about 6,000 men had landed. A Captain Humphreys took the trouble to ascertain the truth of the report. His man found a foreign fishing boat lying in Wakering Haven. The people imagined it to be a Dunkirker, ran away and roused the country. The alarm could not be stayed before the county levies had been concentrated at Chelmsford and preparations made to resist the threatened attack. It was probably in connection with this war with Spain that letters of marque were issued to the owners of the "Pelican" and "St. John," of Leigh, of 40 and 200 tons respectively. At a later stage the Admiralty ordered the warship "Fortune" to cruise between Tilbury Hope and the Estuary.

The Growth of Puritanism.

Shortly after Mary passed away, her successor, Elizabeth, had to grapple with a new religious movement, which later became known as Puritanism. Roughly, it represented a state of mind that cared little for the externals of worship, but was wholly occupied with the internal, or spiritual, aspect. Its very existence was a protest against ornate ritual and the episcopalian theory of church government. From the nature of its teaching it oft-times came into opposition to royal and ecclesiastical prerogative in that day, and for over 100 years its history was the history of persecution, broken only by the Civil War, when the disciplined fanaticism of the Puritan established Oliver Cromwell as Lord Protector. It then waned in power until the accession of William III sealed the victory for religious freedom. There was a strong influence in the Church towards the end of the Sixteenth and in the early years of the Seventeenth Centuries in favour of stricter observance of ritual and more regularized form of worship. It was upon directions respecting the wearing of surplices, the eastward position, and similar questions, that much of the smouldering flame of discontent against ecclesiastical power was kindled

ADMIRAL NICHOLAS HADDOCK.

From a portrait in the Painted Hall, Greenwich Hospital.
By permission of the Lords of the Admiralty.

into active opposition. Benton has given a selection of cases from Benfleet which were dealt with as being breaches of ecclesiastical discipline, and these throw some light upon one of the causes of the prejudice of the people against the clergy. They are taken from the Archidiaconal Registers of London, edited by Archdeacon Hale, and include : "1566—Action taken against the Vicar, because he will not minister in a surplice, and came to the house of Henry Wood, with his bow and arrows, to seek for the said Wood ; 1583—Johan, Ellis Mone's maid, scolded· and cursed in church ; 1598—William Haynes detected for dancing wish minstrels on a green during afternoon service ; 1612—Complaint against Master Balley, the Vicar, for that he is not resident, in so much that sometimes for a month together there is nobody to bury the dead, or to christen ; 1618—Action against Catherine Edwards for a slanderer of her neighbours, a make-hate, and a common liar, which if it be not reformed will make much strife." In Rochford Hundred the spirit was almost entirely Puritan. The Rich family, celebrated as the Earls of Warwick, strongly held to the new belief. They had the right of presentation to the livings of Hadleigh, Leigh, Ashingdon, South Shoebury, Prittlewell, Rochford, Foulness, Hawkwell, Southchurch, Butlers and Shopland. These were often filled with divines of Independent opinion, who largely influenced the feelings of their parishioners. The third Lord Rich succeeded to the estates (including those at Rochford) in 1580, and at once became an avowed Puritan. In 1581 he invited Robert Wright, who had gone to Antwerp to be ordained, to become domestic chaplain at Rochford Hall. At Wright's desire, Lord Rich consented to a church being formed at Rochford. Wright was elected to the oversight of it, and with him was associated John Greenwood, a few years later to become one of the best-known martyrs of the Independent cause. The congregation did not withdraw

G

themselves from the Parish Church, but held their meetings in
the Hall at 8 o'clock in the evening. Lady Bacon, the
mother of Francis, Lord Bacon, wrote to Lord Burleigh
concerning these services thus : " I hear them in their
public exercises as a chief duty commanded by God, and
I also confess, as one that hath found mercy, that I have
profited more in the inward feeling of God's holy will
. . . . . . by such sincere and sound opening of
the Scriptures . . . . . . than I did by hearing
occasional services at St. Paul's well nigh twenty years
together." An effort was made to get Wright licensed to
preach without conforming, and so high did temper run
that Lord Rich and Bishop Aylmer proceeded from argument to blows, and Lord Rich's uncle took the Bishop
by the collar and gave him a thrashing. Elizabeth punished
this unseemly behaviour by commanding that the services
should be forbidden. Wright and a man named Dix were
apprehended and cast into the Fleet Prison, whilst Rich
went into "durance vile" at the Marshalsea. A commission was appointed to enquire into the character of the
services, and the evidence heard included statements by the
Rectors of Southchurch, Leigh, Rochford, South Shoebury,
and the Vicars of Prittlewell and Shopland. It was alleged
that Wright called the preachers that followed the Book
of Common Prayer, "dumb dogs"; that the people listened
to Wright rather than to the beneficed clergy, who were
publicly rebuked for their sermons. Eventually Wright and
Rich were released upon subscribing to the Prayer Book.
In 1585 the minister of Leigh, named William Negus,
was suspended by Bishop Aylmer for refusing to wear the
surplice. He would not promise the Bishop to comply
with the order, and he was suspended until he would give
the required undertaking. Negus hesitated about complying
with the demands of the Bishop, and he was then appealed to
by twenty-eight of his principal parishioners that he should

surrender. They wished with all their hearts that it should not be necessary so to do, but added : "We entreat you as you render our souls, and as you regard that account that you must make unto God for them, not to forsake us for such a trifle." The signatures included those of many well-known Leighmen of that day : Robert Salmon, John William Goodlad, Robert and William Bonner, Richard Chester, Benjamin Cocke. Negus's suspension was recalled, but in consequence of further trouble he was deprived of his living by Bishop Bancroft. He was succeeded by a man named Sym, who also got into trouble with high authority. In 1606 the minister of Little Wakering was presented at Archdeacon Harsnett's (later Archbishop of York) visitation for declining to wear a surplice, refusing to name the holy days, or to read the prayers thereon. The same Archdeacon reported a minister of Great Stambridge for not wearing a surplice and making the sign of the Cross. In 1633, Dr. Aylett, an ecclesiastical lawyer, acting as commissary in Essex for the Bishop of London, made a report to Laud, obviously connected with the agitation against wearing a surplice. He stated that on March 23rd he was at Chelmsford, where he heard Dr. Browning, of Rayleigh, read the whole service in hood and surplice. He made a sermon suitable to the time and occasion, which the clergy present desired to have printed. The Doctor added : "Now that the wheels be set agoing and the people be followed in this kind, they will be as pliable to order as they have been violently against it." Hardly a true forecast. Two years later the same gentleman made a lengthy report upon certain dissenting lecturers in Essex, and among the places referred to was Rochford. In 1634 several local people were before the Court of High Commission. Frederick Waggoner, of Leigh, a physician, was fined £100 for profane speech of the Lord's supper and contumelious conduct towards the clergy. The fine was afterwards mitigated. Thomas Ellis, of Canewdon, and Abraham Crouch, fisherman, of Foulness, were also before the same Court. Sym, the Leigh parson referred to above, was in trouble with Dr. Aylett in 1636. The latter wanted to know why he kept a solemn fast in his parish church on Wednesday in Ascension week, when the people remained all day in the church, fasting and praying, and Mr. Sym preaching. Sym alleged that he was supported in this by the ancient Canons concerning Rogation. Beside the appointed service he preached at two services, with prayer for the cessation of pestilence and for rain. As there were many similar services in the Rochford Hundred, there was evidently a good deal of anxiety among the people concerning the two matters mentioned. Aylett reported Sym's explanation to the Dean of Arches, and termed it "a kind of defence." Upon his death, Sym was buried in the churchyard, and a stone slab marking the spot was broken up in 1848 and thrown away. Aylett, in the same letter, spoke generally of the condition of affairs ecclesiastically, and gave a short but vivid picture of the strife and confusion which was then prevalent. He stated he had caused many of the communion tables to be railed in, so that the people might come up and receive at the rail. This met with great opposition, for the people said there was no such thing in the London churches, and they urged that the article books for Metropolitan visitation supported their argument that they could remove the table at the time of the celebration and place it at the most convenient spot for the parishioners to receive. In some places the ministers had fallen in with the popular demand, and Aylett complained that his work had been undone. Rochford Hundred was greatly concerned in a movement which ultimately flamed into the Civil War, brought about the execution of King Charles, and the triumph of Parliament. .

Ship Money.

Essex was ordered to find £8,000 of the levy popularly known as Ship Money, by which Charles I. sought to procure means to provide and equip a navy and avoid the necessity of calling his Parliament together. In 1634, £6,615 was called for from Essex and Suffolk jointly. Subsequently the area of taxation was enlarged, and on August 4th, 1635, Essex was ordered to contribute £8,000. Its collection occasioned considerable rioting, though by the end of 1636 only £410 of the amount remained unaccounted for. Five towns were separately assessed : Colchester, £300; Walden, £80; Maldon, £70; Thaxted, £40; Harwich, £20. These realized £510, and the remainder was distributed among the Hundreds. This district was called upon to find £308 1s., according to a return prepared by Sheriff Lucas, and preserved in the Record Office; being twelfth in amount out of nineteen. The following are the details of the assessment, which was fully met :—

PARISH.	AMOUNT £ s. d.			NUMBER OF PERSONS ASSESSED.
Prittlewell - (Including Milton Hamlet)	28	11	8	- 68
Canewdon -	28	0	0	- 46
Rayleigh -	26	0	9	- 83
Leigh -	25	8	0	- 85
Foulness Island	22	19	8	- 25
Hockley -	16	2	8	- 47
Wakering Ma. -	15	9	6	- 51
Rawreth -	13	9	10	- 24
Southchurch -	12	10	0	- 26
Eastwood -	12	5	0	- 51
Stambridge Ma.	12	0	1	- 32
Rochford -	11	13	1	- 73
Barling -	11	0	0	- 38
Paglesham -	9	10	0	- 26

PARISH.	AMOUNT. £ s. d.			NUMBER OF PERSONS ASSESSED.
Wakering Pa.	-	8	0 0	- 34
Hadleigh	-	8	0 0	- 27
South Fambridge		7	10 0	- 11
North Shoebury	-	6	10 0	- 17
South Shoebury	-	6	0 0	- 18
Ashingdon	-	5	19 6	- 13
Hawkwell	-	5	12 2	- 25
Stambridge Pa.	-	4	16 6	- 14
Shopland	-	4	6 1	- 9
Sutton	-	3	14 1	- 15
Thundersley	-	2	12 5	- 20
		£308	1 0	878

South Benfleet is not included, because it was then part of another Hundred.

The details given above indicate roughly the relative importance of the parishes in those days. These values alone are not a safe guide, for the tax was largely one on land, and [the size of the parish was an important factor, but taken with the numbers assessed, they are practically conclusive. There are some curious features in the return. As a rule, the christian name and surname only are mentioned, but in Paglesham, not only was a baronet, Sir Philbert Vernant, rated, but also one "Esquire" and four "gents." In the Leigh list appear several well-known names mentioned in other parts of this volume—Pulley, Chester, Goodlad, Waggoner, Bundocke, Breadcake, Harris, Salmon, Bonner and Emery. Barling had the distinction of possessing the only "Doctor of Physick," named Waggoner. In Canewdon a remarkable feature was the absence of christian names. Of forty-six, fifteen of them gave "Goodman" (yeoman) as the initial distinction. Samuel Freeborne, who played a prominent part in the subsequent struggle, was assessed at £1 5s. in respect of property at Milton Hamlet, and Mrs. Judith Freeborne for 18s. 9d. for Prittlewell. The Thundersley contingent was headed by "The Ladye Pooley," whilst the Right Hon. the Earl of Warwick got off with a paltry £1 2s. in respect of his Rochford estate, and £1 4s. for Eastwood. We do not know whether this was the final assessment, but it is certain that Lord Rich complained he had been unjustly treated and did not pay, as ordered, within thirty days. He alleged that his property at Rochford and Eastwood was in dispute at law, but Sir Humphrey Mildmay, the Sheriff, reported to the Privy Council in 1636 that the litigation concerned certain tithes and was no impediment to the payment of the money. At Hockley a curious entry was made in respect of Richard Harris, from whom 5s. was exacted "for his abilitie." Great Wakering had the doubtful honour of the highest individual assessment, viz., that of Sir William Cope, of £6. Southchurch came next with £3 19s. 4d., levied against William Archer. The tax as a rule did not exceed a few shillings, and at Prittlewell the highest was £2 5s. In respect of this latter parish there is a series of entries not made against any other place. It is headed: "The names of those who are rated in respect of theire estates or trades they drive and use, holding little or noe quantitie of land." There are eleven names, and the total of the tax levied £5 18s. The woodland was rated at a penny per acre and only five acres were scheduled. Colchester, as the chief port of the county, was heavily assessed. The ancient borough protested that several seaports between Gravesend and Burnham were not charged at all, and mentioned places in the Rochford Hundred, among others. The result is not disclosed, but evidently Colchester's envy of the assessment of our district was shared by other parishes. Pledgdon, in North Essex, formerly a parish of 600 acres and now a hamlet, resisted a tax of £9 11s. 9d.;

complaining that South Benfleet, with 1,200 acres, had escaped with £9 15s.

Cromwell's Connection with the Hundred.

During the struggle between Parliament and the King Cromwell rapidly rose to prominence, and at this juncture it is interesting to note that he had intimate relationship with the Hundred. Between 1584-7 Thomas Bourchier, a London haberdasher, bought the manor of Little Stambridge off the Cocke family. The new owner did not enjoy his country seat for many years, for he died in 1594 at the age of 56. He was succeeded by his son James, subsequently, as Sir James Bourchier, to become famous as the father-in-law of Oliver Cromwell. The latter married Sir James's daughter on August 22nd, 1620, at St. Giles', Cripplegate, and no definite connection of the Knight with this Hundred had formerly been established prior to 1630. The register of baptisms at Tower Hill showed that six of his children were there baptized and two buried, and historians have generally described him as being of Felstead. No doubt his business connections constantly caused him to live for periods in London, but a return of the county levies furnished to the Privy Council in 1608, recently published, leaves no room for doubt that he was often in this Hundred, too, for in that year he was named as captain of the militia infantry in the Rochford district; being succeeded by Edward Humfrey in 1622. This supports Mr. H. W. King in his suggestion that, although there is no documentary evidence to support it, it is at least probable the future Lord Protector and his wife were visitors at Little Stambridge Hall. Sir James died in 1635, and it is most likely that his daughter and son-in-law were present at the funeral. This, it is thought, took place at Little Stambridge Church (now pulled down), though no gravestone, inscription or other record of it exists. Mrs.

Cromwell profited little by the will, and at the death of her father the connection of the Cromwells with the district ceased altogether.

The Rebellion and its Effect Locally.

The year before the outbreak of Civil War this district felt some of the inconveniences arising from the strained relationships between King and Parliament. Stringent orders were issued to the Fleet in the Thames to stop vessels and prevent the escape of political refugees. The search was so strict that communication was hindered with other ports than those to which these people journeyed. As an instance, the fishermen of Leigh and elsewhere were stopped from following their avocation. When fighting commenced in 1642, Essex was joined with other counties into the Eastern Association, the backbone of the resistance to Charles. For months the issue hung in the balance, but gradually the superior resources of Parliament, coupled with the generalship displayed by Cromwell and others, caused victory to incline to the Puritans. There is no evidence that any fighting took place in this part of Essex. There is a tradition that Cromwell slept at Porter's Grange for a night on his way to reduce Hadleigh Castle, but as this building had been in ruins for some years, and had probably been quarried for stone for the re-building of Leigh and other churches at the close of the Sixteenth Century, the tradition has little of fact to support it. The influence of the Rich family and the Puritan ministry, coupled with the tendency of the people towards independence of thought in religious questions, guaranteed practical unanimity for the Parliamentary cause. The leader of the local trained bands was Lieutenant-Colonel Freeborne, of Prittlewell. He was very active in the cause and a member of the County Committee. Freeborne must have been a man of humour as well as a soldier. He married three times, and over the grave in Prittlewell churchyard of his first two wives (one of whom was a member of the well-known Leigh family of Goodlad) he caused the following epitaph to be placed :

" Under one stone two precious gems do lie,
Equal in worth, weight, lustre, sanctity :
If yet, perhaps, one of them might excel,
Which most, who knows ! ask him who knew them well
By long enjoyment ; if he be thus pressed,
He'll pause, then answer, truly both were best ;
Were't in my choice that either of the twain
Might be returned to me to enjoy again,
Which should I choose ?   Well, since I know not whether,
I'll mourn for the loss of both, but wish for neither.
Yet here's my comfort, herein lies my hope,
The time's acoming, cabinets shall ope
Which are locked fast ; then, then shall I see,
My jewels to my joy, my jewels me. "

The Earl of Warwick (Lord Rich) was placed in command of the Fleet by Parliament in 1642, and he refused to resign it at the command of the King ; taking determined and successful steps to overawe those commanders of ships who differed from him.   He almost succeeded in capturing the Queen as she was crossing from Falmouth to Brest. A year later, when peace with the King was being debated, one of the demands was that Warwick should be made a Duke, but this came to nothing, as the treaty was never concluded.   Blake succeeded to Warwick's command under the Commonwealth.   Rich's son for a time sided with the King, and Parliament seized his estate at Rochford, which had been settled on him by his father upon his marriage in 1633.   He returned to the Parliamentary party later, and his property was restored to him.

The Eastern Association troops were usually clad in the red coat which has since become famous in the annals of the Army.   At the outbreak of the war, Essex contributed some excellent troops, but when the call came in the harvest-time for more men for service in Lincolnshire, the poor character of the levies and the poverty of their equipment was the cause of constant correspondence. Soon after hostilities commenced, Essex contributed weekly a sum of £1,687 10s. towards the expenses, and in the year 1643, in levies, compositions and sequestration money, it paid over £50,664, only excelled by Suffolk from among the five counties. Essex evidently held high place in the opinion of the leaders of the Rebellion, for John Hampden wrote to Sir Thomas Barrington in the extremity of the crisis in 1643 : "The power of Essex is great, a place of most life of religion in the land, and your power in the county is great, too, The difficulties of this war need the utmost of both. Our army wants both men and money. . . . . ."

After the battle of Edgehill, 1642, there was great fear that the King might march upon London. Essex joined with the other home counties in most enthusiastic preparations for resistance. At a County meeting at Chelmsford they "with one consent resolved to unite themselves in defence of both King and Parliament, and at their own cost and charges set out 12,000 men to march towards the Lord General (the Earl of Essex, who was then falling back upon London, with the Royalist army marching in the same direction), desiring that the Earl of Warwick might be made their General, which was condescended unto by both Houses of Parliament, and in pursuance of these, their valiant resolutions, agreed that such gentlemen hereafter named, in the several places of their habitations in the County, should raise what men they could, and have the leading and command of such as they should particularly raise in the places mentioned." For Rochford Hundred the gentlemen nominated for this service were Mr. Thomas King, Mr. Whitaker, Mr. Peck, Mr. Sams and Mr. White. The King did not march on London, however, and the war continued in the provinces until the monarch's capture in 1645, after the defeat at Naseby.

Signing the Covenant at Prittlewell.

When in 1643 Parliament, to secure the aid of the Scotch, ordered that the Presbyterian form of worship should be established throughout the country, Essex was constituted a province and Rochford Hundred a classis. In Prittlewell parish most of the parishioners, standing in the church, their heads uncovered and their right hands uplifted, swore to respect the Covenant. They were led by the Rev. Thomas Peck, the vicar, a Puritan divine of some note. Five years later, however, after the King had surrendered, there was some change of feeling, for the same parishioners expressed their dissent at the attitude of the Army in forcing their grievances upon the attention of Parliament. Both the Covenant and the resolution of dissent, with the lists of signatures, were entered in the parish minute book, and someone subsequently added a note to the latter, "All roundhead villains." Amongst the names of those who signed the documents were : Harvey, Green, Brand, Taylor, Sorrell, Chambers, Wilson, Glasscock, Purchas, Manning, Rule, Westwood, Rayner, Tabor, Burton, Barrett, Eve, Carter, Harding, Spurgeon, Payne, Francis, Dowson and Dilliway ; many of which are familiar to us to-day. At Hadleigh fifty parishioners supported the Protestation against Popery to Parliament in 1641, and later subscribed to a vow to assist the Parliamentary cause and to the Solemn League and Covenant. The signatures included those of Glasscock, Offin, Wood, Salmon, Coke, Norden, Pilbrow, Sorrell and Harvey. At Ashingdon the Solemn League and Covenant was subscribed.

The Second Revolt.

What is known as the Second Revolt in 1648, a Royalist rising, profoundly affected Essex. It first broke out in Kent, but Sir Thomas Fairfax crushed the cavaliers

at Maidstone. Five hundred of them fled across the Thames
on a bridge of boats to Essex, and there they were joined by a
considerable following, headed by the Lucas family, of Colchester. They imprisoned the County Committee, then in
session at Chelmsford. Fairfax followed hard after them;
crossing at Tilbury and taking the road through Billericay.
He chased them with surprising speed, for he was suffering severely from gout. It was not long before he forced
his opponents to take refuge in Colchester. Here he
closely besieged them. The issue was fought out on
both sides with unwearied obstinacy and resolution. After
three months' investment, and the town had been reduced
to starvation (all the cats and dogs having been eaten),
the Royalists capitulated; two of their leaders (Sir C. Lucas
and Sir G. Lisle) being shot. The spot is now marked
by a monument in the Castle yard at Colchester.

Royalist Sufferers.

There were several sufferers for the Royalist cause
either living in the Hundred or owning land therein. Five
ministers were ejected for refusing to support the Parliamentary party; viz., Elizeus Burgess, Canewdon; Roboshobery
Dove, Foulness; John Vicars, South Fambridge; Walter
Holmes, Southchurch; and John Browning, Rawreth. The
most conspicuous case was that of Sir Henry Appleton, of Jarvis
Hall, South Benfleet, an extensive landowner. He was
amongst the prisoners taken at the siege of Colchester.
His lands were sequestrated; a third being allowed to
him for maintenance. He was reduced to miserable circumstances and did not long survive his misfortune; dying
at Baddow. He owed money to a cavalier, named Mildmay,
who took out letters of administration. He was succeeded
in the title by his son, one of those who in 1660
signed at Chelmsford a congratulatory address to Monk
for his efforts in bringing about the Restoration. In 1646

"Henry, son of Sir Henry Appleton, Bart."—it is not quite clear whom of the two above mentioned is meant—compounded for delinquency in bearing arms for the King, and he took the oath not to bear arms against Parliament. He was fined £500, which was afterwards reduced to £456. In 1643, William Monger was consigned to prison at Colchester because the inhabitants of Rochford complained that whilst sheltering amongst them he did not go to church for three weeks, and, what is probably far more important, he tried to persuade the people not to pay money to the Parliamentary cause, "which hindered the public good and peace." About the same time representations were made on behalf of the minister at Paglesham, named Hansley, who was condemned to pay £20, a twentieth part of his estate; it was urged that a fifth part of the £20 was more than he could pay. A man of considerable local importance fell into trouble in 1646. The Salmon family of Leigh, referred to in an earlier chapter, was wealthy and flourishing at this time, and a member of it named Robert Salmon compounded for having been in the King's quarters for a year until the taking of Dartmouth by the enemy. Apparently he consented to take the oath of the National League and Covenant, and was ready to swear the "negative oath." He was fined £120, and a year later he begged to be allowed to stay in the town a month to complete the payment of the composition, for he was required to leave the kingdom. He paid the money in 1650. Anna Goodlad, widow, in 1652, claimed certain of Salmon's lands on the ground that she had purchased them from him. The County Committee ordered the tenants to keep back the rent; some question of the price paid for the property having arisen. The Committee for Compounding, however, granted her the required discharge. In 1651 a Salmon fell foul of the Committee for the Advance of Money, and his estate was sequestrated for non-payment of a charge levied upon him. A year later—the same time as that of the claim made by Mrs. Goodlad—the County Committee reported he could not be found, and directions were then given for a levy to be made on lands at Stanford-le-Hope, Corringham and Leigh, of the value of £43 per annum. In 1646 two Prittlewell residents were heavily fined for enlisting in the King's service. They were both men of fairly substantial means, for one, Edmund Fisher, having interest in farms at Wakering and Canewdon, was fined one-tenth, equal to a sum of £20, and the other, Samuel Reniger, had to pay £22. The entry concerning Fisher raises an interesting point. On May 18th, 1643, Sir Richard Everard wrote to Sir Thomas Barrington asking what he should do with two Royalist captains who came to Prittlewell and plundered, whom he had arrested. One of them was named Fisher, who had a son with the King. Everard was ordered to keep the two captains in custody until he received the instructions of the House of Commons. The outcome of this raid is not disclosed, nor can it be certain which Fisher it was, father or son, who suffered in 1646, as mentioned above. There is little doubt, however, that the family was ardently for the King, and paid the penalty. Frances Mynott, a Rayleigh spinster, was about the same time reported as a recusant. Another notable Royalist who suffered severely for his devotion was Sir William Campion, of "Lambourne Hall Castle," Canewdon. He was ordered to pay £800 by the Committee for the Advance of Money. He took part in the Second Revolt and was slain at the siege of Colchester. Two years later a report was made that his lands at Canewdon, worth £400 a year, had not yet been sequestered, and there were three years' rents in his tenants' hands. Three months later the Committee for Compounding ordered his marshes to be seized, but immediately a man named Catelyne, of Lincolns Inn, claimed he held an interest in the marshes to the value of £200 a year, which had been mortgaged by Sir William for ninety-nine years for £1,500. He was ordered to file full particulars, but the final outcome of the matter does not transpire. Included in the property belonging to the Earl of Northampton, which was seized, was Eastwood Rectory. Immediately several creditors put in claims, and so protracted were the proceedings that the issue was not settled at the Restoration. Edmund Roper Hartlip, a Thundersley property owner, was also condemned as a recusant, and again claims were made of an interest in the income therefrom, which were admitted by the County Committee. In 1654 John Webb, of Fleet Street, owner of the celebrated Mitre Tavern, compounded as a recusant for farmlands in Paglesham and Little Wakering. There were probably many other instances in these parts where the heavy hand of Parliament fell upon those who differed from them, but the records are lost. Sufficient, however, has been given to prove how much men risked in the territory of the Eastern Association in taking up arms on behalf of the King.

Cromwell's Protectorate: Blake and Leigh Road.

The execution of the King in 1649 left Cromwell the most powerful man in Britain, and as Lord Protector he exercised as much power as a monarch. Upon land little of note happened in this district during the ten years of his Protectorate, but in the Thames Estuary there was considerable movement. The Commonwealth Navy frequently anchored off Leigh Road. The rise of the Dutch naval power rendered control of the mouth of the Thames exceedingly important strategically ; and most of the obstinate battles with the Lowlanders were fought within a comparatively few miles of the River.

In 1650, Blake, who had earned renown in the Civil War by his valiant defence of Taunton, was transferred from the land to the naval service and placed in charge of the Commonwealth Navy. He quickly re-asserted the authority of Parliament afloat, rendering it signal aid by his determined chase of Rupert and certain revolted English ships which had taken refuge in Holland. Blake pursued the Cavalier across the Atlantic, scattered his fleet, brought back Virginia and the Barbadoes to allegiance, and within a year Rupert's last ship wandered alone upon the waters. This was Blake's preparation for the greater service of fighting the powerful navy of Holland. Irritation had been growing between the Dutch and English maritime populations owing to the increasing wealth and power of the former, and when Parliament passed its Navigation Act re-asserting the right of search of foreign vessels and ordering the salute of the flag in British seas, hostilities very quickly ensued. The English Channel was the great highway of Dutch commerce, and if this country could successfully obtain control of the Narrow Seas it would seriously imperil the prosperity of the Lowlanders. The series of wars thus inaugurated ultimately resulted in the ruin of Holland as a world power. Right from the start of this bitter and prolonged struggle the Estuary, and Leigh Road in particular, frequently served as a station for the ships engaged in this service. Blake and Van Tromp had an encounter in the Downs in 1652, and on the failure of negociations, Parliament published its declaration of war. Before this formal announcement, however, Blake had set sail for the Dutch fishing fleet off Scotland and attacked their guard of twelve men of war, which he either captured or sunk. A storm, which severely damaged the Dutch fleet, prevented Van Tromp from engaging Blake. He was succeeded in his command by Admiral De Witt, whom Blake defeated off the Kentish Knock, a point not far from the Estuary. Van Tromp was then re-appointed to the command, and met Blake again between Dover and Calais. An obstinate battle resulted in the retirement of Blake, whilst his enemy, flushed

H

with success, sailed the Channel with a broom at his mast-head, as a token that he had swept the English seas. Blake returned to Leigh Road in the Thames to refit. The Council of State represented that it was inconvenient to bring his fleet into the River, and suggested Harwich. Blake persisted in his intention, and for two months he laboured hard repairing and equipping his ships. In February he sailed from the Thames with sixty men of war. Two of the most experienced seamen of the time, Penn and Lawson, commanded his vanguard and rearguard, whilst the fighting men were reinforced by 1,200 soldiers, commanded by Monk and Dean. The fleet was joined in the Straits of Dover by twenty ships from Portsmouth. "It was the most numerous, the best equipped, and the most ably com-manded fleet the Commonwealth had ever put to sea." Blake met Van Tromp in the Channel, and after days of hard fighting the Dutchman escaped to Holland with heavy loss. This did not finish the struggle, however. In June, 1653, Van Tromp had a drifting encounter with an English fleet, under Monk and Dean, from Essex to Dunkirk. It is stated that Blake was fitting out a fleet at Portsmouth, and that his appearance at the opportune moment with thirteen vessels gave the victory to the English. There is a record in the Calendar of State Papers which suggests that Blake was in the Thames and not at Portsmouth, for on June 2nd, 1653, the first day of the fighting, Captain Wildey reported to the Admiralty that Blake had sailed from the Estuary, but, owing to contrary wind, had up to that time not got lower down than Shoeburyness. The Captain added that he went on board the vessels left at Leigh and found them poorly manned ; the crews being taken to complete the complements of other ships. In July the final battle in the first stage of the Dutch wars was fought off the Texel, when Van Tromp was mortally wounded. The Dutch lost twenty-six ships and 6,000 men, whilst the English had two ships sunk and

1,000 men killed and wounded.   Peace was made in May, 1654.

For many years in the Seventeenth Century the Thames Estuary was troubled with pirates, who chiefly came from Dunkirk.   The troubles between Charles I and Parliament, and the consequent disorganization of the naval forces, greatly aided these depredators.   A pirate was captured even in the Thames itself.   One of the first acts of the Commonwealth Government was to protect the seaport towns and their commerce.   In 1649 Captain Henley, of the "Minion," was ordered to ply between Leigh Road, the Gore and North Foreland, to destroy Ostend and Dunkirk pirates who lay there in wait for plunder.   Captain Stayner, of the "Elizabeth," was also ordered to patrol the coast between Leigh Road and Harwich for the same purpose.   Apparently some vessels were taken by pirates from Leigh Road, for on November 29th Captain Coppin, of the "Seaflower," was given instructions to sail to Dunkirk and endeavour to bring back the vessels which had been captured, but first to obtain Admiral Blake's advice thereon.

Dutch Fleet in the Thames: Landing on Canvey Island.

Eleven years after the first Dutch war, when Cromwell was dead and Charles II reigned in his stead, we were again fighting the Dutch, and the cause was largely the same— the bitterness occasioned by fierce commercial rivalry.   Both sides fought with skill and vigour, and although the English won two of the three squadron actions, De Ruyter's entry of the Thames in 1667, his burning of Sheerness, and capture of some of the warships lying there, profoundly alarmed the public mind.   The third of the naval battles above mentioned was fought off the North Foreland.   Leigh Road and the Thames Estuary have an intimate connection with that encounter.   After the four days' battle in 1666, the

English retreated to Harwich, and the Dutch, after re-fitting, anchored in the Gun Fleet, not far from Shoeburyness, on the 2nd July, threatening both the Thames and Harwich. A fleet was hastily collected at the Nore, and in Sir Thomas Clifford's reports to Lord Arlington we have a daily, almost hourly, account of its operations when it sailed to meet the enemy. On July 5th, 1666, Clifford wrote to say he had come to Leigh the previous Tuesday. Scouts had seen signs of the enemy. A fisherman also said they lay at anchor in the Gun Fleet, except some fourteen or fifteen, which were taking soundings. In the evening of that day he again reported a S.W. breeze, which he termed an English wind. He had heard nothing of the Hollanders, and he believed the story about them being seen at the Gun Fleet was a mistake. We do not know how he became convinced the Dutch were in the Gun Fleet, but as Sir Thomas Allen's squadron was ordered to investigate, the latter probably confirmed the truth of the report. A fortnight later Dutch scouts were reported near Margate Road. The English fleet, commanded by Rupert, had reached the Shoe beacon and were weighing anchor when the wind changed. The enemy numbered ninety sail without hoys, and the English ninety-one, in addition to seventeen fireships, beside other vessels which had been left behind. The wind remaining contrary, the men were employed in pulling down cabins and making other preparations for the expected engagement. All faces were reported to be full of courage. At noon the same day the Dutch lay between the Gun Fleet and Long Sands; on the 21st of July they stood out to sea, and on the 23rd, the wind being favourable, the English Fleet passed the Narrows, and at break of day sailed after the Dutch. On the 25th July, Rupert and Albemarle (Monk) came up with the enemy and beat them in the battle which ensued off the North Foreland. Harwich was crowded with the wounded from this engagement, and men who had lost their limbs were reported to be lying in the streets for lack of shelter, with the plague raging virulently. The English Fleet returned to Leigh Road in November, and, to save expense, was laid up for the winter, mainly in the Medway. Owing to lack of funds, and serious troubles consequent upon the non-payment of the seamen, many of them were not commissioned again the following year. De Ruyter took advantage of this, and in June, 1667, he entered the mouth of the Thames. One squadron of light vessels, under Van Gent, was ordered to ascend the river and surprise some English ships lying there. Owing to lack of wind, Gent only got to Hole Haven, at the western extremity of Canvey Island, and anchored there for the night. On the following day a number of the seamen landed on Canvey Island, where they fired several buildings and stole some sheep. They quickly re-embarked, however, and in the afternoon of the same day Van Gent joined De Ruyter, and Sheerness dockyard was captured, together with some of the King's ships. The next day they sailed up the Medway, burnt several big men of war, and also attacked Upnor Castle. Here, however, they were not successful, and retired with some loss, abandoning two of their ships, which they fired. A sad feature of a sad business was that the Dutch had on board many English deserters, who had left their country's service because they could not get their pay. The invaders retired to the mouth of the Thames, and lay there without interference for some days. They then fought an engagement below Leigh with Sir Edward Spragg, but without definite result. When peace was declared the Dutch ships were in the neighbourhood of Harwich. The landing on Canvey Island caused widespread consternation in Essex, and at one time it was reported that Leigh had been fired. On June 10th the King ordered the Lord Lieutenant to send to Leigh such of the Militia as were not employed towards Harwich, whilst Sir John Bramston, of Chelmsford, wrote to a friend at Lincolns Inn that the greater part of a regiment had been marched from Chelmsford to Leigh, the idea being that the enemy would attempt to land at Wakering, Foulness, or some other suitable place. The proximity of Dutch warships was evidently the cause of £15 15s. being spent by Prittlewell parish on firing, pitch and tar for the beacon. The account was placed before the Vestry on March 23rd and not passed, being referred to the treasurer of the county for payment. It is not certain where this beacon was erected. At times the church tower was used, but a beacon was also shown on old maps existing on Milton Hall Estate, near by the thoroughfare now known as Cliff Town Parade.

The Third Dutch War, commenced in 1672, was the result of the secret treaty of Dover between France and England. This had for its object the partition of Holland between the two powers and the conversion of the former country to Catholicism. The navies of both nations joined in attacking the Dutch, but with little success, and Louis the Fourteenth's great army of invasion was checked by the opening of the dykes by the unconquerable Dutchmen and the rise to power of William of Orange, later King of England, under the title of William III. The Thames was again the centre of naval activity; the commander of the English Fleet being the Duke of York, afterwards James II. Early in May, 1672, the English anchored near the "Shoe," with the Dutch very active outside, though not strong enough to attack. De Ruyter, had his whole fleet been ready, intended to strike at his opponent at the Nore, but, owing to delay in his preparations, he could not prevent the junction of the French and English squadrons, and he did not come up with them until they had reached Southwold Bay. The public, however, had not got over the fright of 1667, and at Deal rumours spread of a British defeat off Shoeburyness. This was false; the only event of importance at that time being the grounding of the Dutch Vice-Admiral's ship off Shoebury;

which, it was also asserted, he had deserted and blown up. The battle of Southwold Bay or Solebay, June 2nd, 1672, was indecisive, though it has an interest for us as being the action in which Sir Richard Haddock won great distinction. In September of the same year Charles II paid a visit to the buoy at the Nore to witness the trials of a ship called the "Greyhound." In May of next year Prince Rupert, the English Admiral, suggested to an official that a way should be found of signalling from Leigh when the Dutch Fleet or any ship was in sight of the Forelands, so as to warn merchantmen. In 1673 three drawn battles were fought by the allied squadrons and the Dutch off the Coast of Holland. The first fight took place in June. On April 27th Prince Rupert had ten sail near Hole Haven. He was on his way to Leigh Road to take up pilots for Holland. The companies of Lord Power's regiment quartered at Leigh were ordered aboard the fleet. Complaint was made that thirteen shipwrights from Woolwich were sent to do work to a fireship at Tilbury, but were persuaded to come to Leigh Road, where the fleet lay, and were there impressed. Trinity House asked assistance from the naval authorities to set the Shoe beacon for the better security of the warships, and also for licences to prevent the pressing of men engaged on the work. In May the English Fleet was still off Shoeburyness, but by June it had sailed to fight the three battles above mentioned—the last in the history of the Anglo-Dutch wars. Two years later Van Tromp, son of the old sea dog who sailed the Channel with a broom at his masthead, was royally entertained at Sheerness.

The Estuary was also the scene of other notable events in the closing years of the Seventeenth Century. On the landing of the Prince of Orange in 1688, James II fled from Nottingham to the Isle of Sheppey, in an attempt to embark on a hoy which was ready to convey him to France. Suspecting him to be a Jesuit some fishermen refused to permit him to leave, and he was escorted back to London by a troop of Life Guards. It was not, however, desired that he should be prevented from escaping, and very shortly afterwards he found means of safely embarking for France. In 1690 the Dutch and English Fleets fought the French off Beachy Head. Herbert, the commander, is said to have stood idly by whilst the Dutch were beaten, and at nightfall to have withdrawn to the shelter of the Thames. The position was brilliantly reversed in 1692, when Russell beat the French off La Hogue. In 1694 there was considerable activity in the search for hostile people who were travelling to and from France, where James II had his headquarters. In January a boat was stationed at Leigh to stop small vessels and search for disaffected persons and papers, and a month later a warrant was issued to arrest seven people who were aboard the "Katherine" in Leigh Road.

Press Gangs at Work.

Recruiting for the Navy by force was a familiar method of increasing the personnel in the Seventeenth Century. In 1637 the Deputy Vice-Admiral for Essex (Richard Pulley) wrote from Leigh that the officer of the Navy appointed to impress 150 sailors met with many hindrances. Among other things, Sir Henry Palmer exempted the able-bodied inhabitants of Barling and places adjoining, alleging that it was the desire of the Board of Greencloth that some boats might be free to carry oysters to the Court. Sir Henry, it was complained, granted too many of these warrants. In 1652, when the press gangs were at work to man the fleet engaged in the first Dutch war, orders were issued to the press officers to permit four hoymen of Leigh to keep a crew of two men and a boy each free from impress. The following year—just prior to the final battle with Van Tromp—press officers reported 200 colliers to be in the Swin in Leigh Road, and stated that if five men were taken out of each there would then be enough to make up the deficiency in the fleet. After De Ruyter's raid on Canvey Island, the mouth of the river was carefully watched, and vessels were constantly searched for men to make up the crews of His Majesty's ships.   A Captain Perry was very active in stopping vessels and also in imploring the naval authorities to provide him with sufficient provisions. On one occasion a cask of pork fell overboard whilst it was being hoisted in.   It contained three weeks' supply, and the captain promptly asked for more to replace it.   He met with some success in pressing seamen, for in 1670 he reported he had obtained eighteen single men for the ketch " Eaglet," apparently bound for a voyage to Newfoundland.   He could not accommodate any more because he had no room, and he urged that the " Eaglet " should be sent to receive the men before they studied mischief.   He had but little employment for them, and if rain came on he could not stow either them or their clothes away.   The captain later on reported that the " Eaglet " had taken sixteen men ; two others who were in the Virginia trade being set free to do their business on giving a promise to return.   On a subsequent occasion Perry reported that he had pressed another thirty men, and Captain Bond returned to Hole Haven after having delivered twenty at Portsmouth.   In the third and last series of battles with the Dutch the need of seamen was severely felt.   Leighmen suffered severely at the hands of pretended press masters. Eventually the officer in charge, with the assistance of the soldiers quartered there, arrested the offenders and freed the town from sore trouble.   The press gangs were at work in the Estuary right up to and including the Napoleonic Wars.

The Lawless Court of Rochford.

Volumes have been written concerning what has been described as " the most extraordinary of local tribunals of England "—the King's Court of the Manor of King's Hill, better known as the Lawless Court of Rochford.   Learned antiquaries of the Nineteenth Century took part in an animated controversy as to the origin of this peculiar custom, and whether or no it was formerly held at Rayleigh and had been translated, many years after its origin, to Rochford. It is now generally agreed that the place from whence the custom sprang was Rayleigh, and that it was moved to the market town, somewhere in the Seventeenth Century, at the direction of the second Earl of Warwick, owner of Rochford Hall, probably to suit the convenience of the steward. The reason for its institution has never been definitely settled, and tradition is all that we have to rely upon for guidance. This represents that a Lord of the Manor, on his way home after a considerable period of absence, heard several of his tenants plotting against him. As punishment he ordered that all owing suit on his manor should ever afterwards assemble at cockcrow on the Wednesday after Michaelmas Day and thereat pay his lordship's dues and demands. The manor was an extensive one, for it comprised Scott's Hall, Apton Hall and Lambourne Hall, Canewdon; Rawreth Hall and Trindleys (or Trenderhayes), Rawreth; Lower Hockley Hall, Hockley; Westbarrow Hall, Eastwood; Little or West Grapnells and Great or East Grapnells, Wallasea Island; Down Hall, Rayleigh; Butler's Hamstall and Godfrey Beeches, Prittlewell; and West Hall, North Shoebury. The ritual was fully described by Blount in the Seventeenth Century in his "Fragmenta Antiqutatis": "On King's Hill in Rochford on every Wednesday morning next after Michaelmas day, at cocks crowing, there was by ancient custom a Court held by the Lord of the Honour of Rayleigh, which is vulgarly called the 'Lawless Court.' The Court is called lawless because held at an unlawful hour; the title of it was so in the Court rolls to this day. The steward and the suitors whisper to each other, and have no candles, nor any pen and ink, but supply that office with a coal. He that owes suit or service thereto and appears not, forfeits to the lord double his rent every hour he is absent."

The custom was also enshrined in Latin rhyme, of which the following is a translation :

> This Court of our good lord, the King,
> To name of Lawless answering,
> Shall at the self-same spot unite
> According to an ancient rite,
> When every field is silent found,
> And silence broods the pole around.
> The whisper'd business that is sped
> In dismal charcoal shall be read ;
> And when the cock shall crow his warning
> Of the near approach of morning,
> When the shrill summons sounds at last,
> Atoning for transgressions past—
> The Lawless Court, with humbled air,
> Shall for their monarch breathe a prayer.
> He who comes not here with speed
> Shall repent him of the deed ;
> Quick let him take his secret way,
> The Court may not his coming stay ;
> Yet his hand no light must bear,
> Darkling he must journey there.
> Thus 'mid darkness they alone
> For past errors can atone ;
> Then, 'ere breaks the dawning day,
> Steal silent from the spot away.

The Court, as we have said, is now usually credited with having been first held in Rayleigh. This contention is not only supported by an entry of the time of Edward VI concerning the death of William Lumsforth, of Lambourne Hall, who owed suit to the Lawless Court in Rayleigh, but Weever, who, in 1631, was the first to describe the strange ceremonial, indicates it to be in that parish, for he said that he gathered his information from "a gentleman of the country" whilst riding from Rayleigh towards Rochford, and that the latter showed him "a little hill, which he called the King's Hill." Benton claims that the Court in Rayleigh was held on the Weir Farm, near Thundersley,

at a spot formerly known as King's Hill, and that its transfer
to Rochford was purely a matter of convenience. He says:
"The original meeting place was a mile or so from a public
house, and must have been a most dreary spot, the approach
to which was deplorable, up a miry lane, in a primitive state.
This spot upon a dark and rainy night, surrounded by the
roughs of the district, must have given the homagers attending
the blues, which the punch imbibed could hardly dissipate."
King is more cautious as to the site, and contents himself by
saying : "If it were proper for an archæologist to speculate
or form a vague conjecture, I might be inclined to look for
the King's Hill somewhere in the neighbourhood of Down
Hall, Rayleigh, but I refrain." If Mr. Benton be right,
the situation in Rayleigh might with some appropriateness be
termed King's Hill, but the location fixed upon by Lord
Warwick in Rochford would not support that designation,
and it has been suggested that a more fitting title would have
been King's Plain. The precise spot was near the King's
Head Inn, on the road to Stambridge, and was visible
from the roadside until building operations a year or two back
hid it from view. The post was erected in 1867 and
is of wood ; being about five feet high, with a spike-shaped top
to represent the flame of a candle ; similar in all respects to the
post which preceded it. In 1647 the importance of this
Manorial Court had sadly diminished, for it only existed for
the collection of quit-rents and suit fines, which then
amounted to £6 5s. In fact, as another writer has observed :
"The Court had long lost all forensic importance. For
centuries past no prosecutions and no litigation had taken
place in it. Perhaps, indeed, no prosecutions ever had ; for
its title, 'Curia sine Lege,' has been conjecturally explained
as the 'Court without a leet-day.' And it had ceased to do
conveyancing work ; no demesne lands or copyhold lands
were controlled by it. It had become a mere settling day for
the payment of quit-rents and suit fines." Until the earlier

part of the Eighteenth Century fines were inflicted for non-attendance, but the custom gradually died out, and ere long the dues were paid at the office of the steward during daylight hours. The holding of the Court, however, continued until nearly the close of the Nineteenth Century, and the reason for its survival until that time is shrewdly hinted at in the dinner which preceded the Court at the King's Head. Both the social function and the subsequent mystery have been graphically described by Dr. Kenny, now Downing Professor of the Laws of England at Cambridge University, who visited Rochford in 1878. "A good supper i' faith it was. It was held in the traditional room, with the steward of the Manor presiding in the traditional chair, over the traditional joint and the traditional apple-pie, and, ultimately, with the most traditional of ladles, dispensing the traditional bowl of punch, compiled from a traditional receipt of preterhuman cunningness. A jovial supper it was ; as we ate up and drank up, at our feudal seigneur's bidding, all the proceeds of his quit-rents, and chief rents, and fee-farm rents, and fines of suit and profits of *rendre and prendre.* A pleasant supper it was ; for the scholarly steward turned the talk from topic to topic, and the Essex men told us all the wonders of their country—the 'English Goshen, the fattest of the land,' as it used to be termed in Tudor times. . . . . . Presently Mr. Gregson, the steward, broke in and warned us that, whilst we were talking of our midnight business, midnight was actually at hand. So we got up from our seats and sallied out into the dim passage, and hence into the Market Square. What a surprise it was ! The dark houses scarcely visible in the starlight, but the open square full of men and lads hurrying to and fro with burning torches. The lurid glare fell strangely on their faces, and flashed back every now and then from the windows. The noises of the day were all hushed to silence, and no sound was heard but the constant cock-crowing of the excited torch bearers.

On we sallied through the streets, bearing the steward with us and surrounded by our linkmen, who crowed as they hurried on. The town was soon left behind, and we stood on the so-called King's Hill, close to the wall of an old manor house. Here we gathered round a short post, about a yard high. This post, which replaces a much older one of the same shape, is carved in the close resemblance of a burning candle. . . . . . As soon as we reached this all shouts ceased, and we stood still and silent in the dim torchlight. Then the steward bent down by this little wooden stump, and, in a voice tremulous as if with suppressed emotion at the creepy horrors of the scene, whispered the proclamation, ' O, yes ; O, yes ; O, yes. All manner of persons who owe suit and service to this Court now to be holden in and for the Manor of King's Hill in the Hundred of Rochford, draw near and give your attendance according to the custom of the same manor. God save the Queen.' Then he whispered out the roll of the fourteen tenants of the manor—most of them, if not (as I was assured) all of them, being themselves lords of minor manors held from it. And at every name the crowd vociferously (and utterly unveraciously) cried to him ' Here ! ' and with his burnt stick he made his charcoal entry accordingly. At last the roll was ended ; and the steward bade all who had appeared at this Court to ' depart hence, keeping their day and hour at a new summons.' Then with a wild sense of relief the whole assembly broke the silence of the night and crowed exultantly. The torch bearers rushed forward. Bang, bang, bang went their burning brands against the venerable post till each was extinguished, whilst glowing chips and burning tar came flying in all directions. Then we dispersed and all was over till old Michaelmastide should come round again." The custom has now been abandoned for some years. It had long before lost all meaning, but as a unique survival of the custom of a past age it is a pity that it should have been allowed to lapse.

At Hoketide there was formerly held the Lesser Lawless Court, but this has not been observed for very many years.

Parochial Activity.

The registers of Prittlewell Parish only date from the Seventeenth Century, but the entries from that time onward afford much information as to the parochial questions which exercised the minds of the residents. First in importance was the care of the poor. Each parish, prior to the Poor Law Unions Act of 1834, was expected to provide accommodation for its own poor, with the result that the expenses of administration, of maintenance and care of the poor in parish workhouses, the easy going definition of what constituted a claim to relief, and the costly and bitter quarrels among parishes as to places of settlement, gradually put upon the parishioners a crushing burden, from which they were appreciably relieved by the Act above mentioned. The old methods of succouring distress were very similar to those of the present day, viz., doles to the aged and widows and children, apprenticing of orphans and provision of work. In 1637 the expenses of maintaining the poor were £30 0s. 8d., and in 1648 the allowance to a male pauper was from 1s. 6d. to 2s. per week, and to a widow 1s. A lame boy named William Battle was apprenticed in 1630 to a Leigh resident named Harding for eight years for the sum of £10 ; the order being that the boy should be supplied with a leathern suit, a shirt and a pair of hose and shoes. In 1632 the parishioners considered the question of providing work for the poor, and it was then agreed that four persons should advance 40s. each for the purchase of wool, flax, hemp, etc., obviously to be used in spinning and weaving. Twenty years later Captain Stane —a prominent resident—reported that he had 72lbs. of flaxen yarn in hand. Of this he made 69 ells of cloth, which he sold the next year for £6 6s. ; the weaving having cost £1 14s. 6d. Twenty-one yards of flaxen cloth were also

sold for 18s. 2d.   For attending to a poor person's leg John
Haydon, the surgeon, was paid a noble by Samuel Peck, the
vicar.   Beside the care of their own poor, Prittlewell and
Milton Hamlet were in 1652 compelled by Quarter Session
to contribute £4 14s. 4d. towards the relief of the poor
of Chelmsford, Moulsham and Danbury.   In 1697 the
accounts included the following items :

	s.	d.
Payd Muther Peck for a munth - - -	8	0
Payd ye widdow spenser for ceeping ye garl -	13	0
Layd out at Chelmsford for ye wench at Suten	3	8
Payd a wooman for thre days work - -	1	6
Payd Goodman Barnard for cewring ye girl -	1	0
Payd to ye wench at wilbors - - -	0	6

With the opening of the Eighteenth Century there was either
a large increase of the poor or there was a movement towards
a more definite system of relief, for in 1728 it was agreed to
erect a workshop for the relief of the poor jointly with two or
more parishes, but the records do not state whether the
project was carried out.   However, in 1759 a workhouse was
hired for £3, and the accounts for provisioning that institution showed that a shoulder of lamb and veal cost 3½d. per
lb. ;   quarter of mutton, 22lbs., 2½d. per lb. ;   quartern loaf,
5d. ;   flour, 4s. 8d. per barrel ; cheese, 3½d. per lb. ;   wheat,
15s. per sack ;   sack of flour, £1 3s. ;   flannel, 1s. per yard ;
coal, £1 8s. per chaldron ;   wood and faggots, £1 per 100 ;
dish kettle (probably of brass), 11s. ;   a coffin, 9s. ;   pair of
girl's shoes, 2s.   The parish built a workhouse in 1786 at the
corner of the road leading to Sutton from both Prittlewell and
Southend.   The property continued to be used for this
purpose until the Union was formed, and then was sold to the
Scratton family ; the residence being converted into several
dwellings, which are still standing and are known as Workhouse Cottages.   In 1813 it was resolved that the clothing for
the male inmates should be made of coarse cloth of mixed dark

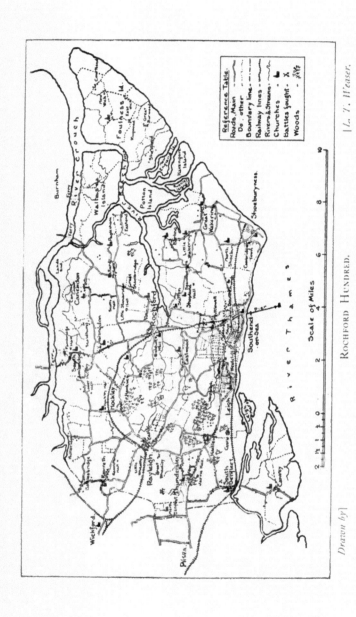

Drawn by]   [L. T. Weaser.

ROCHFORD HUNDRED.

grey colour, marked with a large Roman " P " on the collar of
each coat; the women and girls also to have clothes of this
colour, similarly marked, with strong brown worsted stockings
for both sexes. The poor were kept by the workhouse master
at 3s. per head per week, and were employed in spinning and
carding wool for his benefit. In 1817 the names of all
persons receiving relief were ordered to be posted weekly in
some conspicuous part of the tap rooms of the public houses.

The Rector of Rayleigh has given extracts from the
registers of that parish which throw more light upon the
early Workhouse system than do the entries at Prittlewell.
In 1796 Rayleigh Vestry entered into an agreement with
a Brentwood weaver named John Pearson to " find the paupers
of the parish of Rayleigh, who shall be in the Workhouse,
with all necessary meat, drink and clothing, after being
decently clothed at the parish expense. J. P. shall be
allowed and compelled to keep at work and employ in a
reasonable manner the said paupers in whatever manner he
shall think most to his advantage in the spinning and woollen
manufactures; to be allowed 3s. per week for each pauper,
and also three chaldrons of coal per annum and £2 for each
lying-in; and the parishioners further agree to provide all
necessary furniture and utensils for the use of the house, and
likewise all spinning wheels, etc." In the agreement next
year the conditions were slightly altered, and again in 1812,
owing to the varying prices of goods. In the latter agreement
the governor was to be paid 7s. per week each for the care of
two lunatics. Between 1822-29 thirteen Rayleigh youths
were apprenticed either as blacksmiths, carpenters, cordwainers,
brush makers, tailors, hatters or fishermen.

The cost of removal of paupers from one parish to their
place of settlement in another was enormous. North Shoebury amalgamated with South Shoebury and Foulness Island
for poor relief purposes. In one case it cost £10 10s. to
convey a man and his family from that district to Thriplow,

I

Cambridgeshire, and £17 12s. 4d. for taking two women
from Foulness Island to Suffolk. A curious entry in the
Prittlewell Vestry minutes concerns the payment of £8 8s. by
the overseer to a man named Curry when he married Hannah
Cleve, and 7s. more when the ceremony had been completed.
The local surgeon in 1766 received £6 6s. per annum for
attending to the poor of the parish. There was a gradual rise
in the scale of remuneration, for in 1776 John Arnold had
£9 9s. for acting as surgeon, apothecary and man-midwife,
whilst a year or two later Richard Wren had £10 10s. for
the same duties. In the early part of the Nineteenth Century
the salary had risen to £40 per annum.

Other parochial matters also occupied the attention of
the Vestry. In 1665 the great plague was raging in London,
and there was considerable fear of the contagion spreading to
Prittlewell. The annual fair, "which is only arbitrary and
not by charter," was, therefore, ordered not to be held, "lest
by permitting the same to be kept we should be instrumental
to bring this said infectious disease upon ourselves, which
hitherto, through the mercy and goodness of God, we have
been preserved from." It is not known whether the plague
did reach the parish. The deaths registered in that year were
fewer than usual, though there is a tradition that victims of
the pestilence were buried at Sutton. In June, 1666, Captain
Stane had the highway measurement taken from Prittlewell
Church porch to Rayleigh Church porch, and it was found to
be 6 miles, 144 rods, and by the footway 5 miles, 142 rods.
Ten years later a dispute arose with the owner (Mr. Arthur)
of what was then known as Southend. Mr. Arthur interfered
with the taking of gravel from the sea shore for the repair
of the highways; giving orders to his tenant to stop the carts
of the surveyors from removing the material. The parish
claimed "ancient custom," and instructed the officers to
maintain the privilege by all lawful means, the cost of the
litigation to be borne out of a voluntary rate. There is

no record as to the result of the dispute. These were times
of parochial storm ; for shortly afterwards, in 1678, William
Unthank received the support of Vestry in obtaining an
order to compel the inhabitants of Milton Hamlet, who
claimed to be a separate parish, to contribute towards the
cost of erecting a bridge over the brook in North Street.
This was probably a footbridge, for such a structure was
in existence in 1800 on the side of the road next the pump.
It was pulled down upon the construction of the present road
bridge.

The Oyster Industry.

The oyster has from time immemorial been associated
with Essex. Parts of the coast make excellent breeding
and fattening grounds, and the industry has been so prolific
in supply that 70 per cent. of the world's consumption
comes from the rivers and flats of this county. Prior to
1700 there was little or no scientific cultivation of the oyster.
About that year Colchester began to give attention to the
matter, and as a consequence the oyster trade gradually
reached enormous proportions ; the average annual produce
now being reckoned by millions. The indigenous oyster
at one time spread in banks all over the area of the Thames
Estuary, but ceaseless dredging has rooted them out until only
two banks of any size survive. The private fisheries of
South-East Essex have, however, developed, and until a few
years ago the foreshore opposite Southend and Southchurch
provided important fattening grounds. Writing in 1786,
Morant observed : "The shore against Southchurch is a very
good nursery for oysters, a quality which was accidentally
discovered about 1700. One, Outing, having been out at
sea in his hoy or boat, and having on board some small
oysters more than could be used, he threw them overboard on
this shore. About a year after, being accidentally here at
low water, and seeing these oysters, he opened some and found

them much improved in size and fatness. He got more oysters and tried the experiment again and found it to answer. Upon that he went to Mr. Asser and took a lease of the shore at a low rent, the method of improving oysters by laying them here not being known. By this trade Outing got a great deal of money and built a house near the shore, now inhabited by a dredger. From that time advantageous leases have been granted of this shore, and a great trade in oysters been carried on." The virtues of this coast became rapidly known. The Southend foreshore was also devoted to the same culture, and so continued to within the last fifteen years. Of this Morant wrote: " On this shore is a good nursery for oysters. The oysters are brought hither small from the southern coast of this island, particularly from the coast of Sussex and Dorsetshire, where the dredgers employ the poor people to pick them in baskets in the months of February, March and April, and, putting them in vessels which are ready to receive them, sail back here and lay them in the water till they come to their proper growth, which is about seven or eight months. The owners of the oysters here have their proper limits staked out, and have an advantage over the rest of the dredgers in this county in being so much nearer London ; but, in a frosty season, the oysters here, from the shallowness of the water, are more liable to be killed by the severity of the weather ; the shore being even and dry when the tide is out, and not having the conveniency of the pits and layings about Colchester and Maldon, which are replenished with new water almost at every tide." The reason for the Thames Estuary being a good feeding ground has been attributed by Dr. Murie to "the shallow waters conducing to a congenial temperature. Then their salinity just hits the happy medium, varied by occasional freshets from the rivers. But the great factor of the oysters thriving and breeding so well in the Thames Estuary, and the creeks and waters connected therewith, is the abundance of diatoms, foraminifera and such like microscopic plants and animals. On the muddy clay, when dry at ebb, there is everywhere a coating of olive-brown, slimy-looking material, otherwise a delicate film of diatoms of various species. Now nothing equals the unctuous blue London clay—locally known as 'clyte'—together with brackish water, for the fostering of these lowly organized algæ. Add to this a substratum of gravel and shelly sand, with just sufficient superficial deposit, teeming as it does with microscopic life, and you have a choice home for the sedentary oyster and its molluscan fraternity." Beside the Thames there are other rivers connected with the Hundred which have also become famous oyster grounds. The River Crouch, the northern boundary, contains one of the largest fisheries of its kind in England. It is worked by a private company, which normally employs ten boats and from forty to fifty men. Another fishery, which has a more intimate connection with the countryside, is that of the River Roach, which takes its rise in Eastwood, and flowing through the greater part of the Hundred enters the Crouch near the sea, forming the western boundary of Foulness Island. The Roach is unique among English estuarine waters as a spatting ground, and this property has been ascribed to the action of the tide, by means of which much of the spat brought in on the flood is retained in the river. The Roach Company employs about forty men and boys, and its annual sales have exceeded a million and a half, but ordinarily they are less than a million annually. There are other smaller private fisheries in the same river. Self-raised oysters have been regularly taken in fair numbers in recent years on the Leigh and Canvey shores. Before it was worked and cultivated as it now is, several Leighmen managed to make a living by picking up native oysters in Hadleigh Ray, and at Southend Pierhead they used to be obtained in plenty. An oyster was found to have developed in a sea-water tank used for flushing purposes high up on a building at the end of the old Pier.

Of late years the prosperity of the oyster trade has been seriously affected by the liability of consumers to contract enteric fever from oysters which had become contaminated by sewage containing the specific organism. In the Crouch and the Roach this danger is not great, though in respect of the latter river the Company have had to complain occasionally of alleged pollution by Rochford sewage, and steps have been taken to remedy the trouble. In the Thames, however, the possibility of disease arising from this cause, owing to the growth of large populations on both sides of the river, may result before many years are over in the extinction of the industry on the northern bank. The several fishery founded on the Southend foreshore, having been purchased by the Local Board, was subsequently extinguished by the Corporation. In 1906 the Town Council were defendants in an action brought by an occupier of oyster nursery beds in Hadleigh Ray, named Hobart, who alleged that sewage from Southend's system was carried up stream into the Ray and polluted his stock, which was mostly obtained from America, France and Portugal. The issue was tried before Mr. Justice Buckley in the Court of King's Bench, and he awarded the owner £1,500 damages, with costs, in addition to granting an injunction. The case was taken to the Court of Appeal, when a compromise was effected, whereby the injunction was dropped and the Corporation had to pay damages and costs. As a result of this litigation, which cost the town nearly £10,000, a new sewerage scheme has been devised by which the sewage is to be treated before discharge. The proposal received the sanction of Parliament in 1909.

Growth of an Educational System.

The disendowment of the Guild of Jesus in the reign of Edward VI, and consequent abolition of the chantry priest, whose duties included the instruction of poor children of Prittlewell, left the parish, so far as we know, without an

organised system of education, though no doubt there were
private agencies at work to supply the deficiency.   It was not
until nearly 200 years later that an attempt was made to organise
a public school for the parish.   In 1727, mainly owing to the
exertions of the Rev. T. Case, rector of Southchurch and at one
time curate of Prittlewell, Mr. Daniel Scratton, lord of the
manor, was prevailed upon to convey to trustees some acres of
land lying near the bridge in North Street, known as Glynds,
a garden near the pathway leading from Prittlewell Priory
towards Prittlewell Church, and a small parcel of garden
known as Mill Croft, part of which was occupied by the
schoolmaster, and the other part let by him, and the proceeds
devoted to his support.   There was some educational work
going on prior to this time, because Mill Croft was stated to
be "then in the occupation of John Coles, schoolmaster."
There were trustees named, but Case appointed the schoolmaster during his lifetime, and after that his son had
the same privilege.   Upon the latter's death the school
was carried on by trustees, who comprised the vicar,
lord of the manor, and the vicar's warden.   The condition
attached to the grant of the land was that the schoolmaster should teach ten poor children of the parish to
"read and write, and instruct them in the catechism and
principles of the Christian religion according to the usage
of the Church of England."   He was to pay a nominal rent
of 9s. a year, and keep the school-house and premises in
repair at his own cost, "at the yearly inspection and order
of the trustees."   In 1739 Scratton made a further grant
of land, making a total of nearly twenty-one acres, and the
number of children to be educated free was increased to
sixteen.   The Parliamentary Commissioners who conducted
an enquiry into the charities of the country between 1819 and
1837 thus described the school building: "The premises
consist of a house of lath and plaster, situate in the village,
near the bridge ; it comprises a schoolroom of about 30ft. in

length and 20ft. in breadth, and several other rooms which are appropriated to the use of the schoolmaster." An additional schoolroom of brick was built in 1817 by Robert Scratton on part of the land belonging to the Charity. This was devoted to the exclusive use of the boys, and the old schoolroom appropriated to the instruction of the girls. In the same year, in order to extend the advantages of education to a larger number of children, Dr. Bell's system was introduced. The schoolmaster in 1836 received £23 per year from the endowment, the use of a house and premises, and a sum not exceeding £30 per year, which was raised partly by subscriptions in the parish and partly by a collection after a sermon annually preached in the Parish Church for the benefit of the school. The master was also allowed to receive a penny per week from all the children in attendance excepting the sixteen free scholars; he was also at liberty to take private pupils upon his own terms. His wife was schoolmistress, but received no salary; her only emolument being derived from the proceeds of the sale of the needlework of the children. The scholars were admitted on the nomination of the trustees from among poor parishioners who were members of the Church of England; the age of admission being fixed at seven years. The boys were instructed in reading, writing and ciphering, and religious knowledge; the girls being taught the same, with the addition of needlework. Books and stationery and a chaldron of coals were annually supplied by the trustees from voluntary contributions. There were between forty and fifty boys in the school and between thirty and forty girls, and a desire appeared to be generally felt by the poor parishioners to avail themselves of the educational advantages provided. The growth of Southend—it was made a separate ecclesiastical district in 1842—resulted in the erection by subscription in 1855 of a National School, near the Castle Inn, Lower Southend, controlled by trustees, consisting of the Vicar of S. John Baptist, the churchwardens and the lord of the manor. The site was granted two years before by the last named. A clause was inserted in the trust deeds providing that if a change were made in the original scheme of management the grant would become null and void, and the land and buildings revert to the lord of the manor. The British School, in High Street, the head-quarters of the Congregational body, had been established to afford facilities for educating the children of parents who were not of the persuasion of the Church of England. The school accommodation thus provided did not long satisfy the rapidly growing necessities of the town. The difficulty was emphasized by the temporary closing of the Southend National School through financial troubles. Early in 1876, therefore, notices were published by the Board of Education, which had been established as a result of the Education Act of 1872, calling attention to the need of extra accommodation, and if it were not provided within six months " the Lords of Educa-tion" would cause a School Board to be formed. The existing accommodation was then given as : Prittlewell Church of England, 175 ; British School, 233 ; Miss Felton's Infants' School, 7, Grosvenor Place, Lower Southend, 54 ; leaving 220 to be provided for. If, however, the Southend National School were re-opened under a certificated teacher, it would afford accommodation for 152 children ; still leaving a deficiency of sixty-eight places. Angry meetings of parishioners followed the publication of the notice, and determined attempts were made to prevent the establishment of a School Board. It was sought to control the fortunes of the Southend National School by a public committee, but the lord of the manor (Mr. Daniel Scratton) spoilt this scheme by pointing out that the grant of the land for the school was made on the understanding that the present trustees should have entire and sole management, and it was his pleasure they should continue so to act. Any alteration such as proposed would

cause the loss of the land and of the school buildings
thereon. If the present school was not properly supported,
he (Mr. Scratton) would use his influence in the right
quarters in favour of a School Board. Foiled in this direction, the parishioners were summoned to another public
meeting to protest against the Board of Education's threat.
"I abominate School Boards," said one, and "School Boards
are a bugbear and a disgrace to the country," piped another.
An effort was made to meet the necessity by voluntary
contributions, but it was a failure, the extra accommodation was not provided, and Prittlewell School Board
came into being in 1877. The Rev. S. R. Wigram
(deceased 1909), Vicar of Prittlewell, was the first Chairman.
Prior to this the Prittlewell Church of England School
had been removed from its old position near the village
pump and housed in new quarters in East Street, near
the church. The building is still used. The first act of
the School Board was to provide new schools for 500
children, which were opened in June, 1879, and upon which
the British School in High Street was closed. These premises,
greatly extended, are now called London Road Schools.
Up to the present there have only been two head masters,
viz., Mr. W. H. Norman and Mr. George Reed; the latter
gentleman still holding the position. The new school met
all requirements for a considerable number of years until
the development of the town towards the east caused the
erection of Brewery Road School in 1892. This was
followed at intervals by other schools in various parts of
the town. Leigh Road School was opened in 1897, and has
since been increased by the addition of a fourth department.
The next school was Southchurch Hall, of four sections, which
was occupied in 1904. Bournemouth Park School (two
departments) opened its doors in 1907, and the present year
(1909) records the building of Chalkwell Park School.
There are now provided ten Council and Voluntary schools

(including the parish of Southchurch), accommodating 7,500 scholars, in addition to a centre for manual instruction, cookery and laundry, and a class for mentally deficient children. By the Education Act of 1902, the Prittlewell School Board was dissolved and replaced by an Education Committee, appointed by the Town Council, consisting partly of members of the latter body and partly of nominated members.

The Science and Art Department was established about 1867, to provide technical and secondary education by means of science and art classes, principally held for young artizans in the evening time, but it was not until 1882 that the movement reached Southend. Two classes were then opened at London Road School for instruction in art subjects and animal (human) physiology. The instructors were Mr. J. H. Burrows (who was largely responsible for the initiation of the work) and Mr. W. H. Norman ; the movement also having the vigorous support of Mr. W. Gregson. In 1883 magnetism and electricity took the place of physiology, but little interest developed. Although the classes were never strongly supported, they had a stimulating influence on the life of the Institute, which had been started in an upper room over a shop in High Street. It was felt that this organization should foster the new educational effort, and for that and kindred purposes a building was erected in 1883 in Clarence Road, now utilized entirely as Town Council Offices. University Extension Lectures were then added to the Science and Art Classes. Owing to the devotion of the "Whiskey Money" to purposes of technical instruction in 1890 means were provided for carrying on the work on a more extensive scale. The late Mr. R. Langton (for many years Clerk to the School Board) moved the Local Board to obtain a grant of money from the County Technical Instruction Committee, and in April, 1891, a local committee was formed, consisting of representatives from the Local Board, School Board and the Institute Committee. The growth of the effort caused the purchase of the Institute building by the Town Council in 1894, and its enlargement by that body to better equip it for purposes of instruction. In 1895 legislation, prompted by the Minister for Education, made it possible to establish a Secondary Day School (Mixed), a movement which was earnestly supported by Mr. F. Gregson (at that time Chairman of the Technical Instruction Committee), Mr. R. Langton, Mr. W. Gregson, Mr. J. H. Burrows, Mr. H. T. Cox, and Mr. E. H. Draper. The school opened on September 2nd with twenty scholars; Mr. J. Hitchcock, who still occupies the post, being appointed head master. The success of the venture necessitated the provision of more accommodation, and the Town Council were persuaded to order a scheme to be prepared for the utilization of a corner site in London Road and Victoria Avenue for the purposes of municipal offices and school premises. As a result of a competition, judged by the late Mr. J. M. Brydon, the designs of Mr. H. T. Hare were approved. Additions were made to the Clarence Road School, but the continued increase in the number of scholars necessitated proceeding with the school portion of Mr. Hare's design, which was adapted to the London Road frontage of the site. A grant of £5,000 was made by the County Committee, but the remainder of the cost of erection and furnishing, totalling £20,000, was met by the Town Council. The foundation stone was laid by Lord Avebury, and the opening ceremony was performed by the Countess of Warwick in 1902. In the building were grouped the Secondary Day School, the School of Art and Evening Classes. Growth still continued, and in 1905 an extension was carried out, costing £5,000, and affording increased accommodation for the Day School up to 400 pupils. The property is now leased by the Town Council to the County Council (as the Higher Education Authority under the Act of 1902) for a term of years expiring in 1911. From 1890 to 1903 there were, under the County

Committee, three local sub-committees in the Hundred for the direction of secondary and technical instruction, but as a consequence of the Act of 1902, one representative sub-committee was appointed by the County Education Committee. In 1906, Professor M. E. Sadler, in reporting upon secondary and higher education in the county, wrote of the Southend Secondary Day Schools: "The most striking points about this school are its evident popularity in the neighbourhood, the excellent planning and equipment of its buildings, the spirit of serious work which pervades it, the skill and practical character of the teaching, the attention paid to the physical development of the pupils, and the success with which, under somewhat novel conditions, the corporate life of the school has been built up."

Visits of John Wesley.

Leigh in its religious life was much quickened in the Eighteenth Century by a series of visits from the Rev. John Wesley, the founder of the Wesleyan Methodist Connexion. When Wesley discovered that he could not conduct his evangelizing effort within the Church of England, he organised a mission of his own, and for the remainder of his life made constant pilgrimages to all parts of the country. His experiences have been recorded in a voluminous journal. He paid six visits to Leigh between 1748 and 1756, and his comments upon his excursions to this part of the county are extremely interesting. They present not only vivid pictures of the trials and troubles of travelling in those days, but also glimpses of the life and circumstances of the little fishing town. Its commercial prosperity had departed, and in his first note concerning Leigh, November 12th, 1748, Wesley says: "Here was once a deep, open harbour, but the sands have long since blocked it up and reduced a once flourishing town to a small ruinous village." The great preacher's journey was rendered exceedingly difficult by a hard rain,

which was succeeded by a sharp frost, so that most of the road
was like glass.   He preached to the inhabitants in the evening
and again the next morning, when he rode back to London.
Wesley does not mention it, but the local tradition is that he
stayed on all or some of his visits with Dr. Cook, physician,
a prolific contributor to the "Gentleman's Magazine,"
and a well-known man of that day.   Dr. Cook's house was
situated on the south side of the railway, and his garden was
taken by the Company on the construction of the line.
There is a quaint story regarding the house that a troubled
spirit haunted its precincts, and that at one time it was closed
owing to the state of public alarm.   Dr. Cook died in 1777 ;
leaving references to the spirit world in his will which
indicated him as a forerunner of the modern spiritualistic
movement.   Wesley's next visit was paid a year later, December 18th, 1749.   His comment upon it was very brief : " I
rode to Leigh in Essex and spoke in as awakening a manner as
I could.   On Wednesday, December 20th, I left the little
flock in peace and love and cheerfully returned to London."
He came again in 1750, when he found "a little company
seeking God, and endeavoured to encourage them in provok-
ing one another to love and good works."   There was an
interval of three years before he was next there.   On
November 12th, 1753, he set out in a chaise for Leigh and
preached in an extremely draughty room, and at the close he
said his feet felt as though he had been standing in cold
water.   The house where he stayed (from its description
apparently Dr. Cook's) was even more cold, so that "with a
large fire I could not keep myself tolerably warm, even when
I was close to the chimney."   Wesley had been very unwell
prior to his visit, and on driving back caught cold again.
When he arrived home he had a pain in his left breast, a
violent cough, and slow fever.   However, under medical
advice, he soon got better, and was preaching within four days.
On October 27th, 1755, he was at Leigh again, and in his

diary Wesley gives a graphic picture of the difficulties of travelling. "We set out for Leigh, in Essex, but being hindered a little in the morning the night came on, without moon or stars, when we were two miles short of Rayleigh. The ruts were so deep and uneven that the horses could scarce stand, and the chaise was continually in danger of overturning; so that my companions thought it best to walk to town, though the road was both wet and dirty. Leaving them at Rayleigh, I took horse again. It was so thoroughly dark that we could not see our horses' heads; however, by the help of Him to Whom the night shineth as the day, we hit every turning, and without going a quarter of a mile out of our way, before nine we came to Leigh. Wednesday, 29th, I returned to London." Whilst on this visit Wesley read for the first time "Lord Anson's Voyage," and remarked upon it: "What pity he had not a better historian; one who had eyes to see and courage to own the hand of God." A year later, 1756, he made his last recorded journey, and on that occasion succoured a woman and two little children who were starving and ill with ague; whilst he kept up his wide range of reading by studying Voltaire's "Henriade." The work which the great divine started in so humble a way never died out, and now Wesleyan Methodism is a progressive movement in the chief centres of population in the Hundred. In 1811 the little church at Leigh leased a piece of ground for sixty-one years, and upon it erected their first chapel. This was compulsorily acquired by the Railway Company in 1854, and as compensation they built another structure in New Road. This was succeeded in 1880 by a more commodious church, and then in the closing years of the Nineteenth Century an additional cause was started upon the hill (Wesley Church) to serve the growing population. In 1810 Leigh was constituted a circuit by itself, but from 1823 to 1846 it was linked with Chelmsford. From 1847 to 1853 it was attached to Maldon. The Leigh people refused to be joined to the Sheerness circuit, and were again constituted a separate organization, with a young minister, whose stipend was £55 per year. At that time there were only two chapels in the circuit, at Leigh and Rochford. Work was occasionally carried on at Southend, but it was not until 1860 that regular services were established there. They were held in a house near the Army and Navy Inn ; forty persons comprising the membership. It was decided to build a church, but some of the trustees objected to the control of the Wesleyan Conference. . They had their way, and as a consequence the Free Methodist Chapel was built, with Mr. Michael Tomlin as minister-in-charge. In 1868 the remnant faithful to Conference commenced services in a tent on Runwell Terrace Green (now occupied by houses). This was subsequently blown down, and occasional services were then held at private houses until the liberality of Messrs. Baxter and Cater enabled the Society to erect the present chapel in Park Road in 1872, at a cost of £2,500 ; the minister's house and schoolroom being added later. The premises have been greatly extended of late years. There are now two other Wesleyan Churches in the Borough—at York Road and at Prittlewell. The cause also prospered in other parts of the Hundred, and churches were opened in the principal towns and villages at intervals, chiefly during the latter part of the Nineteenth Century.

Shortly after the Primitive Methodist cause was founded, about 1810, a church was started at Prittlewell. For years the sole representative of this Connexion in the Hundred was the Primitive Methodist Church at Great Wakering, attached to the Maldon Circuit. Then a little church developed at Barling. Independently, the Southend church in Pleasant Road was built, and later other branches were established at Westcliff, Leigh, and Shoeburyness. The whole of the churches in the Hundred are now united in a single circuit, with headquarters at Southend.

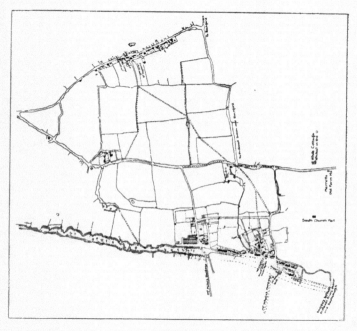

EXTENT OF SOUTHEND BEFORE THE PIER WAS BUILT (ABOUT 1830).

Reproduced from a plan in the possession of Mr. W. J. Foot.

Mutiny at the Nore.

The mutiny of the seamen employed upon the warships stationed at the Nore in 1797 was fraught with grave peril to the defence of the country. Lord St. Vincent had recently fought the battle of St. Vincent, and preparations were being made to destroy the Dutch Fleet, which was threatening commerce in the North Sea. The British Fleet, under Duncan, lay off Yarmouth, watching the enemy's movements, and the ships collected off the Nore were intended as a reinforcement. On April 15th the men of the Channel Fleet at Spithead refused to obey the signal to put to sea until their grievances were remedied ; these chiefly concerning a demand for an increase of pay and better treatment by the officers. After various delays Parliament voted the additional wages and removed 100 officers against whom complaint had been made. The men were pacified on the Portsmouth station, and the fleet put to sea. On May 22nd, however, the spirit of disaffection, encouraged by the vacillation of the Admiralty Commissioners, broke into active mutiny among the ships at the Nore. The demands of the men went much farther than did those of the Channel Fleet, and many were of a nature which it was impossible to concede. The crews elected a number of delegates, who controlled the conduct of affairs, and they were led by a man named Parker, who had formerly been an officer in the Navy. For various reasons he became reduced in circumstances. He was incarcerated in Edinburgh gaol for debt and volunteered for the naval service as a means of escape. He was sent to the Nore and there was entered as a seaman on board the "Sandwich." Upon the outbreak of the mutiny, all the ships, twenty-one in number, were ordered by Parker to drop down to the Great Nore. The three or four vessels suspected of still being loyal were moored in the centre, among them the "St. Fiorenzo," which was specially fitted out to take the Princess of Wurtemberg to Germany. Lord Spencer, head of the Admiralty, came

J

down to Sheerness to pacify the men, but without success. The "St. Fiorenzo," by a bold manœuvre, escaped to Sheerness, but the gravity of the situation was deepened by the arrival of part of Duncan's fleet from Yarmouth, which had also mutinied. The brave old Admiral was left with only two ships, but this did not prevent him sailing over to Holland to watch the Dutch Fleet; determined, if they came out, to fight them. Happily the enemy were unprepared, and the battle of Camperdown—at which Duncan annihilated them and earned an earldom—was not fought until the mutiny had been finally crushed. The mutineers dispossessed the officers of command, a line of ships was drawn across the Thames from Southend and Sheerness, and the merchant shipping stopped. Parties of mutineers frequently came ashore in the Old Town and visited the Ship Inn. The "Lion," a sixty-four gun battleship, was commanded for the time being by a brother of Mr. John Renneson, who kept the Library at Southend. He had little sympathy with the mutiny, and was pressed into the post by the men against his will. There were several attempts by ships to escape and firing was frequent. An old resident of Leigh, named Goldspring Thompson, who died in 1875 at the age of ninety-seven, had been taken by the press gang, and was on board one of the rebel ships. He had no liking for the situation, however, and with a companion determined to escape. They rowed away in a small boat, pursued by another with a crew of six. The latter gained on them rapidly and they took to the water, letting their boat drift. Thompson tried to make for Leigh, but the tide carried him to Canvey Island, where he landed. He hid himself in a wheat field whilst his clothes dried, and then saw a boat coming towards the spot where he was concealed. He watched his pursuers for three days, meanwhile living on corn and ditch water. He then made his way to Barking, where he joined the crew of a fishing smack, and stayed on board till the danger was over.

Thompson subsequently came to live at Leigh, and remained there until his death. His companion also had the good fortune to escape. The spirit of the mutineers gradually weakened. First they allowed trading vessels to pass, and then, deterred by the active preparations of the Admiralty to reduce them to submission, the increasing lack of provisions (in search of which they had to raid the farmhouses on both shores), and the impossibility of sailing away owing to the removal of the buoys, the sailors submitted to the naval authorities at Sheerness. On June 14th the "Sandwich" was brought under the guns of the forts and Parker was surrendered. He was tried by court-martial and hung at the yard-arm of his ship. He met death with great fortitude, and begged that his life might be the only sacrifice ; if the rest of the men were pardoned they would return to duty with alacrity. About forty more of the mutineers were condemned to death and others were ordered to be flogged. The death sentence, however, was only carried out upon eighteen. Several of the ships subsequently formed part of the British Fleet which shattered the Dutch Navy at Camper-down ; the spirit and gallantry of the men being highly praised on that occasion.

Napoleonic Wars: Fears of Invasion.

The outbreak of war with a Continental power always brought alarm to the inhabitants of the Essex Coast, owing to the possibility of invasion. The threat to land an army on our shores has happily rarely been carried out ; the chief annoyance being to the British merchant fleet through the depredations of hostile warships and privateers. Upon the rupture with Republican France in the closing years of the Eighteenth Century and during the long, harassing naval and military operations which ensued when Napoleon rose to power—a struggle which lasted for twenty years—plans were developed for the invasion of England, and the peril then was real and menacing. Much controversy has arisen as to whether Bonaparte ever seriously intended to invade this country when he established his enormous depôt at Boulogne. Whatever the proper conclusion may be, however, there is little doubt that whilst Napoleon may have had no definite plan, had it been possible for him to secure command of the sea, and had the European situation been favourable, he would have thrown troops into England and sought to capture London. His genius for war and extraordinary powers of organization were menace enough, in spite of the difficulties he had to encounter. Apprehension was felt along the coast of Essex, and in every scheme that was carried out the defence of the county and the Thames Estuary figured prominently. There was, of course, no actual fighting hereabouts, but a brief sketch of the preparations for resistance and the difficulties that were encountered must be interesting. In the present day the possibility of invasion is again being seriously discussed. In respect of the safety of our immediate shores, we have the advantage of the opinion of Nelson himself, who knew the Estuary intimately, and who, in 1801, studied the problem anxiously and carefully on the spot. Whilst attached to the "Triumph" at Chatham, Nelson, as a young man, was frequently out with the ship's boats, and thus, in his own words, "By degrees I became a good pilot for vessels of that description, from Chatham to the Tower of London, down the Swin, and the North Foreland; and confident of myself amongst rocks and sands, which has many times since been of great comfort to me." In 1801 he was appointed to the command of a "Squadron on Particular Service," whose duty chiefly lay in the protection of the Thames Estuary and South Eastern Coast. Mahan states in respect of both St. Vincent and Nelson: "Neither of them had, nor was it possible for clear-headed naval officers to have, any substantial, rational fear of a descent in force; yet the vague possibility did, for the moment, impress even them, and the liability of the populace, and of the commercial interests, to panic, was a consideration not to be overlooked." Nelson's mature opinion was, after considerable reflection, "Our first defence is close to the enemy's ports," and it was this grasp of the truth of the strategical situation that ultimately led to Trafalgar and the destruction of the French Navy.

In 1801, however, Nelson's duty was to devise a scheme for the protection of the coast line within his charge. Shortly after taking command he drew up some memoranda on the defence of the Thames, etc. Alluding to the probable intentions of the enemy, he observed: "Besides the stationed ships at the different ports between North Foreland and Orfordness, as many gun vessels as can be spared from the very necessary protection of the coast of Sussex and of Kent to the westward of Dover, should be collected, for this part of the coast must be seriously attended to; for supposing London the object of surprise, I am of opinion that the enemy's object ought to be the getting on shore as speedily as possible, for the dangers of a navigation of forty-eight hours appear to me to be an insurmountable objection to the rowing from Boulogne to the coast of Essex. It is, therefore, most probable (for it is certainly proper to believe the French are coming to attack London, and, therefore, to be prepared) that from Boulogne, Calais, and even Havre, the enemy will try and land in Sussex, or the lower part of Kent, and from Dunkirk, Ostend, and the other ports of Flanders, land on the coast of Essex and Suffolk, for I own myself of opinion that, the object being to get on shore somewhere within 100 miles of London, as speedily as possible, that the flats in the mouth of the Thames will not be the only place necessary to attend to."

His scheme of defence was to create three flotillas of gun boats and flat boats; one near Margate and Ramsgate; the second between Orfordness and North Foreland; and the

third in Hollesley Bay.   Floating batteries were to be
stationed at all the different channels of the Thames, which
would act as supports to the lighter vessels.   For a month or
two Nelson worked vigorously in carrying out his proposals,
but the Peace of Amiens came at the end of 1801.   He went
on leave, and was not recalled to the flag until 1803, when he
was appointed to the command of the Mediterranean Fleet,
and entered upon the long watch of the French ships which
ended at Trafalgar.   Whilst alarm was felt upon the water
there was equal apprehension among the military chiefs on
shore.   The east coast as far as Norfolk was surveyed
by Brigadier-General John Moore—afterwards victor at
Corunna—who reported in 1798 to Sir William Howe, commanding the district including Essex, Suffolk and Norfolk,
that "the coast from the Thames to Harwich is the most
vulnerable."   The Marquis Cornwallis, Master General of
Ordnance, was very anxious about Essex, which he said was
"a most difficult county to defend with inexperienced troops,
unaccustomed to move against a most active enemy, who have
derived confidence from their extraordinary success against the
most powerful and warlike countries of Europe."   The Duke
of York, as Commander-in-Chief of the Army, issued complete
instructions for dealing with the invaders.   The enemy, as
soon as he had quitted the coast, was to be surrounded in
front, flank and rear, and obliged to fight for every article of
sustenance.   Everything useful within his reach was to be
destroyed without mercy ; in any event, cattle and horses
were to be removed.

On the re-opening of the war in 1803 the fighting spirit
ran very high in England.   Volunteers were enrolled by
thousands.   The East India Company gave twenty armed
ships for the protection of the Thames, and several block-
houses were built at the entrance to the river.   Three military
divisions of Essex were created—Colchester, under General
Sir James Craig ; Chelmsford, under Major-General Finch ;

and Danbury, under Major-General Beckwith. Working parties of the Guards were engaged in erecting a line of batteries on the heights of Moulsham for the defence of Chelmsford, and it was ordered that every thoroughfare in Essex should be broken up, with the exception of the turnpike roads, directly intelligence was received of the landing of the French. The Rev. J. Wise, curate of Rochford, was appointed captain pioneer in Rochford Hundred, to direct the inhabitants in retreat wherever the Government ordered them to go. Drivers of cattle and guides on horseback were selected, whilst a captain of every company of fifty men was ordered to be paid 5s. per day on service, and every leader of twenty-five men 3s. per day. General Dumouriez, the celebrated French refugee, was asked to report upon the condition of defence in which the British Isles had been placed, and he was of opinion that Colchester Camp well served to resist an invasion into Essex, and that the Isle of Sheppey was the pivot of the defence of the Thames. He, however, was doubtful whether Napoleon did intend to invade these shores, and George III in 1804 insisted that the danger of invasion lay in Dorsetshire and not in Essex, Kent or Sussex.

The commencement of hostilities in 1793 made the need of men very urgent, and this district, in common with others on the coast, was called upon to contribute a certain number. Thus in 1795 Prittlewell sent three volunteers into the Navy, whose bounty expenses came to £94 2s. 6d., whilst next year two men were despatched at an expenditure of £70 16s. 2d., which included a payment of £5 17s. 6d. to a man who afterwards absconded. The operations of the press gang were also severely felt. In 1798 signal stations were established at Foulness Island, Wakering, Shoebury and Southend. The circumstances of the time, however, rendered it necessary that the countryside should do more than assist in finding crews. In the early part of 1797 the outlook was grave. Ireland was in revolt; the discontent which had culminated in the mutiny at the Nore was still smouldering ; the French were over-running Europe and the Battle of the Nile had yet to be won. At this juncture a new force was ordered to be enrolled called the Sea Fencibles. Its purpose was to provide for coast defence ; the personnel to be composed of fishermen, boatmen and others of the seafaring population, who were not liable to impressment, paid at the rate of 1s. per day and controlled by officers from the Navy. In 1798 there were two districts in Essex—the first from the Stour to the Blackwater, with one captain, five lieutenants and sixty-five men ; the second from the Blackwater to the Lower Hope (in the Thames), with one captain, six lieutenants and 187 men. A year later three districts were formed ; the headquarters being respectively Harwich, Brightlingsea and Southend. In the latter case Leigh provided twenty-two men and Southend twenty-nine. Fears of invasion became acute in 1801, owing to the preparations made by Napoleon at Boulogne, and by this time the number of Essex Sea Fencibles had risen to 1,205 ; the northern portion of the county providing the greater number. There was, however, always a great difficulty in persuading the men to come forward for training, though there was no doubt of their readiness to serve as soon as the enemy actually appeared in sight. Of the Essex force only 248 volunteered for training service afloat, the fear being that they would be sent to the East or West Indies. Upon this, Captain Schomberg, who was in command of the Southend district, wrote to Nelson : " Notwithstanding the number of men who have volunteered to go afloat, it is inconceivable the difficulty I find when the time arrives to persuade them to embark. The people, who are mostly smugglers and wreckers, object to go on board the revenue cutters." The volunteers from Leigh all withdrew from the service. By this time Nelson and the district captains came to the conclusion the force was nearly useless ; and shortly afterwards it was disbanded.

A Leigh resident fought at Trafalgar in 1805, and upon the centenary of the victory there was placed in Leigh churchyard a memorial stone with the following inscription : "On the Centenary of Trafalgar the four surviving sons of Captain A. W. Brand, who was buried here, have placed this stone to record that, as midshipman of H.M.S. 'Revenge,' he was one of those who, in the momentous battle of October 21st, 1805, so amply satisfied their country that they had done their duty.   During the ten years of almost ceaseless warfare, following Nelson's victory, Captain Brand bore a gallant part in many dangerous engagements and enterprises, distinguishing himself by devotion to duty, daring and seamanship worthy of England's naval traditions.   In the period of his country's great struggle, Captain Brand's father, himself formerly in the Navy, gave four sons to her service, one to the military and three to the naval forces.   Of the latter, Lieutenant George Rowley Brand lost his life in action in 1806 under circumstances publicly recognised as of heroic gallantry, going down in H.M.S. 'Unique,' which he commanded, with colours flying, and himself covered with twenty severe wounds."

In Rochford and district some hundreds of volunteer soldiers enlisted, particularly on the outbreak of the war in 1803.   At Rayleigh and Rochford infantry detachments were raised, and in 1803 Jonas Asplin, of Wakering, recruited a troop of volunteer cavalry.   The captain at Rochford was John Barrington, and his lieutenants were Thomas Swaine and John Vanderzee.   The corps in 1803 was made up of the three officers above mentioned, four sergeants, three corporals, two fifers, two drummers, and eighty-four privates.   The rate of pay for non-commissioned officers and men was 1s. per day. In 1804 the remuneration was as follows : Sergeants, 1s. 6d. per day ; corporals, 1s. 2d. per day ; drummers and privates, 1s. per day.   In 1806 the cost of uniform for each man was put down at £1.   The corps put in twenty-six days' exercise in that year, for which they received £1 6s., and the drill sergeant £13 13s. for 182 days' work. On August 22nd, 1803, John Mill was authorized to form a company of sixty-three men at Prittlewell. His lieutenant was John Watehurst, and the ensign William Hardwick. There were three sergeants, three corporals, two drummers, and fifty-four privates. Four years later John Lodwick was captain. There was no lieutenant, but forty-four of other ranks. Rayleigh also had a volunteer infantry company in 1801-2, with William Dobson as captain and R. Goodman and J. Bell as lieutenants. There were twenty-six of other ranks, including one sergeant. In 1813 the company had grown to sixty-six non-commissioned officers and men (three of whom were sergeants), under the command of Richard Goodman, with James Ford as lieutenant. The offer of Mr. Knapping to raise a similar force at Great Wakering in 1803 was refused, as a company could not consist of less than sixty, whereas the men proposed to be enrolled were only about fifty. Knapping must have surmounted the difficulty, for later a company was formed, with Joseph Knapping as captain, John Knapping as lieutenant, and P. L. Burchell, ensign. There were three sergeants, three corporals, two drummers and sixty privates. Some humorous incidents were related about the local troops. At Southend a rumour spread that the French were coming. The commander paraded his men upon the beach and exhorted them in glowing language to be true to King and country, only to find at its conclusion that there had been a false alarm. Of another captain of volunteers it is related that finding two young men were courting his maids, he had them delivered to a press gang, and put on board the guardship at the Nore. They were detained there for a week, when the captain, finding that he had exceeded his powers, obtained their release. Another commander found huge sport in a journey upon the sails of a windmill! Jovial volunteers fired into the old Town Hall at Rochford, which at the time contained a prisoner. Luckily he escaped by lying down. The bullets were observable in the building until it was pulled down in 1861. This structure was erected about 1707, upon the model of the Cinque Ports Court House. It consisted of wood and plaster, with a tiled roof. On the ground floor was a receptacle for pigs, which place later served as a barber's shop, whilst above was a large room used for wool weighing. With the victory of Trafalgar the fear of invasion passed away, but the subsequent military operations in Portugal and Spain, and the brief campaign which ended at Waterloo, created an urgent need for soldiers, and this Hundred supplied its quota under the various measures which were adopted to stimulate recruiting. The following advertisement, taken from a county journal published in 1806, supplies a typical instance of the means adopted to secure men: "Additional Force Act. Wanted one man to serve for the Parish of Rayleigh, in Essex, for whom the full bounty will be given. N.B.—Apply to the Parish Officers."

Smuggling Incidents.

The whole district is honeycombed with traditions concerning smuggling. Situated most favourably for trips to the Continent, with a seaboard population knowing every inch of the creeks and waterways, it follows that when the stress of high duties was linked with Napoleon's effort to keep our commerce out of Europe, the watermen of the Estuary and the Crouch found a lucrative occupation in "running" illicit cargoes of brandy, tea, etc. Smuggling was not, however, solely connected with the struggle with Napoleon. It had its roots deep in the past. Warfare with the French upon the waters often made the smugglers' voyage a daring one, though, it is said, Napoleon ostentatiously encouraged them on account of the information of the enemy's movements that could be gleaned thereby. The English men of war made similar use of these outlaws of the seas. Along the shore the struggle between the preventive service and the smugglers was waged with desperate tenacity on each side. The passage of years has begun to tint the episodes of this long drawn conflict with the old gold of romance. To the traditional adventures of these times has been added the skill of the novelist, who has graphically described the mystery of a dark night, a silent creek, a long row of waiting ponies, and the pervading air of tense excitement lest the revenue officers should disturb the night's operations. Kipling has best expressed something of the glamour which is associated with these extinct desperadoes in the warning lines addressed by a mother to her little girl :

> " Five and twenty ponies,
>   Trotting through the dark—
>   Brandy for the Parson,
>   'Baccy for the Clerk ;
>   Laces for a lady ; letters for a spy,
> And watch the wall, my darling, while the Gentlemen go by."

Probably if the experiences of those days could be repeated in this Twentieth Century the sordid aspect of smuggling, the brutality, the licence and the perpetual conflict of law and disorder would render it a nuisance of which we should be glad to be rid.

Smuggling was not unknown in Essex over 450 years before the Napoleonic era. As far back as 1341 complaint was made of the illicit export of wool and cloth. In 1707 members of the staff at Tilbury Fort were denounced for illegal practices. A few years later, upon the discovery by customs officers of concealed tea in a Colchester farmyard, the people re-secured possession of their goods by force, and took the officers prisoners. In 1748 a gang of armed men broke into the Colchester custom house and rescued 1,500 pounds of tea that had been stored there. Although the numbers of men engaged in running contraband were not so large as in some other counties, right through the Eighteenth Century there was an increasing amount of Essex smuggling.

The illicit traffic was secretly connived at by every person of consequence in the Hundred, and every creek from Benfleet to Battlesbridge afforded friendly shelter to the smuggler. It is said that the belfries of most of the churches were used for the purpose of concealing smuggled liquor and wreckage. The tower of Rochford Church was utilized as a store for gin, hollands and tea, and the cavity under the pulpit was known as the magazine. Magistrates employed their servants and horses in transporting the goods from the boats to the hiding places. The chief centres of the illegal industry hereabouts were at Leigh upon the Thames and Paglesham upon the Crouch. Leigh, at the end of the Eighteenth Century, had sadly fallen from its former importance as a port. It was then mainly dependent upon fishing and such revenue as might result from smuggling and wrecking. The population was under 600, housed for the most part in little wooden dwellings of only one storey, lining the water side. The means by which the Leigh smugglers disposed of their contraband were accidentally found after the fire, in 1892, which burnt down the "Peter Boat" public house in the High Street, a Seventeenth Century building. A large underground room with entrance from the waterside was discovered, together with material evidence of the use to which it had been put. This inn adjoined the Alley Dock, from which a narrow path once led up the hill and across to Daws Heath, a hotbed of lawlessness right down to living memory. The settlement of this latter district is attributed to some discharged soldiers who served in the Peninsular war. Upon the heath land they built themselves small huts, and by some means or another managed to obtain a precarious livelihood. Here possibly smuggled goods were concealed until a favourable opportunity enabled the owners to dispatch them to London or through bye roads into the centre of England. The chief place for deposit in the Estuary was a small island known as the "Gantlebor," near the Yantlet Creek on the Kent side.

In an action, Rex v. Montague and others, which was tried in the High Court in 1824, concerning the destruction of a roadway leading from Stoke to the Isle of Grain, a considerable amount of evidence was given by men who had been smugglers that one of their methods of disposal was to land liquor and other goods at Leigh or Southend, transport them to Yantlet Creek, thence to Colemouth Creek, and so to the Medway. About 1786, John Loten, a collector of customs at Leigh, knew of ten vessels of from ten to thirteen tons which carried on illicit traffic. He armed a small vessel with three guns and with her made many seizures. Another customs officer at Leigh made captures every day in July, 1802. There lived into the Twentieth Century an old fisherman who used to say that many years ago upon a dark night he would sail in a small boat down the Estuary, meet ships from the Continent and return to Leigh with his secret cargo. Although suspected he was never caught. Canvey Island was also a haunt of smugglers. Its church is said to have been a favourite temporary store for liquor, and a humorous story is related of a farmer who was in league with the runners of contraband. He complained that his house was haunted by an evil spirit, and so one day the parson was prevailed upon to visit it in company with others to make an investigation. He was entertained with a whole catalogue of dreadful sounds and mysterious sensations, but whilst examining the phenomena men were busily occupied in removing from the island church a store of smuggled goods !

In the Crouch, Paglesham was the rendezvous; the traffic being chiefly the export of wool and the import of liquor. In one year no less than 13,476 gallons of Geneva and brandy were imported. Until a few years ago many cottages were pointed out as having been receptacles of goods, and three pollarded elms near East Hall had, so the story runs, £200 worth of silk at a time secreted within their cavities. Benton has quoted considerably from a book called "Struggles

Through Life," written by a magistrate named Harriott, who resided at "Broomhills," Great Stambridge, a prominent man in this locality in that day. His volume affords considerable information respecting the habits of the smugglers. On one occasion in 1786 he was travelling in France, and wishing to return to England he sought out the smugglers at Dunkirk, as he knew he could be landed by them within a few miles of his own house. At the inn he became acquainted with some of the Kentish men, who informed him that the leaders from Paglesham were expected at every tide. He was invited to sit down with them and drink to the destruction of all revenue laws and officers. This he objected to and was fiercely assailed. Ultimately he betted a bowl of punch with the chairman, who proposed the toast, and a bottle of the best Burgundy with the others, that he was right and they were wrong. The bets were accepted, and he then enquired if in wishing destruction to the revenue laws and officers they did not mean there should be neither one nor the other. "Certainly," was the answer, and Harriott went on to show that if they were abolished so would smuggling be. "Lost," said the chairman. "Here goes, revenue laws and officers for ever." The men from Essex subsequently arrived, Harriott sailed at midnight, and was landed within a mile and a half of his own door. The leaders in this traffic were named Blyth, Emberson, Brown and John Dowsett. The latter equipped a cutter called the "Big Jane," which carried six brass six pounders. He had several conflicts with the Government vessels. Upon one occasion Blyth, who was a son-in-law of Dowsett's, was boarded by a party from a revenue cruiser. As the tubs were being transferred from one vessel to the other a good deal of drinking went on, with the result that the King's men quickly became drunk. As fast as the tubs were put down the cruiser's hold others were handed back to the cutter, and when the vessels parted Blyth was able to land a considerably increased cargo ! At another time Blyth was taken prisoner at sea, but the vessel got ashore on the Goodwins. Blyth was below in irons, and the captain appealed to him for his advice. He at first refused, but upon being promised his liberty he saved the ship and was set on shore a free man. When at home the men often engaged in their spare hours at a game of cricket, taking the precaution, however, to have loaded pistols and cutlasses close at hand. One day they were playing in the Church field when a bull, with a reputation for ferocity, charged down upon the players. Blyth caught up a cudgel in one hand, seized the bull by the tail in the other, and belaboured its ribs so strenuously that it turned and fled. Blyth held on as it cleared hedge and ditch, and the animal becoming completely exhausted, dropped and died. Blyth was a man of much reputation in other affairs. Drink seemed to have no effect on him, and he is reported to have eaten and swallowed two wine glasses. He subsequently became churchwarden of the parish, and kept a small grocer's shop in the village, where he used the leaves of the parish books and registers as wrappers for butter, bacon and other goods. On his death in 1830, after having had a chapter from the Bible read to him and he had repeated the Lord's Prayer, he expired with the words, " Now I am ready for the launch."

The coastguards' system was inaugurated in the early years of the Nineteenth Century, and this, with the abolition or heavy reduction of duties, quickly put an end to the traffic. Mr. Arthur Morrison, in his novel "Cunning Murrell," has made a plot to land a cargo of spirits and conceal it in a chamber at Hadleigh Castle the chief incident in a story of mid-Victorian life in Rochford Hundred. There is, however, little doubt that long ere that smuggling and smugglers of the old school had ceased to be.

The Crowstone.

A good deal of speculation is aroused among residents and visitors by the Crowstone—an obelisk of granite situated

on the beach off Chalkwell Esplanade, and forming a
notable mark along the shore.   No satisfactory evidence has
been forthcoming to account for the name Crow Stone, but
the purpose served is well known and fully authenticated.   In
the year 1197, Richard I, being in want of funds to equip
his expedition to the Holy Land, sold the rights of the Crown
in the River Thames to the Lord Mayor and citizens of
London.   In 1285 a statute was passed concerning the
preservation of fish in the river, and an Act of Richard II
ordained that the Mayor of London for the time being should
have the powers given under the earlier statute.   This is a
probable explanation of the reason why the date 1285 was
prominently inscribed upon the stones which, placed at
Crowstone, Yantlet Creek (Kent) and Staines (Middlesex)
marked the limits of the jurisdiction of the Corporation of the
City of London.   In 1746, Griffiths, in the course of an
essay written to prove that the jurisdiction and conservancy of
the River Thames were committed to the Lord Mayor of
London, stated: "Leigh, or Lee, is of little or no account,
otherwise than that it is well stocked with fishermen and
seamen, and likewise that about two miles below this town
the jurisdiction of London on the Essex side of the river
terminates at a place called Crow Stone, where there was a
mark stone, but by some accident it has been lost for these
several years past," so that it seems certain a stone was
used for the purpose indicated from early times.   The
stone was replaced some years after Griffiths wrote by a
square pillar of granite little more than seven feet high.
Upon it was inscribed 1285 and the words, "God Preserve
the City of London," whilst the following names of Lord
Mayors were added at various intervals : Brass Crosby, Esq.,
1771 ; Richard Clark, Esq., 1785 ; William Gill, Esq., 1789;
William Curtis, Esq., 1796 ; Sir John Eamer, Kt., 1802 ;
Charles Flower, Esq., 1809 ; Matthew Wood, Esq., 1816 ;
William Heygate, Esq., 1823; the Right Hon. William

K

Thompson, M.P., 1829; and the Right Hon. William Taylor Copeland, 1836. On the western face there are also marks, but they are undecipherable. These inscriptions are accounted for by the custom that once in seven years or thereabouts the Lord Mayor, accompanied by the Recorder and other City dignitaries, used to inspect these mark stones, and their visits were the occasions of festivity. At Southend the Mayor and Aldermen were "bumped" with much ceremony, and for thus being made free of the water they had each to pay the watermen two guineas, whilst the children were entertained with scrambles in the waves for money. Alderman Copeland's name was the last inscribed on the small stone, for by that time its surface could contain no more, and a much larger obelisk was erected to the north of the existing stone, fourteen feet high. Upon it were carved the names of Alderman Copeland, Sheriffs John Lawson and David Salomans, and various aldermen, members of the Common Council, the City Solicitor, Water Bailiff and Common Crier. In 1842 the name of Sir John Pirie, Bart., was added, and that of Sir James Duke in 1856. This was the last, for in 1857 the Thames Conservancy Board was formed by Act of Parliament, which transferred to them the rights and privileges of the City of London. The Crow Stone still formed the visible sign of the limit of the Conservancy's jurisdiction seaward, but by an Act of 1908 this authority was superseded by a Port of London Commission, whose powers were extended to embrace an area reaching to Havengore, at the eastern extremity of the Estuary.

Rochford Hundred a Century Ago.

Before dealing with the development of modern Southend, it is interesting to glance at the social, political and moral condition of the countryside a century ago. The movement which was developing for more liberal methods of government, more humanity in the administration of justice, and better educational facilities was hindered and repressed by concentration on the grim struggle with Napoleon, and the troubles of the people were added to by the constant demand for men for the Services and the increased taxation which was imposed to meet the cost of the war. The pressure of the times was severely felt, and the feeling of discontent was deepened by special local circumstances.

The system of plurality which prevailed in the Church was responsible for many of the parochial livings being held by non-resident clergy; the roads were mere tracks or ruts, intolerably dusty in summer and quagmires in winter; smuggling was practised everywhere; wreckers were not unknown along the coast; highwaymen were frequently met with; horse and cattle stealing were very prevalent; the administration of justice was slack and inefficient, and many of the justices too ignorant to efficiently carry out their duties. In some parishes the residents formed themselves into societies for their own protection. At Rayleigh, for instance, eight guineas were paid by an association for the apprehension of a thief who had stolen wearing apparel; a sum of £8 13s. 2d. was expended upon securing a purloiner of peas, and £3 5s. upon an unsuccessful pursuit of a horse stealer. The high price of corn, whilst it severely afflicted the homes of the labourers, made the landowners and farmers prosperous and also led to the inauguration of the last great series of land enclosures for the cultivation of wheat, which has left its mark on many of the roads in the Hundred. Land was taken from common and wayside and either added to the adjoining fields or the original hedgerow left and another planted; thus making a long narrow belt of cultivated ground and leaving clear traces of the manner in which it had been acquired.

The religious life of the Hundred was quickened by the advent of the Rev. James Pilkington, of Rayleigh, in 1797. He was urged not to come—the whole country was ripe for rebellion. Shops and public houses were open in the town all day on Sunday, and there was constant rioting in the streets. He steadfastly refused to heed these warnings; replying: "I am aware that I am liable to be cast into prison, but if you will leave me alone I will begin and leave myself in the hands of the Lord." Mr. Pilkington not only established the Baptist Church at Rayleigh, but carried on a vigorous ministry throughout the Hundred. He materially assisted the Congregational cause; aiding in the formation of the churches at Great Wakering and Canewdon, and doubtless also helping in the establishment of a branch at Southend.

There was considerable interest taken in hunting, racing, cricket, pugilism and other forms of active recreation and amusement. In 1808 the Foulness men, by advertisement, challenged any other parish to a game of cricket for any sum of money. "The Foulness Champion" (John Bennewith) was a famous pugilist in his day. He commenced boxing at the annual fair in 1810, and among his subsequent victims were "The Infant," "The Giant," "Bullock's Bones," etc.; some of whom he defeated with one hand. He refused to be scientifically instructed in the art, and on occasions was dreadfully punished for his lack of knowledge. He fought at Wakering, Hadleigh, Sheerness, Woodbridge (Suffolk), Rettendon, Cricksea and Southminster. At Rettendon he found a well-known man named Joshua Hudson. There were over 2,000 present, including nearly all the inhabitants of Foulness Island. Bennewith was knocked out in two rounds. At Southminster he was nearly beaten until roused by the promptings of his wife, who acted as bottle holder, when he pulled himself together and settled the issue by fracturing his opponent's ribs. Foulness churchyard was a favourite spot for pugilistic encounters.

For the purposes of a Parliamentary election the Hundred voted with the remainder of Essex for two knights of

the shire. The arrangement usually made was for the election
of one Whig and one Tory. In August, 1830, a dissolution
of Parliament ensued upon the death of George IV, and at
this contest the Hon. W. Pole T. L. Wellesley, a nephew of
the Duke of Wellington, unable to secure nomination otherwise, entered the lists as an independent candidate. His
struggle excited keen interest in this Hundred, as his wife was
owner of Temple Sutton estate. This local connection
secured him the strong support of the freeholders. He was
a man of dissolute habits, who spent not only his own fortune,
but also that of Miss Tylney Long, his first wife, who was
described at the time of her debut in society as heiress to an
estate worth £30,000 per annum and £200,000 in the funds ;
making her the richest female commoner in England. The
fight was bitterly personal and unprecedented in many particulars. It was the only one that continued for the full period
of fifteen days, and the number of objected votes (900) was
a record. The voters were divided into indwellers and
outdwellers. The latter were almost as numerous in Rochford Hundred as the former, and came from such far off
counties as Hampshire, Rutlandshire, Somersetshire, Surrey
and Sussex, with an extensive list from London and Middlesex.
There were 225 votes cast from this district (the poll took
place at Chelmsford), and of these Wellesley secured no fewer
than 152 ; Mr. Weston, the Whig, 81 ; and Colonel Tyrell,
the Tory, 60. This expression of opinion was not sus-
tained over the county, and Wellesley was defeated by both
the other gentlemen named. In Prittlewell there were
twenty-four indwelling voters, the majority of whom polled for
Wellesley. Their names included Asplin, Barnard, Bragg,
Fairhead, Francis, Heygate, Lacell, Lindsell, Mason, Scratton,
Thorne, Vandervord, and Wood. There were thirty-one
freeholders from Rayleigh, twenty-seven from Rochford, eleven
from Leigh. All the last named, with the exception of
one, voted for Wellesley, whilst at Great Wakering Mr.

Alfred Wedd was staunch to his principles by only voting for the Whig nominee.

Some light on the methods of transit for goods is thrown by Dr. Murie, who has written that the catch of the Leigh fishermen was sent to Billingsgate by boat, though occasionally a cart was employed. Sheerness and Chatham also received consignments. In 1820, however, Mr. James Cook commenced to run vans nightly from Leigh to London. The vehicles were large four-wheeled open conveyances, adapted to take the shrimp pads—oblong lidded baskets, holding from eight to ten gallons—and other catch. The service usually started from the Billet Wharf between 6 p.m. and 7 p.m., through Hadleigh, via Wickford and Shenfield to Billingsgate, where the waggon would arrive between four and five next morning. Mr. Cook accidentally broke his neck, and Mr. W. R. Hay bought the business. A rival firm sprang up, named Surridge and Hong. The latter soon left, and Hay and Surridge joined hands ; the former taking the trip between Leigh and Shenfield, and Surridge from Shenfield to London. After the opening of the line fish was transmitted by rail, and at the same rates as were obtained by the old carriers. In February, 1909, an effort was made to obtain a cheaper fare. A private firm tendered at a lower figure, which caused the Railway Company to reduce their charges by half, but the fishermen decided to stand by the people who made the first offer.

South-End: Its Early Days.

In 1768 a scheme was set on foot to make Southend— the southern extremity of Prittlewell parish—a resort for sea bathing ; "the situation being esteemed the most agreeable and convenient for the purpose on the Essex Coast." The idea caught on to some extent, and by 1780 the number of houses had increased to fifty-one. Eleven years later the erection of leasehold residences known as Royal Terrace and hotel was commenced, but financial difficulties ensued and for a time the buildings remained unfinished. They were subsequently completed, and in 1793 were ready for tenants. Two years afterwards the syndicate controlling the property failed; five of the houses being unoccupied. In 1800 the estate was sold and some of the houses were purchased by Mr. J. T. Hope, Sir T. M. Wilson, Bart., and Lady Langham, but the greater part of the interest was secured by Mr. James Heygate. "New Southend" was picturesquely described in the "Gentleman's Magazine" for 1794 by a writer of flowery prose, who was astonished to find the great change which had taken place in four or five years. He wrote: "From the shore ariseth a bold declivity mantled with evergreens and the gayest shrubs of summer; various walks intersect each other; meandering along the side of the hill through shades where seats are placed, secure from the sun's heat, for the accommodation of visitors. . . . . Should the impending cloud, apparently teeming with rain, deter those delighting in rural walks from taking their diurnal exercise, even though defended by an umbrella, the day may not be lost; for the romantic library, the elegant card, assembly and coffee rooms all combine against the ennui of a summer afternoon's gloom. . . . . . Old Southend emulates, in a less degree, the conveniences of its new neighbours; the humble cottages of the fishermen interspersed with a few houses neatly built and furnished as lodging houses have an agreeable effect upon the eye; whilst the inns afford viands and wines not at all inferior to those at the Grand Hotel, and what may be equally acceptable to many of the visitors, on much more reasonable terms." At that time the two turnpike roads to London, one through Rochford and the other through Hadleigh, were much improved. A daily coach service was inaugurated, and there was a postal delivery four times a week. Southend received great advertisement in 1801 by the visit of Princess Charlotte of Wales for the purposes of sea-bathing, which had been ordered by her physicians for the benefit of her health.

She was then five years old, and one day, meeting the then
Bishop of London, Dr. Porteus, she asked for and obtained his
blessing upon going to reside in his diocese. Whilst in this
district her Royal Highness stayed at Southchurch Lawn.
She patronised the bathing machines of Mrs. Glasscock, and
also spent a considerable part of her time upon the beach.
On one occasion, at Southchurch Lawn, she ran across the
road in front of a horse and narrowly escaped being seriously
injured. The Princess attended service at Southchurch
Church, where she sat under the Rev. T. Archer, curate at
Southchurch and South Shoebury, a noted character, who had
also occupied the same position at Prittlewell, and subsequently
became Rector of Foulness. He was a great hunter, and
when week-day service clashed with a hunting appointment he
would wear his surplice over "the pink." Once, whilst
marrying a couple, the hounds passed near the church, and he
broke out with "Tally ho, Tally ho." Upon another occasion
at Foulness he hurt his leg. The church was shut up for
twenty-eight weeks, and upon a colleague going over to take
service, he found Archer dressed in an old red nightcap,
smoking his pipe and resting his limb on the kneading trough.
When burying a near relative at Prittlewell, he stood over the
grave and observed : " Good-bye, God bless you, you were a
good wife, farewell ; thank God Who has enabled me to do
this. I daresay there will be observations made, but by not
employing a brother clergyman I have saved the fees and a
hatband." He was, despite his eccentricities, a well read
man, and published several literary contributions, which were
appreciated. The Princess died in child-birth in 1817, an
event which opened the way to the throne for Queen Victoria.
In 1803 Princess Caroline of Wales, the unfortunate wife of
the Prince of Wales and mother of the Princess Charlotte,
stayed for three months in two houses on the Terrace, and it
is from this circumstance that the term Royal became attached
to Hotel, Terrace and Library. At the enquiry in 1806

Particulars

AND

CONDITIONS *of* SALE

OF

A Leasehold Estate,

AT

NEW SOUTH END,

IN THE

COUNTY *of* ESSEX,

LATE THE PROPERTY OF

Mr. THOMAS HOLLAND;

CONSISTING OF

The CAPITAL HOTEL & ASSEMBLY ROOM,

WITH ALL ITS APPURTENANCES,

AND

Fifteen Substantial Well-Built convenient Houses,

WITH

GARDENS, enclosed by Brick Walls,

COACH-HOUSES AND STABLES,

Delightfully situated on a noble Promenade (enclosed with Post and Chain) gently inclining to the Sea with full Command of View of the Nore, the Rivers Thames and Medway, Sheerness, and the County of Kent; the Scene momentarily enriched by the passing and repassing of the Shipping that form the principal part of the commerce of the world

A Gothic Building, intended for a Public Library,

A RANGE of COACH HOUSES and STABLES, and TWO HOUSES adjoining,

Two good Houses in High Street,

EIGHT HOUSES IN MARKET STREET,

TWO GARDENS,

A large Quantity of LAND to Build upon (part on a Line with the Terrace)

AND

A Nett Annual Ground Rent of £76 9s

Which will be Sold by Auction,

(By Order of the Commissioners named in a Commission of Bankruptcy against the said THOMAS HOLLAND,) and with the Consent of the Mortgagors and Assignees,

By Mr. CHRISTIE,

AT HIS GREAT ROOM, PALL MALL,

On FRIDAY, JUNE 20, 1800, at One o'Clock,

IN FORTY-ONE LOTS.

The Estate may be Viewed till the Sale Plans may be seen on the Premises, and in Pall Mall

Particulars and Plans may be had as above; at the Black Boy, Chelmsford, at the Crown, at Billericay, at the Rose, at Sittingbourne; of Mr GILBERT JONES, Attorney, Salisbury Square; of Messrs DAVES Angel Court Throgmorton Street, of Messrs GREGG and CORFIELD, Skinners Hall; of Messrs MANLEY and LOWE Temple, of Mr DENNISH, Assignee, Tilliers Street, at the Rainbow Coffee House, and in Pall Mall

Printed by JACKSON & SON "Kentish Independent" Office, Woolwich

---

FACSIMILE OF PARTICULARS OF SALE OF ROYAL HOTEL, TERRACE
AND OTHER PROPERTY, AT NEW SOUTH END, 1800.

See page 171.

PLAN ACCOMPANYING PARTICULARS OF SALE.

into the conduct of this Princess, it was stated that irregularities occurred at Southend, but the allegations were disproved. The Princess subsequently separated from her husband, lived for many years on the Continent, and died in England in 1821, after an unsuccessful attempt to obtain an entry into Westminster Abbey, to claim her right to be crowned with her husband, King George IV. It was in those days that it was written of the town : "Sometimes the company is pretty numerous, and they are mostly of the superior ranks of Society ; the lower orders of the community not having as yet intruded themselves into Southend as into many other places of this description." A theatre was erected in 1804. Previously performances took place in the stables of Lawn House. The need for a more permanent building was supplied by a Mr. Trotter, who erected a theatre near the Castle Inn, described "as a very small house, but neatly divided into boxes, pit and gallery." The "Globe" newspaper frequently published reports from various watering places, and by means of extracts from the file for 1806 it is possible to give a detailed description of the incidents attending a "Season" at Southend, which lasted then, as now, during the months of July, August and September. The first reference to the town was at the end of June, when it was said to continue daily to improve, and was the resort of many people of the first rank. Most of the houses on the Terrace were taken. Admiral Rowley was a prominent figure in the social life, and took the lead in the patronage of local drama. The company then staying at Southend included the Hon. General and Mrs. Henniker, Lady Cotton, the Right Hon. Mr. and Mrs. Turner, Lady Elizabeth Richardson, Lady Charlotte Denys, Lady Rowley, etc. ; several naval officers coming from Sheerness to join in the festivities. The theatre was reported to have undergone complete repair, and would open the next week with several performers from London. On August 19th it was

stated : "Since this place was first called into notice it never
before attracted such a numerous assemblage of company as is
here at present. The lodging houses are very full, and
the inns, or hotels, as they call themselves, exceedingly
crowded. Yet, what in these speculative times appears very
strange, is that notwithstanding the extraordinary encourage-
ment given to the place for some years past, no additional
accommodations are provided, and the only new building
erected since the last season is, perhaps, one of the least to be
expected in a watering place, viz., a Methodist Chapel. It
was, yesterday evening, most numerously attended." This
reference to the chapel provoked a lively controversy. On
August 20th another correspondent wrote that it was not a
Methodist place of worship, and added : "It is connected
with a denomination of Protestant dissenters, called Inde-
pendents, a sect which is quite as far removed from the
Methodists or from enthusiasm of any sort as the Church of
England herself." The original writer retorted with spirit :
"I observe that a correspondent of yours has taken some
offence at the mention made of a Methodist Chapel at this
watering place when he should have been glad to avail himself
of the opportunity of correcting a very general mistake here,
as I never heard this little conventicle called by any other
appellation. I am happy to find that he has given so
satisfactory an explanation ; and if I profit by his rebuke it
will perhaps be the first benefit found to result from its
establishment." The chapel referred to no doubt belonged to
the Congregationalists. They held services at irregular
intervals in Southend prior to 1799 in a room at No. 3, Grove
Terrace, but in that year a rev. gentleman named Austin,
then living at Leigh, commenced regular services, and subsequently removed to No. 1, High Street (now forming part of
the Royal Hotel). The growth of the cause brought about the
erection of a chapel in 1806 upon land in High Street, given
for the purpose by Mr. James Heygate, who also gave the

necessary ground in 1816 to provide for an enlargement. The preachers were supplied for three years by students from Homerton College. . In 1809 a resident minister was appointed, and except for a short interval the pastorate of the church was regularly filled by ministers. In 1864 a project was formed to acquire a site upon the Cliff Town Estate, and the negociations were so successful that in 1865 the first steps were taken to erect a building which, with its subsequent extensive enlargements, is still known as Cliff Town Congregational Church. The "Globe" correspondent on the 19th August, 1806, also commented upon the "elegant display of company" exhibited upon the Terrace, beach and adjacent walks. Although the visitors were numerous there was then only one lady of title, viz., Lady Brisco, who resided in the house upon the Terrace occupied last season by Lady Hamilton. "The absence of this latter lady, who was the soul of everything cheerful and elegant, was deservedly lamented by all those who have any taste for gay and rational amusement, which seems to have fled the place this summer, as you may suppose, when I inform you that though the place never was so full before, there has not yet been a single ball or assembly since the commencement of the present season." There was, however, considerable activity at the theatre, where Mrs. Powell, a well-known actress of the day, performed in the early part of the season, and was expected again at the conclusion of her engagement at Windsor. Upon one occasion a special performance was given by desire of Captain Lodwick, who commanded the volunteers in the neighbourhood. At the end of August the correspondent reported the weather to be so bad that many visitors had left the place, but there were still an ample number remaining. The theatrical news was given at considerable length. "Cory concluded his engagement here last Saturday in Penruddock in the 'Wheel of Fortune,' which he performed in a very respectable manner ; after which the vivacity of Mrs.

King was much applauded in the performance of Roxalana in
the 'Sultan.' This night the company will perform the
'Castle Spectre' and 'Tom Thumb.' The theatre has
received many improvements since last season, when it was
not thoroughly completed ; but notwithstanding the liberality
and unremitting exertions of the manager to give every
satisfaction, the house does not appear to receive that
encouragement which might be expected from the great
number of visitors in the place. What makes this more
strange is that there is no other evening amusement, except
what may be obtained at the Library, which either for taste
in its arrangement or attentive civility in the ladies who
conduct it is not inferior to those at any other watering
place." Among the arrivals at that date were Mr. Baron
Thompson, Lady Baynes, Sir Thomas and Lady Wilson, Mrs.
Lambert and others. News contributed on September 1st
reported the weather still wet, though the town did not
suffer any diminution of visitors. The West India Fleet had
passed up the river a few days previously, and one of the ships
got aground nearly opposite to Southend. Several barges and
boats went immediately to her assistance. The vessel was
heavily laden, but the Spring tide of the next morning was
sufficient to float her, and she pursued her journey with
no other injury than a slight straining. Upon this occasion
the correspondent concluded with a sporting note : " The
neighbourhood of this place abounds so much in partridges
that one can scarcely walk half a mile in any direction without
flushing some covies of them. Of course, this would prove a
place of carnage to these feathered victims were they not
carefully protected, as I am told they are, by Mr. S——n,
lord of the manor, whose effort is to have an asylum against
sporting gentlemen, however poachers may try to ensnare
them pro bono publico, for I have not heard a gun fired this
morning except one, which burst in the hands of the gentleman without any material injury to him." September of

1806 opened with fine weather, and there was a great influx of visitors. The comedy of "The Rivals" was performed one evening at the theatre at the desire of Admiral Rowley, and attracted one of the most numerous and brilliant audiences of the season. The success of the entertainment resulted in an incident which the correspondent noted at length: "Before the commencement of the play some confusion and disturbance arose in consequence of some parties, from coming in rather late, or the impatience of others, who were regardless of ceremony, having lost their places. One gentleman in particular was outrageously violent at the disappointment of himself and party until Admiral Rowley, with that urbanity and politeness characteristic of the British officer, consented to accommodate them in one of the side boxes, and the general harmony was restored." The visitors at the time included Lady Lambert and Miss Canning. On September 4th an account appeared of an exciting bathing adventure. "A young gentleman from the City, who was also a young swimmer, having ventured some distance from his machine, began to doubt whether he should be able to return to it. Proceeding then to sound whether he was out of his depth, he felt himself embarrassed and found it difficult to emerge. After floundering, however, for a few moments, he felt his head above the water, and was enabled to cry out for help. Fortunately for him the sea was calm and the exclamation reached the ears of some ladies on the beach, who immediately screamed out, and it was equally fortunate that a boat passing at the moment picked him up without his having suffered anything but the fright." Licensing troubles were not unknown in those days, hence the note which was added: "A very extensive hot and cold bath has been erected here for some time past, but as the undertaking did not succeed to the expectation of the proprietors, they have adopted the plan of converting it into an hotel, and this being the licensing day at Rochford the case is now under discussion

before the magistrates; the inn keepers of the place and the
neighbourhood opposing the strongest opposition to it." The
"Victory," which refitted at Chatham after Trafalgar, lay off
Southend during the month, and presented a "magnificent
appearance." By September 7th the number of visitors had
rapidly increased. "Beside the frequent arrival of post
chaises, the stage coaches daily pour in fresh reinforcements,
and as the houses here are already full, many families are
obliged to seek for accommodation in the neighbouring farmhouses and villages." In 1806 a British force had been
landed in Calabria, Italy, to assist the peasantry in resisting
the encroachments of the French troops. At the battle of
Maida, in July of that year, the French were defeated at the
point of the bayonet, a brilliant combat, which shook the
confidence of Europe in the superiority of Napoleon's infantry.
The correspondent of the " Globe " thus described the
reception of the news at Southend: "The victory of our
gallant troops at Calabria, which caused so great a sensation in
the Metropolis, was also announced here by the firing of
cannon from Sheerness, the Nore, and the men of war in the
river. The cause of it was not generally known till the
arrival of the papers in the evening, but while this annuncia-
tion was going forward the spectators here were further
gratified by the appearance of fourteen of the China Fleet,
then sailing up the river." The arrivals at that date included
Lady Smith Burgess, Mr. and Mrs. Bellamy and others.
A despatch of September 11th announced great preparations
for a ball at the Royal Hotel, and an account of the benefit
performance of Mrs. Powell, at which " Romeo and Juliet "
and " The Children in the Wood " were performed. At the
end of the programme Mrs. Powell "delivered with great
feeling and effect some very affecting and impressive lines in
commemoration of the brilliant services, as well as lamented
but glorious death of the heroic Lord Nelson. Such an
address could not fail in any place, but particularly in this, of

producing enthusiastic applause, especially from the naval
officers who attended the evening's representation. She could
not ·possibly have selected a theme more gratifying to the
feelings of the audience, and her tones and manner were such
as irresistibly to produce all those strong-emotions which such a
subject was calculated to excite." A special performance was
given at the theatre on another evening at the request of Mr.
Jonas Asplin, and it was reported that visitors were still
arriving. As the correspondence closed at this juncture it
may be assumed that the "Season" had nearly run its course,
and by the end of September Southend had been deserted by
its patrons.

To commemorate the Jubilee of George III in 1809,
Lady Langham planted and enclosed a little grove of trees
at the western extremity of what is now known as the
Shrubbery. The following inscription was painted upon a
board and preserved for many years :

"Preserve, my countrymen, this little grove,
  Planted in honour of our glorious King,
'Twill show your loyalty, as well as love,
  And future ages will your praises sing."
"King George III entered into the fiftieth year of his reign on
this day, October 25th, 1809."

Three years later a correspondent, writing in the
"Gentleman's Magazine," praised Southend as a watering
place, though noting some deficiencies in its requirements.
The roads were good ; it was a modern bathing place which
was not known or accounted as such "forty summers ago";
there had been a considerable amount of building, and though
it was still without the advantages of a town or the sufficient
competition of tradesmen, it possessed several conveniences.
Eight or ten machines were used with awnings, and "the warm
baths, though confined in accommodation, are not objectionable, otherwise than the attendants do not abound in official
assiduity." The writer proceeded to refer to Old Southend

and New Southend, terms which were often used at that time to distinguish between the town lying at the foot of Pier Hill and the Royal Terrace and adjoining property perched upon the summit. He was careful to add: "The distinction between Old Southend and New Southend involves no distinction of gentility or fashion. More privacy may, indeed, attach to the lower town, while the Terrace is the scene of greater observation. The company of this place chiefly consists of families who live in the contiguous part of the country, and of those who migrate for a short time from the Metropolis. Mr. Baron Thompson is the most distinguished person that annually visits Southend." It was in 1812 that Samuel Jerrold, who had been manager and lessee of the Sheerness Theatre, took the Southend Theatre from Mr. Trotter, and worked it as a summer resort. He was, however, a loser by the transaction, but his short tenancy enabled Southend to have some connection with his well-known son, Douglas William Jerrold, the dramatist and wit. Jerrold, whilst staying with his father at Southend, was under the tuition of James Glasscock, who contrived to make ends meet by the varied occupations of a schoolmaster and tailor. In 1818 another testimonial was written of the town, which ran: "Southend has within the last twenty years obtained some repute as a bathing place, and has since continued to rise in importance. The air is esteemed very dry and salubrious, and the water, notwithstanding its mixture with the Thames, is very clear and salt." A very important addition to the transit facilities was inaugurated in 1819, when steamboats began to ply. There was considerable inconvenience in disembarkation, for travellers had to be transferred into small boats from the corn hoys and steamers. When the keels of the boats grazed on the sand passengers were carried either on the backs or arms of the sailors to their destination. The "hards" used for landing purposes were maintained by the landlords of the Royal and Ship Hotels.

In 1824 a much more ambitious guide to the town was published than that which had been issued in 1806. It numbered well over sixty pages, with several illustrations. Although it was of modest dimensions, it is questionable whether during the many years which have elapsed a more complete or better informed guide has been written. The book recognized that Southend's good reputation as a health resort was a first essential to its continued success. An opinion was obtained from a medical gentleman "of great respectability," who wrote: "Southend has long been considered aguish, and at this time great prejudice exists against it. That this arises from prejudice I am well convinced, having conversed with several eminent medical men who have visited this place, and their decided opinion, as well as my own, is that it is not aguish. During several years' practice I have not been called in to one visitor who has been attacked with this fever, although some of the families have resided here the whole year. The late Mr. Mosely was in the habit of visiting this place for several years, and he had so favourable an opinion of it that he always strongly recommended it. Sir James McGregor, Dr. Birkbeck and other eminent men appear to concur with Dr. Mosely's opinion by visiting Southend with their families." In the same guide there is a minute description of the appearance of the town, which is quoted below, as it presents a graphic and interesting sketch of Southend as it existed almost a century ago:

"The Lower Town is an irregular line of houses facing the "sea, and was the site of the original village, but of late "years some handsome houses have been added, between "which and the beach a small parade has been partly "enclosed and covered with turf. In the centre of the "street stands the Ship Inn, the principal hotel of the "Lower Town; it is a large and commodious building, "with every possible convenience, and during the season

L

" is generally full of company. There are also two
" secondary inns, the Hope and the Castle.

" Eastward of these there is a large brick building called
" the Hall, belonging to Mr. Vandervord, the proprietor of
" the barges which regularly sail between this place and
" London ; and it is here that the manor courts are held.
" There are several neat rows of dwelling houses in this
" part of the town, the principal of which are Jubilee Row,
" Upper and Lower Grosvenor Places, Wellington Place,
" Argyle Buildings, etc. The Post Office and most of the
" shops are also situated in the Lower Town as well as the
" theatre, which is at its eastern extremity. It is a very
" small house, but neatly divided into boxes, pit and
" gallery, and is visited every season by a company of
" performers, who have lately met with much encourage-
" ment, but, as is generally the case in all summer retreats,
" they are perhaps more indebted for their success to the
" generosity and liberality of the visitors than to the
" amusements they have to offer. However, they are
" certainly not inferior to such as are usually to be met
" with at places of this description. At the west end of
" the Lower Town there are some particularly good
" dwelling houses ; that immediately at the turning of the
" ascent to the Upper Town is the property of Lady
" Charlotte Denys. There are good bathing machines,
" and a warm bath at the Ship Inn for the accommodation
" of the inhabitants of the Lower Town.

" The New Town of Southend has far the advantage of
" the Lower Town both in point of situation and style of
" building, and in every respect may be considered the
" fashionable end of the town.

" The Terrace is a handsome range of buildings standing
" on a bold and commanding situation, fronting the sea,
" and finished in a neat and uniform style. The centre
" houses are ornamented with pilasters and surmounted

" with a pediment, and the whole are planned with a view
" to comfort and convenience in a far superior manner to
" the accommodation usually afforded in houses of this class,
" and particularly at the seaside. They have likewise the
" advantage of good coach-houses and offices.

" Adjoining the Terrace is the Royal Hotel, the principal
" inn in Southend. It is a spacious and convenient
" building, containing, besides a pleasant coffee room and
" many good suites of rooms for the accommodation of
" families, a handsome assembly room, 60ft. by 24ft., with
" a music gallery, supper and card rooms, and is ably
" conducted by Mr. Miller, whose assiduity and attention
" to strangers render him truly deserving of the patronage
" he meets with. Indeed, the concourse of guests in the
" summer and autumn has been sometimes so great that
" even with the addition of two houses adjoining his hotel,
" he has not been able to find apartments for them.

" Opposite the Royal Hotel is Rennison and Tarry's
" Library, a fanciful building in what may be called the
" semi-gothic style, with a circular front. It has a good
" reading room, and is well supplied with London and
" provincial papers, periodical publications, etc. This is
" the only library in the town, and is well attended,
" particularly in the evenings, when there are raffles and
" other amusements of the same kind.

" Adjoining the Library is the Billiard Room, which is
" light and in every respect well fitted up, having a very
" good, full-sized billiard table.

" Near the Library, and almost in a line with the Terrace,
" there is another neat row of houses called Grove Terrace,
" at the end of which a long avenue leads to Grove House,
" which is sufficiently extensive to hold two or three
" families. On the western side of the avenue there are
" several neat houses, as well as in High Street, which
" divides the Royal Hotel from the Library and joins the

" London Road. In this street there is a large, roomy
" chapel for the use of dissenters. In the front of the
" Terrace there is a fine broad gravel promenade, and
" between this and the sea is the Shrubbery, which, with a
" little care, and at a very small expense, might be made a
" most delightful resort. It extends the entire length of
" the Terrace, the descent from which to the beach has
" been cut into intersecting walks, and planted with a
" variety of trees, the whole being enclosed with a light
" fence of posts and rails, with gates and seats at convenient
" distances. Unfortunately this pleasant little enclosure,
" which, with a little attention, might be made an orna-
" ment and an object of attraction, not only to the houses
" on the Terrace, but to the town itself, has been allowed,
" in a great measure, to fall to decay, and now deserves
" more the name of a wilderness than any other appellation ;
" but it is still an agreeable spot, and it is hoped the
" increasing fame of this sea bathing place will soon induce
" those who have it in their power to turn the great natural
" advantages of the Shrubbery to more account.

" In the Shrubbery there is a neat cottage, exceedingly
" well fitted up with warm baths, which are constantly
" supplied by means of machinery ; and near this retired
" spot are stationed the bathing machines for the use of the
" visitors of the Upper Town."

A note was appended that a movement was then on foot
to preserve the Shrubbery, which in later years was placed
in the care of a body of trustees, by whom it is administered
at the present day. At the same time attention was called to
the encroachment of the sea upon the cliff forming Pier Hill,
and regret expressed that steps were not taken to better
protect the shore.

Reference has been made to the daily coaches which
ran from London to Southend. These vehicles used to
start from Whitechapel Church, thence by Mile End to

Stratford, Ilford, Chadwell Heath, Romford, Warley, Brentwood, Shenfield, Billericay, Wickford, Rayleigh, Hadleigh,
Leigh, Milton Hall to the Royal Hotel—a journey of forty-
one and a quarter miles. The coach occasionally turned
to the Rochford Road from Rayleigh instead of going via
Hadleigh. The trip by water was made daily by steam
packets from St. Katherine's Dock, the passengers landing at
the "New Pier," at that time probably a jetty opposite the
Royal Hotel, which had been erected in 1802 by Sir Thomas
Wilson. An auction sale of a farm called Snell's, in Milton
Hamlet, advertized in 1827, particularly referred to the
advantages it derived from being "within one and a half
miles of that increasing fashionable bathing place, Southend."

When he was attracting attention as a brilliant novelist
and giving little promise of the distinguished political career
which lay before him, Benjamin Disraeli (afterwards Lord
Beaconsfield) in 1833 and 1834 stayed at Porters Grange,
and enjoyed his visits very much. On one occasion he
wrote : " I can answer for Southend being very pretty.
I am staying at an old Grange with gable ends and antique
windows, which Mr. Alderman Heygate turned into a
comfortable residence, and which is about half a mile from
the town—a row of houses called a town." At another
time Disraeli wrote that he had hunted with Sir H. Smythe's
hounds, upon an Arabian mare, the best mounted man on the
field. He nearly killed the animal, he said, for he stopped at
nothing in a thirty miles run. Later on he again wrote in
praise of the town : " I live solely on snipe and ride a good
deal. You could not have a softer climate or sunnier skies
than at abused Southend. Here there are myrtles in the open
air in profusion."

In the early years of last century the water side labourers
found considerable employment in picking up hard stones,
called "cement stones," which were found along the cliffs at
Leigh, Southend and Shoebury. They were collected and

despatched to a factory at Leigh to be crushed and then formed into a material called Roman cement, which, until Portland cement came into general use, was largely utilized in construction of sea works. The stone was found by means of big iron rods which probed the soil, and the destruction which ensued caused a great deal of alarm to the landowners. Litigation followed, which succeeded in stopping the practice.

The Pier.

In 1830 a syndicate obtained an Act of Parliament for the construction of a Pier, together with the rights of levying tolls on water-carried merchandize landed on the foreshore three miles on either side of the Ship Hotel. The passing of the Bill was received with much enthusiasm, and when Sir William Heygate, an ex-Lord Mayor of London, returned to Southend with the news, the horses were taken out of his coach and he was dragged in triumph to his residence. The first stone was laid by Lord Mayor Thompson in 1829, when he visited the Crowstone. Fresh powers were acquired in 1835. Only one section of the Pier, something approaching half a mile, was at first completed. The full length of a mile and a quarter was not constructed until 1846, and it was upon the need for completion of this project that Dr. Granville commented, when writing upon his visit in 1841 : "The wooden jetty at present in existence, and the only convenient place people have to land upon, extends only to about half a mile, and is always left dry at low tides. It is then followed out by a line of shingle, projecting perhaps a quarter of a mile farther, and called the Hard. Then follows a space of clear water, even at low tide, which divides the termination of the Hard and a cluster of piles in the sea called the Mount, on which a hut is built of two rooms, inhabited by people deputed to take care of a pharo-light for the safety of vessels at night. To this Mount, when it is low water, the Gravesend and Southend steamers land their passengers in the summer, who are then boated over to the Hard, and thence walk to the jetty. At high water, and when the weather is not boisterous, the steamers land their passengers at the jetty itself. The question of the extension of the latter has engaged the various clashing interests in the place for the last ten years, and there is as little probability as ever that this much-desired continuation will ever be accomplished ; without which accommodation, however, it will be in vain to hope that the company at Southend should increase ; for as to the land journey, even with the advantage of rail-conveyance as far as Brentwood, it is so fatiguing and inconvenient, compared with the facility and rapidity of a down course by steamers on the Thames, that to expect people will prefer that line of communication is absurd." In the same chapter the worthy Doctor criticized the cost of staying at Southend ; exclaiming : "No matter whether you be among the fishing smacks of Southend or the dons of Brighton, there is no getting decent food and lodging for less than your hundred shillings a week." The Pier had cost £42,000 to construct. In 1846 it was sold by the Public Works Loan Commissioners, who had taken possession as mortgagees, for £17,000 to Mr. David Waddington. He resold it to Sir Morton Peto, of whom Mr. Thomas Brassey purchased it for £20,000.

The great achievement of the Local Board during its life of twenty-six years was the purchase of the wooden Pier and the erection of the iron structure, which still exists, with the later additions of a steamboat extension, the new head and the tramway passing place. In December, 1873, the old Pier was offered to the Local Board at £12,000 ; the net income being given as £550. The Board offered £10,000. The owners refused, and the Board had to pay £12,000. A large majority of the ratepayers signified their assent to the bargain. Improvements were immediately commenced, including the widening of the approaches and the laying down of the horse tramway. A prolonged struggle took place as to the merits of the low and high level methods of approach ; the respective champions being the late Mr. C. Woosnam and the late Mr. T. Dowsett. The high level system favoured by the latter was eventually adopted, but to the day of his death Mr. Woosnam never departed from his belief. It may be explained that if the low level system had been agreed upon, the approach to the Pavilion would have been about on a level with the present shore end of the Pier tramway. A Provisional Order was secured empowering the Board to extend the Pier, but it lapsed through effluxion of time. Local opinion remained very divided in respect of Pier affairs, and in the middle of 1880 a decision was come to either to let or sell the property, and for nearly a year the Board negociated un-availingly with prospective lessees. In connection with this project an experiment in the nature of a referendum was tried. The Board sought the advice of leading townsmen, and at a meeting of the Local Board and ratepayers, held in July, 1881, at which about eighty attended, the Rev. P. H. Droosten (Vicar of All Saints) carried a resolution approving of the proposed terms, and suggesting the penalty portion of the agreement be not insisted upon. The Board agreed to do as the ratepayers desired, but in a few weeks negociations ceased. In January, 1882, the Board con-sidered another proposal for letting the Pier. These negociations progressed rapidly, and in the following August agreements were exchanged and a sum of £500 obtained as deposit. The lessee found himself unable to proceed with the arrangement, and by the Spring of 1883 the deal was finally off, the Board retaining the deposit. On the motion of Mr. (now Sir) Lloyd Wise the Board in 1883 resolved to obtain a report upon the desirability of constructing a new Pier. A fortnight later a favourable opinion was received from its Committee and adopted, and with great rapidity plans for a new approach and toll house were approved. In August, 1885, it was decided to build a new Pier; the late Sir J. Brunlees being appointed engineer. Powers were obtained by an Act of Parliament, and then the new project slept awhile. To infuse a little more energy into the movement a "new Pier Committee" was formed, the leader being the secretary of the L.T. and S.R. Company (Mr. H. C. Newton). The proposal grew in favour, and on September 18th, 1888, a contract was signed with Messrs. Arrol Bros. for the main structure, followed by another contract in the next year for the superstructure, including the Pavilion. By the summer of 1889 it was possible to use the shore end of the promenade. In April, 1890, the late Dr. Hopkinson reported upon the proposed electrical tramway (the first laid down upon a pier in England), and the contractors, Messrs. Crompton, had completed it sufficiently to enable it to be used on the following August Bank Holiday. The settlement of the various matters in connection with the Pier took time and caused much trouble, and at one stage considerable litigation was threatened. By the eastern side of the old Pier was a small structure used as a loading pier. Upon the carrying out of the new scheme the loading pier was re-constructed near Castle Terrace.

In 1894, owing to the continued silting up of the Swatch, formerly an important waterway, and the need for more accommodation, the necessity was realized for making further provision at the Pier head. An Act of Parliament was obtained conferring power to carry out the work, and then great controversy arose respecting the merits of two schemes which were advocated. One section of the Town Council urged an enlargement of the Pier head, with the provision of better facilities for promenaders and steamboat passengers, whilst the other section proposed to build an extension from the main head to the deep water channel to provide ample depth of water for the steamboats. There were also statements made as to the possibility of attracting Continental traffic, but nothing came of the suggestion. The advocates of the longer Pier, however, had their way, and the new work was completed in 1897 for less than the original estimate. A scheme for a tramway passing place at the centre of the Pier, rejected in 1896, was revived in 1898; in May of that year the Local Government Board held its enquiry, and on July 28th the official trial took place—one of the quickest pieces of work ever carried out in the Borough. Before the Kursaal, in Lower Southend, was built, the Pier Pavilion was the scene of the chief social events of the year, and led to an agitation for protection from the vagaries of the climate. The guests had to walk from the toll house gates to the Pavilion entrance either without any roof at all or under a temporary canvas screen. At one time it was seriously proposed to cover in the entire approach, but the project never received much support. In 1901, however, the present wind screen, with protecting roofs on either side, was constructed, and is held in many quarters to have quite spoilt the noble promenade from the Pier gates to the Pavilion. In 1908 the first instalment was opened of an extensive scheme for the improvement of the new Pier head, and the speculation has proved successful and popular. Including the cost of purchase, the local authority have spent over £128,000 on the Pier undertaking, and there have been transferred from the revenue account in relief of the rates nearly £40,000; the best years being 1904 and 1905, when £4,000 each were handed over.

The old Pier only once suffered serious damage through vessels colliding with it, during the great gale of January, 1881, but the new structure has had to be extensively repaired on three occasions from this cause. In December, 1898, a rent of fully 100 feet was made by a ketch going through a portion of the promenade in the height of a gale. During a hurricane in December, 1907, the barge

"Robert," of Stanford-le-Hope, laden with hay, broke adrift from her moorings west of the Pier and cut a great gap in the side close to the old head. Almost a year later, in November, 1908, the Thames Conservancy hulk "Marlborough," which had also been moored to the west of the Pier, was carried by the force of a stiff nor'-wester straight into the promenade connecting the old and new heads. It cut through the piles and planking and was carried by the force of the wind to the Nore lightship before the crew could obtain control of her. Upon the last two occasions the gaps were spanned by temporary suspension bridges until the damage was repaired, and in this way the entire length of the Pier remained open to promenaders. Apart from these serious accidents there have, of course, been several misadventures caused by small craft breaking from moorings.

In 1894 competitive schemes were invited for the best method of utilizing a piece of waste ground stretching from the Shrubbery to the toll gates. One of them, labelled "Prosperity," was accepted and the work carried out at a total cost of £18,713; involving an annual loss of £200, notwithstanding the Pier Committee, on behalf of the Town Council, work the sea water baths situate therein at a gross profit of £250. The Corporation sanctioned the erection in 1902 of a water chute by a private syndicate upon the east side of the Pier, with an entrance from the Pavilion promenade. The venture was a complete failure and was dismantled; the concrete basin, built to retain sea water, being the only portion still in existence.

The Vicar and the Bell Ringers.

Dr. Frederick Nolan, an erudite theologian and Bampton lecturer of Oxford University, was Vicar of Prittlewell from 1822 to 1864. He was a man of somewhat eccentric habits, and in June, 1840, came into collision with his parishioners as to the hours of bell-ringing. Originally he allowed it to commence at 5 a.m., and then wished to change the hour to 8 a.m. This was resisted, and feeling became so intense that on Sunday morning, June 14th, between nine and ten o'clock, whilst the bells were being rung, the Vicar entered the belfry and tried to cut the ropes with a carving knife. Summonses and cross-summonses were issued. The Vicar employed police to prevent entry into the church. The parishioners retaliated by breaking his windows, and the Doctor armed his wife and himself with pistols for their protection. Notwithstanding every hindrance, the men obtained access to the belfry by mounting the roof and passing through a door there. Shots were fired from the vicarage, followed by groaning and shouting. A scene of much confusion ensued. Five of the ringers were summoned to appear before an ecclesiastical court at the instance of Dr. Nolan, and the parishioners retorted by burning his effigy at Prittlewell. The men failed to put in an appearance and heavy fees became due. One of them was arrested upon warrant and imprisoned at Moulsham (Chelmsford) for thirteen weeks, until the costs had been paid by subscription. He and the others were bound by oath not to further molest the Vicar. Songs and skits were published in this matter, one of the best known being sung to the tune of " The Mistletoe Bough." The song ran—

The Village had long been quiet and still,
The Parson had always enjoyed his will,
And all his Parishioners feared his frown,
Looking with awe as he pass'd through the Town.
The Children all curtesied or made a bow,
As every Child to a Parson knows how.
Angelina looked bold as she gazed around,
Triumphantly striding in haste o'er the ground.
                    But Oh, poor Freddy is done, Oh.
This had long been the case, and 'tis known by us all,
Each day as they strutted to Middleton Hall.
But time alters all things, and so it has here,
Although the poor Doctor himself thinks it's queer;

For whenever he strutts or parades through the place,
He is hooted and hissed by each child to his face,
Though a bludgeon he carries the young brats to chastise,
They still will continue increasing their cries.

But Oh, &c.

Now the cause is quite clear, tho' the Doctor can't see,
And yet it has long been detected by me.
The Sermons he preaches are threadbare and stale :
Tho' attentive you listen to hear him you fail.
Then his brogue, tho' not Irish, none can understand,
Although he's a native of dear Paddy Land;
And should a Friend die, or your Father, or Son,
You must have him buried exactly at one.

But Oh, &c.

To be so respected what Parson could bear?
So resolves he will leave, and thus end the affair;
But a Curate must have, by his rules to abide,
If one can be found will consent to be tied,
That the Bells shall not ring except on condition
The Churchwardens ask of the Curate permission.
And if none can be found will consent to this plan,
We still must put up with poor Freddy Nolan.

But Oh, &c.

Now the Church is deserted, and the Pews nearly bare,
Yet however unwilling, ('tis truth I declare,)
The Bells shall not ring, and no Church Rate shall be,
Until from the Prison James Beeson is free.
Since this is determined, and must be our plan,
When a Meeting is called pray all come to a man;
Be firm, stick to this, and the means may not fail,
For why should a Ringer be shut up in Gaol?

But Oh, &c.

" Punch's " Satire.

If Southend had ardent admirers, it had also those who disparaged it. Others there were who joked about it, and the chief of these was "Punch." In 1848 there appeared an article upon the town by the "Buoy at the Nore." The writer first remarked that there were many peculiarities to be picked up at Southend. The greatest was its size.

"You would scarcely believe it, but it has nearly as many bathing machines as houses—that is to say, there are four of one, I think, and five of the other. The whole place may be packed comfortably, Library and all, in the Thames Tunnel, and leave room for a Bellevue Cottage and a Mount Pleasant to spare. It is a mere shrimp of a sea-town ; Erith is a mighty lobster compared to it. . . . . The postman passes the spot repeatedly without being aware of it, and letters are frequently carried back to London with the libellous inscription, 'No such place to be found.' The inhabitants are so few that there is a legend that when they had occasion once to shout for the Queen they were obliged to send over to Sheerness to 'lend them half a dozen voices' before they could raise a single 'Hip—hip—hurrah.'" The longest peculiarity was its Pier—"instances daily occur of a husband being at one end and a wife at the other and then never seeing one another for hours." Another peculiarity was its extreme quiet—"this may partly arise from there being no one to make a noise; but I half suspect it is strictly forbidden for anyone to laugh or cough. I certainly never heard a sneeze the whole time I lodged there. . . . . The inhabitants, too, seemed as if they were practising to be somnambulists. I never heard them speak—I suppose they do occasionally—but they looked uncommonly like a set of deaf and dumb people that had come out to have a regular good holiday. I had occasion to whistle once, and ten windows were actually thrown up to see what was the noise. The wind is the only thing that takes the liberty of making itself heard, and then it is only in the softest whispers." The writer concluded with the sarcastic comment: "Southend is well worth seeing—with a microscope."

Advent of the Railway.

The town continued to develop slowly until the middle of the Nineteenth Century, when its growth received a great impetus from the construction of the London, Tilbury and Southend Railway. This line was made by the Eastern Counties and London and Blackwall Railway Companies under powers obtained by Acts of 1852 and 1856, and incorporated into a separate Company in 1862. It was leased to Messrs. Peto, Brassey and Betts (who developed the Cliff Town Estate) for twenty-one years from July, 1854, at 6 per cent. on the share capital and payment for debenture interest. Upon the termination of the lease in 1875 the Company took over the line and have since worked it themselves. The track, which started from the Gas Factory Junction, near Bow, and from Forest Gate, on the G.E.R., ran through Barking, Grays, Tilbury and Pitsea to Southend. In 1884 the line was extended to Shoeburyness, chiefly to convenience the military authorities, and in 1888 the Company opened a shorter route through Barking, Upminster, Laindon and Pitsea to Southend. In 1894 the Midland system was connected with the L.T. and S.R. via East Ham. This service and the formation of a branch line of the G.E.R. via Shenfield to Southend in 1889, an event which caused great rejoicing in the villages connected up, enable Southend to be served by three Railway Companies, each possessing good rolling stock and a reputation for punctual travelling. The opening of the L.T. and S.R., in particular, with its cheap season tickets and efficient train service, placed a great opportunity for development before Southend, and the last fifty years illustrate how greatly London residents have appreciated the opportunity of living by the seaside within an hour's journey from London. About the same time as this railway was opened a Water Company was formed by the Brassey interest. The enterprise started modestly with one reservoir in Milton Road, but now the Company control nine reservoirs, supplying a population of nearly 70,000, whilst the water is gathered over an area of ninety square miles. The authorised capital is £983,333, of which £542,969 has been raised. The Company give a constant supply. In 1908 a special examination of the water was undertaken by Dr. J. C. Thresh, the medical officer for the County of Essex, and he reported : "Both the samples are soft and free from any signs of contamination, in fact they are of the highest degree of organic purity. They contain very few bacteria and none which indicate pollution with objectionable matter. They were quite free from visible suspended matter. They are, therefore, waters of excellent character, well adapted for all the purposes of a public supply." The Gas Company established works in 1854 upon a portion of the present site in the Lower Town. The price then charged was 10s. 6d. per 1,000 cubic feet, and in 1856 the total revenue derived from sale of gas, coke, tar and fittings was the modest sum of £382 18s. 4d. In 1881 the output per day was 55,000 cubic feet; the carbonizing capacity of the works being then about 70,000 cubic feet. At the present date the output is about 1¼ million cubic feet per day, and when certain extensions have been completed the producing capacity will be four million cubic feet per day. In the year 1908, 320,774,000 cubic feet of gas were sold. The present selling price is 3s. 6d. per thousand for domestic supply, 3s. 2d. per thousand for power purposes, and 3s. 0⅛d. for public lighting.

Hockley Spa.

In the early years of last century a mineral spring was discovered at Hockley for which great medicinal virtues were claimed. An attempt was made to convert the village into a fashionable watering place. The project was boomed for some years, but eventually it came to nothing. The spring was found at a cottage situated in a bye-lane, just off the main road, which now forms the approach to Hockley Station. Dr. Granville, in his "Spas of England," 1841, gave an exhaustive and detailed description of the water and the circumstances surrounding its discovery. He said : "Mr. and

Mrs. Clay (his host and hostess) had determined upon building for themselves a cottage in this elevated region, after having escaped the relaxing and weakening effects of a long residence in Cheltenham. A well was sunk for water, for the convenience of the cottage, when in throwing out the sod, a hard stone was found, about a foot in diameter, which, when exposed to the air, fell in pieces. It was hollow within, about the size of a two quart basin, in which was fine clear water. Proceeding further down, a kind of ragstone and gravel appeared, and clear spring water flowed. Mrs. Clay, who had been asthmatic all her life, and subject to cough, except when she drank Cheltenham water, after drinking of the new well's water for some little time, found that she lost her difficulty in breathing, and her cough became less troublesome. At the end of a twelvemonth she was so much better in both respects that she was inclined to attribute her recovery to air and situation only. A visit, however, to some friends in London on one occasion, and somewhere else on another, having taken her away from the well, her constitution became heated, the cough returned, and asthma began to plague her again; all which symptoms disappeared on returning to Hockley Cottage and beginning the water once more. This awoke surmises as to the said water possessing medicinal properties. The notion having once gone abroad, it was immediately seized upon by many in the neighbourhood, who used the water, which was most liberally supplied to them; and in the course of three more years such was the healing reputation of Hockley Well, that not only was the water sent for from all parts of Essex, but from greater distances still, and many people of the better classes of society applied on the spot to drink it. Lastly—by the end of the fourth year from the accidental discovery of the source, a regular Spa was constituted, where I noticed in the book of arrivals that several persons of consequence had employed and derived benefit from the water. . . . . Mr. Richard Phillips'

M

experiments led him to the conclusion that the water contains four distinct ingredients, namely, common salt, bicarbonate of lime, sulphate of magnesia, or Epsom salts, and sulphate of lime. The object for which my services were required was, first, to ascertain to what class of disorders the water might be deemed applicable, and in what quantity it ought to be drunk; and, secondly, what disposition and arrangements ought to be made to render the well more available to patients, and the locality more generally suited to the purposes of a Spa." Dr. Granville found the water beautifully limpid and colourless as crystal, with very minute bubbles of air rising in it. Upon drinking, the first impression on the palate was rather sub-acid and pleasing, but the general and continuous taste was that of pure spring water. "When boiled and poured into a glass there is a manifest turbidity, the surface becomes covered almost imperceptibly with a whitish powdery deposit or cream, which, on tilting the glass, will adhere to the surface. After this experiment, the water no longer tastes sub-acid, and the very minute bubbles of air rise even more abundantly. Placed in contact with metals it throws down a copious precipitate. It corrodes lead and iron rapidly and the solder of all metallic vessels. If put into a bottle it will not deposit any sediment, but if a crack exists in the bottle its edges will presently be furred with sediment. If a large quantity of the water be boiled, and allowed afterwards to cool, a large proportion of a white magnesia-looking precipitate falls down." The water of the well was never frozen, and no land spring seemed to affect it. Dr. Granville ascribed marked alterative virtues to the water when taken in small and divided doses. It would also act as an aperient in quantities of a pint and a half, drunk four times in the morning, and as an antacid in stomachic complaints, as well as in cases of lithic disorders of the kidneys. The water had to be drunk cold and immediately after being drawn from the well. It was claimed that rachitic weakness of the bones of a child had been cured, and for diseases of that class, ricketty and bandy legs and weak ankles, the water was recommended. After commenting most favourably upon the high and healthy situation of Hockley, the Doctor suggested the building of a first-rate hotel. The inn as it then existed, with a more showy front and some internal re-arrangement, would do for the present, and in addition detached cottages, with south-easterly and southern aspects, could be erected. The Spa-house should be enlarged by a pump room and a series of four bath rooms. A testimonial from a lady correspondent was appended to the above observations. She wrote: "I feel very sanguine as to the success of the Spa, provided it be forwarded by men of enterprise and spirit. If interest could be made with Mr. ——, the lord of the manor of Hockley, the common might be built upon at an easy rent (or rather quit-rent), no doubt. A few pretty villas, to begin with immediately, would be desirable. If the pump-room is to be built for the coming summer, it should be set about instanter; and I know some gentlemen in the neighbourhood who, having a little land thereabout, would be inclined to erect cottages. Hockley is a remarkably healthy village, and the neighbourhood improving very fast." The pump-room recommended by Dr. Granville was soon supplied, for in 1845 Hockley Spa was advertized below an engraving of a fine building, the remains of which for many years looked gaunt and ugly in their decay until rescued quite recently by a private gentleman and converted into a palatial billiard-room. The water was described of the "most valuable service" in cases of asthma, affections of the lungs, chronic complaints of the digestive organs, indigestion, affection of the liver, kidneys, and bladder, and all inflammatory diseases of the viscera, and particularly gout. It was beneficial in cases of weakness, softening of bones, or rickets in children, in scorbutic and other eruptions of the skin. It was a pleasant, mild, alterative aperient, and, by a steady perseverance in its use, would remove all obstructions in the bowls and internal organs. In order to meet the wishes of numbers who constantly drank the waters, the proprietors had been induced, at great outlay, to have it brought to London, in an aerated form, which far surpassed soda water. It was to be obtained at the Spa, Hockley, at the depôt, 55, Jewin Street, Cripplegate, and at Cheltenham. Hockley and its neighbourhood were declared to be the Garden of Essex. The venture, however, failed, and Hockley did not emerge again from sylvan solitude until the opening of the Great Eastern Railway Company's branch line to Southend caused several residences to be erected for the convenience of season ticket holders.

The Peculiar People.

The Peculiar People—a sect principally confined in membership to Essex—have occupied of late a considerable amount of public attention, owing to the prosecution of members of that body for the consequences ensuing from their refusal to call in medical aid to their children. They had their origin towards the middle of the Nineteenth Century, through the preaching of James Banyard, of Rochford. His teaching had a marked influence upon the agricultural population, and during the course of the last fifty years it may be said to have entirely changed the thought and habit of hundreds of the men and women of South Essex. The Peculiar People are honest, sober, and industrious, caring for their own poor. They are mostly cultivators of market gardens or agricultural labourers, though in the towns many have entered into business, and some have become possessed of considerable means. It is said in respect of one district, Daws Heath, Thundersley, that they found it of evil repute, and by their missioning zeal and industry transformed it into one of the most prosperous agricultural communities of the County. James Banyard's father was a ploughman at Rochford Hall, and as he grew up the son followed a similar vocation. He fell into loose habits, was caught poaching and sentenced to a term of imprisonment. Whilst in gaol he obtained a knowledge of shoemaking, by means of which he made a living in later years. One of Banyard's greatest friends at that time was an old smuggler named Layzell. They frequented public houses, where Banyard was a popular figure, owing to his skill in topical rhyme and mimicry. As years passed he became devout and joined the Wesleyan Methodist body, to whom he rendered service as a local preacher. In 1838 a hat block maker named William Bridges, of Gravel Lane, London, stayed for a time at Rochford with his sister, and there met Banyard. An intimacy sprang up, and the men had many talks together upon religious topics. Banyard subsequently visited Bridges in London, and the result of the further interchange of views was that the former returned to Rochford and commenced preaching, according to one of his biographers, "Right of liberty; that there is no sin in Christians; no doubts in believers; that we must be born again and receive the Holy Ghost from Heaven, for to know our sins are really forgiven is the first step in religion." Banyard came into conflict with the Wesleyan authorities and had, as a result, to continue his work outside that body. He preached for a time in the Square at Rochford, holding prayer meetings at his house, until the growth of the new denomination enabled him to rent a building known as the Barracks, near the Marlborough Head Inn. A church was formed, and Banyard laid down the following rules for its government: "We will have a prayer meeting at five o'clock in the morning before we go to work; and on Tuesday and Thursday evenings at seven. On the Lord's Day we will meet at six and half-past ten in the morning; at half-past two in the afternoon; and half-past six in the evening. When we meet to worship the Lord let no vain or worldly thoughts enter your hearts, but keep your minds on the Lord, fall on your knees and ask the Lord to meet with us and bless us. At all meetings brothers and sisters may offer their thanks, praises and requests to God the Father and His people, except Sunday afternoons and evenings, when the leaders will preach from the Word of God. We will accept no money for preaching, make no laws, have no book of rules but the Word of God alone. For unless one knows his sins are forgiven, and that his name is in the Lamb's Book of Life, we will not accept him as a member of the Church of God." Banyard continued his open-air preaching, and was much persecuted therefor ; one bitter assailant being his old friend Layzell. Filth of all sorts was thrown at him, and he was frequently drenched by pails of water. Within a short time of its foundation the sect adopted the practice with the sick of laying on of hands, anointing with oil, and offering up prayer for the restoration of the invalid. This principle of faith was based on St. James v., 14 : "Is any sick among you ? let him call for the elders of the Church and let them pray over him ; anointing him with oil in the name of the Lord ; and the prayer of faith shall save the sick and the Lord shall raise him up." The practice of faith healing came about in this way. A member named William Perry, suffering from consumption, declared that the Lord had spoken to him through this passage of Scripture, telling him that if he attended to the directions there given, he would be healed. Two fellow members brought him to the chapel and the offices were performed upon him, with the result that Perry apparently completely recovered strength, walked some twelve miles the same day, and the next day went to his work ; living in good health for many years afterwards. Another cure reputed to have been accomplished was that of a man suffering from liver complaint. After several years' practice of this tenet, Banyard's child fell sick and he called in a doctor. This caused dissension among the People and they separated from the founder, who died in 1863 and was buried in Rochford churchyard. After this disagreement a meeting was held at Maldon, at which four Bishops were appointed; the chief of whom was S. Harrod, a Thundersley market gardener, who was henceforward known as "Bishop" Harrod. It was upon that occasion, also, they adopted the name "Peculiar People"; believing, if they carried out their profession, they became God's peculiar choice. The advent of the order to Prittlewell has been described by Elder Isaac Anderson in his life's history, published in 1896. In 1848, when he was fifteen years of age, considerable excitement was caused by the death of a child of a member of the new sect, then known as "Banyardites." In accordance with his belief, the father refused to call in medical aid. An inquest was held, and the feeling of the countryside became very bitter against him. Bills were posted about the village and verses composed and sung in ridicule of the belief, and the curate of the Parish Church announced a sermon in denunciation of the doctrine. Anderson says : " I went to hear him with a number of others. The demonstration was so great afterwards that Banyard had to be guarded out of the village by the police. He was, however, determined to go on preaching, and straightway announced a Sunday for reply to the curate and in defence of the doctrine he and his followers held so dear. The service took place in Rochford Chapel, which was packed to over-flowing. Banyard took the same lesson as the curate and spoke on it, and it appeared to me Banyard turned the sword into the curate's own bosom." In 1850 a chapel was hired in North Road, Prittlewell, and there the leaders of the movement preached on various occasions. Anderson attended these meetings, and in his biography narrates the change that took place in his spiritual life, which aptly presents the cast of thought among the members of this body : "A special meeting was held at Rochford in 1851. I set my mind on going and went five miles; leaving my father at work on Southchurch Hall Farm. As I was walking along the road I had a fearful struggle with my feelings. I was tempted not to go, and not to carry out my purposes, but at length, after great battling with myself, I reached the chapel and was baptized with water by James Banyard and admitted into the Church and recognized as a member. The following day I went to the Hall Farm to work, and while busily engaged there came a blessed power upon me, which cleared away all doubts and assured me I was born again. I was satisfied it was the Holy Spirit of God descending upon me to keep me from sinning and to help me to please God, which hitherto I had not been able to do. On Sunday I met with the friends at Banyard's chapel, Rochford, and it seemed to me as though Heaven had commenced below while praising God in the highest. I was filled with joy unspeakable." Some years before "Bishop" Harrod's death, which occurred in 1897, a division of opinion took place respecting certain acts of his, and, as a consequence, another Church was formed; one branch being known as "The Peculiar People," and the followers of Harrod as "The Original Peculiar People." Later, as the vigilance of the authorities became severe respecting the calling in of medical attendance to their children (several members serving terms of imprisonment), yet another division ensued, and those who held that the passage from St. James did not prohibit medical aid for their little children, who for themselves could not have faith, formed a separate Church, known as the "Liberty Section." The cause, as a whole, is strong in Southend; worship being conducted in buildings in Milton Street and Wallis Avenue.   The other chief centres in the Hundred are at Rochford, Thundersley, Rayleigh, and Great Wakering. The leader of the last-named Church was for many years the late Caleb Rayner, described by contemporaries as one of the finest natural orators the County of Essex has produced. The service is simple, consisting of prayer, reading of Scripture, address, and hymn singing. The last named is a prominent feature, and religious fervour often runs high.

Establishment of Shoeburyness School of Gunnery.

The need of an experimental and training station for artillery was constantly urged by the highest military authorities prior to the establishment of the School of Gunnery. When Shoeburyness had been finally decided upon as the site for the work, land was purchased there in 1849, and it was gradually added to until, in 1859, 200 acres had been acquired, an estate which since has been extensively increased, and now includes the Maplin Sands, concerning which there was lengthy and costly litigation before the Crown acquired ownership. During the above-mentioned ten years the Royal Engineers and Artillery were busily engaged in the work of preparation. In " Early Recollections of the School of Gunnery," by "An Old Essex Parson" (thinly disguising the personality of the late Rev. J. Montagu), a highly interesting sketch of the condition of affairs in the early days is given. "The ground purchased was mostly a wild, rough common, honeycombed with rabbit holes. I have seen snipe and woodcock shot there. The rabbits enticed the cats, and there was a certain gunner, who shall be nameless, a noted shikari against the tabbies, and who had, I think, a hearthrug of their skins. Soon after the purchase, about 1844 (?), Lieutenant A. A. Fisher, R.E., was sent down with ten men of that corps. I knew him early. I was with him when he was superintending the laying down of the first platform for a gun—a mere popgun of a 32-pounder. He had taken up his quarters at the old Coastguard station. These comprised simply two rooms. Calling on him one day he pressed me to stay and partake of his dinner. Now Fisher was in sole charge, consequently commandant, and his home was the Shoebury mess, so I may say that I was the first person who, as guest, dined at the Shoebury mess. How often did I afterwards experience their hospitality! Fisher was a delightful fellow, a wonderfully speedy runner, second only to that all round Eton cricketer, Joe Thackeray (really the Rev. F.

Thackeray), so well known in this part of Essex. Fisher
distinguished himself in after life at the taking of the Peiho
Forts in the China War of 1859 by his skill in draughtsmanship,
and won his ribbon as a Chevalier de la Legion d'honneur.
While at Shoebury he won and married Carry, the charming
daughter of the Rector of Leigh, afterwards Bishop of Moray
and Ross. The Peiho swamps eventually killed him, from
marsh fever contracted there." It was on April 1st, 1859,
that the School of Gunnery was officially established. In that
year the Army estimates contained provision for the expenditure of a sum of £1,500 upon its formation and maintenance.
Mr. Sidney Herbert (afterwards Lord Herbert of Lea), the
Secretary of State for War, in Committee on the Army
estimates in July, pointed out that the amount allocated under
the heading of civil buildings included the establishment of a
School of Gunnery, adding: "The House will not, I am
sure, grudge anything which improves the skill of the Army,
and renders that great arm, the Artillery, more efficient, and
this School is absolutely necessary to afford that branch of the
service the means of practice." In the order issued by the
Adjutant General the staff was formed of a commandant, a
field officer, chief instructor, three instructors in gunnery,
a brigade major, and sixteen other officers, storekeepers, etc.
In 1909-10 the staff had grown enormously, and included,
beside the commandant, chief instructor, five instructors in
gunnery, sixty-nine of other ranks. In addition to these, the
troops in garrison consisted of the Adjutant's detachment and
a company of Garrison Artillery; there being two companies
of the latter until 1908. The station has always been used
extensively for experimental work, and guns, shells, fuses,
and other material from Woolwich and private establish-
ments employed by the Government are tested on the
ranges. An experiment which aroused the greatest popular
interest was that with an 81-ton gun from Woolwich,
an innovation in gun making not altogether a success.

Montagu, the author previously quoted, stood behind it when it was fired, and he records that the explosion produced little effect on those in the rear of the gun, but the men who were at right angles to it were rendered more or less deaf, and in some the seeds of permanent partial deafness were sown. His narrative proceeds: "Then we had O'Callaghan's 'Jack-in-the-Box'—a lot of six and eight inch plates built up around an awful lump of gun cotton. O'C.'s experiment was quite a success. As the proposer and contriver he was invited to mount on the top, with instructions to tell them—when he came down from sky high—what was the temperature at the elevation he might reach. Then all retired with hasty strides to the shelter. O'C., notwithstanding his eager thirst for scientific knowledge, followed their example. And presently there *was a noise!* Well, it was as though Jupiter Tonans was blowing up his butler for negligence in the compounding of his Ambrosia." On another occasion some rocket trials were being held in the presence of the Duke of Cambridge. The rocket, instead of going out to sea, came inland, causing a general stampede and a masterly retreat of the large crowd of civilians present from Southend. It was whilst experimenting with shells on February 6th, 1885, that an explosion occurred which caused a profound sensation throughout the country. A squad, under the command of Captain Goold Adams, was firing from a breech-loading gun in order to test some fuses. The experiments were almost completed when a fuse would not fit into its place in a shell. Goold Adams ordered Sergeant-Major Daykin to tap it, and he did so for a little while without result. He had just resumed his work when the shell burst with shocking results. The explosion killed or mortally wounded Colonel Fox Strangways (Commandant); Colonel F. Lyon (Superintendent at the Royal Laboratory, Woolwich); Captain Goold Adams, Sergeant-Major Daykin, an examiner of fuses from Woolwich named Rance, and two gunners, and injured other officers and men.

Major Bally (later to become Colonel Commandant and also
Major-General commanding the Artillery at Gibraltar) was
wounded in a peculiar way. A shell splinter passed over the
smith's shop and struck him on the right side, breaking a rib
and severely lacerating his hip ; a book in the Major's side
pocket saving him from further serious injury. Alarm was
instantly raised and assistance was quickly at hand. A special
train was despatched from Southend with medical stores and a
contingent of local doctors, comprising Messrs. Deeping,
Phillips, Jones and Morris, and they rendered invaluable aid.
One of the saddest incidents concerned Mrs. Goold Adams,
who was a daughter of a former Rector of Shoebury. She
was out walking with her little child within about 100 yards
of the scene of the catastrophe. She noticed a man running
into the smith's shop with his uniform on fire, and at once
made for the gun. Her husband was lying on the ground.
She clasped her arms around his neck and would not leave
him until he was taken to his quarters, where he died.
Mrs. Goold Adams had a painful experience in earlier days,
prior to her marriage with Captain Goold Adams, when
her fiancée died suddenly, within a fortnight of the wedding,
from the effects of a wetting received in a pond adjoining his
house. The Commandant, although shockingly injured,
heroically refused to be attended until the others had been
treated, and whilst he lay dying caused letters to be written
to the injured enquiring after their welfare. Colonel Strangways was buried at Rewe, near Exeter, and Colonel Lyon at
Warrington, Cheshire, but the other victims, with the exception of the fuse examiner, were interred in South Shoebury
churchyard. The funeral was attended by an extraordinary
expression of public sympathy. Business was suspended in
Southend and Shoeburyness ; not a shop being open. On the
outbreak of the Boer War, No. 10 Company, Royal Garrison
Artillery, then at Shoebury, was despatched to the front.
Artillerymen from all parts of the British dominions have

been trained at this station, and on the occasions of the celebration of Queen Victoria's Diamond Jubilee and the accession of King Edward VII, the Colonial and Native Artillerymen who took part afterwards went through a course of instruction at Shoebury. For a long time the National Artillery Association's annual meeting was held there, at which the King's and other prizes were competed for. Within the last few years, however, that camp has been removed to the practice grounds upon the southern coast of Kent. Shoebury is still extensively utilized for the training of the Territorial Army, and Artillery units from all over the kingdom annually make it their camping ground.

Growth of the Baptist Cause.

The Baptist faith in all its branches has a strong following at Southend. There are five churches, viz., Avenue, Clarence Road, East Street, Prittlewell (Particular Baptist), Leigh Road and Southchurch. The oldest fellowship is that at East Street, the story of the origin of which is of more than ordinary interest. As far back as 1823-4, a few people met at the house of Mr. Warren, at Prittlewell, and service was held once a fortnight. In 1854, John Sutton, of Islington, came to Southend for the benefit of his health. Riding over to Prittlewell one day, he enquired of the barber where the truth was preached. He was referred to church and chapel, but he was not satisfied and pursued his investigations at the shoemaker's. The man replied to his question with "The truth, sir, truth, sir, if you are searching for that, you will not find it in Prittlewell ! If you go to Southchurch, about two and a half miles from here, you will find a few poor people who meet in a room and one of the brethren speaks to them." He ended his statement by asking "Sir, are you a speaker ?" to which Sutton retorted, "No, I am only a poor groaner." The next Sunday Sutton went to Southchurch and found a small congregation presided over by Anthony Smith, thatcher and gardener, of Shopland, a self-taught man, who was sub-sequently pastor of the Prittlewell church. Sutton's religious quest immediately ended and he became a great supporter of the cause. At the first service he placed eight half crowns in the collection, which were used to buy the minister a suit of black. Under Sutton's encourage-ment the church was erected in East Street. He endowed it with five cottages, one for the minister to live in ; the rents of the other four to be applied to the repair of the chapel, and the overplus to be given to the poor of Thundersley and Prittlewell Baptist Churches. The property cost £300. The first six trustees were James Finch, of Ray-leigh, gentleman ; William Westhorp, Great Wakering, grocer ; Samuel Frost, Great Wakering, baker ; Joseph Pease, jun., Rayleigh, farmer ; George Sneezum, Rayleigh, baker ; William Webb, South Benfleet, grocer. Smith found his income insufficient to live upon, and was forced to earn additional means by carrying water about the town. The brethren were not satisfied with this state of things, and his salary was raised to such a figure as would allow him to devote his whole time to the ministerial office. It is said of Smith that he preached in a skull cap, had a sounding board hanging over his head, though the ceiling of the chapel was very low, and often sat down in the pulpit after having spoken for a few minutes, declaring that the matter ceased to flow. Mrs. Emma Windle, of Forest Hill, was a great friend of the Society, and at the death of Smith she caused a memorial to be erected to his memory in the churchyard in 1874 ; recording the fact that Smith had been pastor of the church for twenty years. In 1893 the chapel was pulled down and a new building erected at a cost of £527. Thirteen years later an enlargement was made at an expenditure of £400.

The first service of the Baptist cause in Southend proper was held on June 6th, 1875, at the old Public Hall (the site is now occupied by the Empire Theatre). A year later a church was formed by the Rev. J. T. Wigner, of London, and thirteen joined hands in fellowship. Three weeks after the first meeting of members took place at No. 8 Belmont Villas, Cambridge Road, and in August of the same year a building at the corner of Hamlet Road and Princes Street was purchased for £650 of the Rev. T. W. Herbert, the Vicar of Southend. The rev. gentleman had opened an Episcopalian Mission Church there, but the effort was not well regarded, and so he sold the property, despite the vigorous protest of the then Bishop. A month after the purchase the Baptists opened it for public worship under the name of the Tabernacle. The first baptismal service was held on March 5th, 1877, when six persons were baptized. On June 25th, 1878, the Rev. J. E. Wilson, of Pastors' College, was recognized as the minister of the little body. After four years of successful effort a division occurred. Wilson espoused the cause of open membership, and the deacons held to the trust deed in favour of close membership. The minister vacated the pastorate and took a considerable number of the members with him to the Public Hall, where he commenced services. From this effort sprang the Clarence Road Baptist Church. The deacons of the Tabernacle kept steadily to their purpose, the church gradually recovered from the blow of separation, and in October, 1882, the Rev. H. W. Childs, of Sudbury, Suffolk, accepted the pastorate. It was during Mr. Childs' ministry that a more permanent building was erected at a cost of £950, and opened for worship on December 16th, 1885, by the Rev. Charles Spurgeon, son of the famous preacher. In 1886 the land was purchased upon which a schoolroom and caretaker's house were built. After some years of work, Mr. Childs went to America, and in 1889 the Rev. E. Dyer entered the pastorate ; being succeeded in 1896 by the Rev. J. McCleery, who still holds the position. In 1900 a large piece of land was purchased at the corner of Milton Road and Avenue Terrace, where a block of buildings was erected at a total cost of £8,000, known as the Avenue Church, the largest building in the Borough devoted to the Baptist persuasion. The Tabernacle was purchased on behalf of the Church of England ; a Mission Church being established there under the title of St. Mark's.

The Volunteer Movement: A Great Sham Fight.

Enthusiasm for volunteer soldiering waned after the peril of Napoleon had been removed, until the revival of an invasion scare in the middle of last century brought about the resuscitation of the force upon lines which proved to be popular. Regiments were raised in Essex, and a company of infantry volunteers had its headquarters in Rochford. In 1863 some important manœuvres were carried out at Southend, which were fully described in the "Illustrated London News" of that time. The graphic account of the operations stated : "A sham fight took place at Southend on Monday week, May 25th, 1863, in which the Volunteers were opposed to the blue jackets and marines of the Royal Navy. From an early hour the usually quiet locality of Southend was the scene of great activity and excitement in consequence of the large number of visitors who arrived by each successive train of the London and Tilbury Railway, and also by steamboats, to witness the spectacle of an attack by a naval squadron and Royal Marines against a defensive force of Volunteer Artillery, Engineers, and Rifles. At twelve o'clock the 3rd Essex Administrative Battalion of Rifle Volunteers, under the command of Lieutenant-Colonel John Coope Davis and Major Octavius Coope, marched to the parade ground fronting the Ship Hotel, preceded by its excellent regimental band of sixty performers ; a series of battalion evolutions, which occupied about an hour, were carried out by the force, which comprised the following corps, viz., 1st Essex (Romford), Captain Champion Russell ; 2nd Essex (Ilford), Captain Commandant William Cotesworth and Captain Henry M.

Harvey; 3rd Essex (Brentwood), Captain Hill; 7th Essex
(Rochford), Captain Arthur Tawke; 15th Essex (Hornchurch),
Captain Peter E. Pearblock; 18th Essex (Chipping Ongar),
Captain Philip J. Budworth; 19th Essex (Epping), Captain
Loftus W. Arkwright; 21st Essex (Brentwood), Captain
William J. Burgess; and 24th Essex (Woodford), Captain
Commandant George Noble. At the termination of the
evolutions this battalion marched to Cliff Town, which was
the great centre of attraction, and the vast extent of open
ground immediately adjacent to the heights facing the sea was
thronged by immense multitudes of spectators; the most
excellent arrangements having been made for the safety and
accommodation of the public. The defensive artillery force to
resist the landing of Royal Marines consisted of two 40-
pounder Armstrong guns, which arrived from the garrison at
Shoeburyness in charge of a detachment of the depôt brigade,
Royal Artillery, and the West Essex Yeomanry Artillery,
under the command of Lieutenant-Colonel George Palmer.
The guns of this regiment, comprising six 6-pounders of the
smooth-bore pattern, were placed in excellent position immediately on the summit of the cliff facing the points of attack;
the officers in immediate command of the battery being
Captains S. Bolton Edenborough, J. Jessop, and Lieutenant
Edenborough. The two 40-pounder Armstrong guns, each
drawn by eight horses, took up a position on an elevation
considerably to the rear of the 6-pounder battery; these guns
being supposed, on account of their superior range, to combat
the attacking squadron when far out from shore. At half-past
two o'clock the entire volunteer force had assembled on the
ground and formed in review order; comprising, in addition
to the 3rd Essex Administrative Battalion, the following
corps, viz., the 15th Essex (Heybridge) Volunteer Engineers,
commanded by Captain Edward Hammond Bentall; the
1st Administrative Battalion of the Tower Hamlets Rifles,
commanded by Lieutenant-Colonel C. Buxton, and comprising

N

the 3rd (Spitalfields), Captain Commandant Sir T. F. Buxton ; 5th (Mile End), Captain G. E. Ludbrook ; and 10th (Mile End Gate), Captain Davies ; the 38th Middlesex, Captain Commandant H. W. Phillips ; detachments of the West Middlesex, London Artists', and other Metropolitan corps ; the 5th Essex (Plaistowe), Colonel Commandant Charles Capper ; the 22nd Essex (Waltham Abbey), Captain William Leask ; and the 23rd Essex (Maldon), Captain James A. Hamilton. The reviewing officers, Colonel W. M. P. McMurdo, C.B., Inspector-General of Volunteers, Brevet Lieutenant-Colonel C. P. Ibbetson, Assistant Inspector, and staff, were received with the usual salute by the entire line, and the force subsequently marched past, and carried out various battalion evolutions. Shortly after three o'clock the most interesting portion of the proceedings of the day commenced. A squadron of five steam gun boats was seen rapidly approaching the Southend coast from the opposite shore ; the bugles of the Volunteers sounded the alarm ; an excellent disposition was made of the resisting force by the commanding officer, and each of the guns was well manned and ready for action. The attacking squadron, having got well in position fronting Cliff Town, opened a terrific fire, which was well responded to by the batteries on shore ; and during the cannonade, under the protection of the guns of the squadron, a force of about 300 rank and file of the Royal Marine Light Infantry, under the command of Captain Butcher, left the vessels, and were rowed rapidly in small boats towards the promenade at the bottom of the cliff, by seamen of the fleet. A landing was effected in gallant style, under the superintendence of Vice-Admiral F. W. Hope Johnstone, K.C.B., Commander-in Chief at the Nore, who had charge of the squadron, and Captain Butcher, of the Marines. Arrived on terra firma the attacking force formed and prepared to reach the level plain by advancing up the cliffs. Their progress was, however, opposed by the Volunteers, who had thrown out a party of skirmishers, who were supported by a line prepared for volley firing, which was carried out by the right of companies. The gallant Royal Marines at all hazards continued to advance, and with some difficulty ultimately reached the summit of the cliff by means of a bayonet charge; rushing up at various points of the declivity, and re-forming, in spite of all opposition, on the plain above. The volunteer skirmishers and advance force retired to the main body, and the Royal Marines advanced in direct échelon of companies at quick march to the scene of action. The attacking force then confronted the entire line of the volunteer army, and a very brisk series of file and volley firing was kept up for several minutes. The volunteers subsequently changed front, the battery guns were brought to bear upon the invading force, and, after various other movements of attack and defence, the bugle sounded a retreat and the Royal Marines retired to their boats. The proceedings terminated about half-past four o'clock, and the several corps of volunteers, having formed into square, were addressed at some length by the commanding officer, Colonel McMurdo. The gallant colonel observed that, in consequence of the limited space at the point of landing, it had been found necessary to alter the arrangements as to some of the evolutions. He was highly gratified with the entire proceedings of the day, and considered it was important that the volunteer force should become practically acquainted with the best means of resisting an enemy. He was pleased to find that the whole of the corps present were in a most efficient state; and he must, in the name of the volunteers, return his sincere thanks to the gallant Admiral and the officers and men of the gallant corps of Royal Marines, by whose kind assistance the proceedings had been brought to such a successful termination. Three cheers were given for Colonel McMurdo and Admiral Sir W. J. H. Johnstone, K.C.B., in which the spectators heartily joined; thus pleasantly bringing to an end a most agreeable and picturesque field-day."

Local interest in the volunteers was maintained by the summer encampment of the Honourable Artillery Company at Southend in the early Eighties, but it was not until April 23rd, 1888, that a company of the Essex R.G.A. Volunteers was formed. The first recruits were sworn in at the London Hotel, before Mr. W. G. Brighten, a local solicitor, also a captain in the Honourable Artillery Company. The head-quarters were established at the Ship Hotel, and there the second batch of recruits was admitted into the service. The men included several bearing well-known Southend names such as Absalom, Bacon, Berry, Bonbernard, Burles, Bowmaker, Brewer, Cotgrove, Darke, Dunnett, Dowsett, Forbes, Garon, Guiver, Giggins, Harvey, Hemmann, Ingram, Kingsbury, Pawley, Peters, Potton, Robinson, Shipton, Underwood, Vandervord, etc. The first captain was Dr. E. E. Phillips, with Dr. Dempster and Mr. J. P. White (now lieutenant-colonel of the regiment) as lieutenants, Dr. Albert Morris as surgeon, and the Rev. T. O. Reay, R.D., as chaplain. The company at first ranked as No. 13 Company, 2nd Essex R.G.A. The first annual training took place at Harwich ; next year at Landguard Fort, and later on at Shoebury, which has ever since been the rendezvous. About 1890 Captain Phillips left the town for Bath. Other changes took place, and for some time the company was left with only one officer, until Captain Baldwin, then in a militia regiment, was gazetted to the command. It was during this officer's term of service that the company was re-numbered and became No. 2 Company, 1st Essex. Upon Captain Baldwin becoming Major in a Welsh militia regiment, Captain Leaver assumed command. In 1900 the corps, which had been heavily over-strength, was converted into two companies, No. 2 (Captain Leaver) and No. 9 (Captain Bayly). Both officers subsequently left the town, and Captain F. J. Tolhurst took the command until his departure some years later, when Captain F. G. Ensor was gazetted in his place. A few years ago an Artillery Company was formed at Leigh, but under the new scheme of organization of the Territorial Army, which, came into operation in 1908, the three companies were amalgamated into one double company of the Essex and Suffolk Garrison Artillery, under the command of Major Lloyd. The Southend company sergeant-majors have included Messrs. Foskett, Hutson, Burles, Fox, Forbes, and Glasscock. At first the Southend corps was instructed as garrison artillery, but upon the two units being formed they became siege companies and were trained upon 5-inch guns and the like. In 1907 they were sent two 15-pounders and were treated as field artillery, but in 1908 the new Territorial Company reverted to garrison artillery. The local volunteers have always had a reputation for efficiency and smartness. Their most conspicuous year was 1906, when a group of No. 2 Company, under the command of Lieutenant J. Weston Clayton, brought home the Prince of Wales' Prize from the meeting of the National Artillery Association at Shoeburyness. The regiment oftentimes won the King's Prize by means of gun teams drawn from headquarters companies, but this was one of the few occasions when a provincial gun group was a powerful competitor for the chief award. The local men, however, had to be content with the Prince of Wales' Prize. This carried with it the Dewar Cup for the year. The successful team was: Gun group commander, Lieutenant Weston Clayton ; No. 1 gun : Sergeant Burgess, Corporal Everett, Bombardiers Hearn, Cogger, Briscoe, and Gunners Clarke, Sneezum, and Flack. No. 2 gun : Sergeant Bines, Corporal Deer, Gunners Ennis, Tarling, Lee, Winslow, Wakeling, and Page. At the close of the Boer War (1899-1902) a Yeomanry Regiment was formed for Essex, and Southend was made the headquarters of D Squadron, recruited mainly from the Rochford and Orsett Hundreds, with Major F. H. D. C. Whitmore in charge. In 1908 a company of Infantry was raised, under the command of

Captain H. L. Cabuche; being known as H Company of the
6th Battalion, Essex Regiment. There was also sanctioned in
1909 a detachment of the Army Medical Corps, Major
Mowatt commanding.

Development of the Town: Establishment of the Local Board of Health.

From the time of the opening of the L.T. and S. Railway
line the town slowly grew, and as the end of the century
approached the pace quickened. The Cliff Town Estate
was developed at about the same time as the railway line was
constructed by the great contracting firm of Brassey, Peto,
Betts and Co. The roads were wide, and the rows of houses
were built upon a regular plan which is superior to many
estate plans subsequently adopted in the Borough for extensive building operations. Some years later the locality to
the north of Southchurch Road, known as Porter's Town,
was built, followed rapidly by the Park Estate (from Princes
Street to Milton Road) and Alexandra Street (1869-72), with
an effort on behalf of the Brasseys to make a high-class
suburban retreat of the Hamlet (Milton Road to Hamlet
Court Road); the building restrictions being severe. In the
early Seventies of last century Warrior Square was laid out,
and in 1879 commencement was made of a direct road to
Prittlewell; the first portion only extending, however, to the
present approach of the G.E. Railway station. Early in the
Eighties some building went on along Southchurch Beach, and
in 1887 York Road and adjacent streets were laid out and
rapidly built upon. The vacant portions of High Street
were filled up, and Clarence Street and Weston Road
came into being; the Local Board also completing the
new road to Prittlewell, known as Victoria Avenue, under
powers conferred by a special Act. Land lying immediately to the west of the L.T. and S.R. station, called
the Magdala Estate, was quickly utilized, and then the

extensive acreage stretching eastward from All Saints' Church came into the hands of the builder. The district now known as Westcliff was a very profitable and popular speculation, and with the laying-out of the Chalkwell Hall Estate, early in the present Century, the town was linked with the Seaview Estate, which had been developed at the extreme western limit, and so the Borough of Southend stretches in one long line of buildings to the neighbouring parish of Leigh. Houses were also rapidly erected along Southchurch Road and adjoining thoroughfares, and quite recently a scheme was formed to convert the spot known as Thorpe Hall Bay, at the eastern end of Southchurch, into a high-class residential resort. The only thing needed to make growth in the Southchurch district still more rapid is a railway station. Negociations have taken place on several occasions between the railway company and the landowners, and it is expected that a station will shortly be erected.

The agitation which preceded the establishment of the Local Board of Health in 1866 was chiefly caused by the sanitary needs of the town. The Cliff Town Estate was drained, but the rest of Southend had no system of sewerage, save that the refuse was carried by pipes to the fore-shore and there discharged by means of numerous outfalls. As the agitation strengthened, the town became divided into two camps, representing respectively the Scratton and Heygate interests. Daniel Scratton was the last of the family who permanently resided at the Priory, and as the Lord of the Manor held a large quantity of land, which he ultimately disposed of at extremely profitable prices, and then retired to Ogwell in Devonshire. He was champion of the forward movement. The Heygate family were extensive leaseholders, and they were strongly opposed to the change. Mr. James Heygate led the fight with all the vigour that he and his family could throw into it, but he was beaten. He accepted defeat and became chairman of the new Board;

his influence being paramount until his death in 1873. The area under the jurisdiction of the authority was at first only a small one, comprising the ecclesiastical district of St. John Baptist, the parish church of Southend. The membership was fixed at six, which was increased in 1875 to nine. In 1877 Rochford Board of Guardians suggested to the Local Board that the Prittlewell district (including what are now the ecclesiastical centres of St. Mary's, All Saints', St. Alban's, and St. Saviour's) should become part of the urban district. At the close of the year Prittlewell was associated with Southend, and became a ward with three representatives; the membership of the Board being raised to twelve. In 1880 there was strained feeling between the two wards, owing to the obstructive policy of the Prittlewell representatives, and a movement was initiated with a view to separation, but it came to nothing.

The Local Board first met on the 29th August, 1866, at the Royal Hotel. All six members attended, and appointed Mr. William Gregson, jun., to be clerk at a salary of £40. It was later decided to employ a surveyor and inspector of nuisances at a salary of £20 per year. They made a rate of 6d. in the £, which was estimated to realize £264. The cost of the adoption of the Act and the first election was only £34 12s. 9d., or less than a penny rate. For many years the advocates of strict economy held the upper hand, and, consequently, there was considerable agitation at various times in favour of more progressive methods of government in respect of roads, sanitation, the pier, cliffs, etc., the embers of which were not quite extinct when the Local Board was succeeded by the Town Council.

The main work of the Local Board may be divided under three headings—Health, the Cliffs, and the Pier. The two former are dealt with below in their order; the history of the Pier having been sketched in a previous chapter.

In a health resort the question of sanitation is always uppermost. The early years of the Southend Local Board cannot, however, be associated with much activity in this respect, and their attitude may, perhaps, be best expressed in a resolution which they passed in 1873: "Resolved that as the Board considers the duties of the office (medical officer) will be practically a sinecure, except as to the annual report and except in case of an epidemic (an event which the Board considers unprecedented and improbable), the salary be fixed at £5 5s. a year." Seven years later the amount was raised to £15, and though the figure was increased to £50 several years afterwards, it was not until the close of 1891 that the annual payment became £100. The death rate of the town was always favourable, because of the gravel subsoil upon which it is mainly built, the influence of tides and tidal winds, the large amount of sunshine, and the small rainfall. The sanitary conditions, however, needed attention. In 1872 the prevalence of "Summer diarrhœa" was noted, and two years later anxiety was caused by cases of fever. A further period of two years elapsed, and then the Local Government Board wrote to the urban authority respecting some deaths from diarrhœa which occurred during that summer. In 1879 typhoid fever reappeared, and a year afterwards Dr. Thorne Thorne, a Local Government Board inspector, personally investigated the conditions, but little was achieved as a result of his report; increased ventilation of sewers being the specific. The experiences of 1886 alarmed the medical officer, and he made a special report upon the matter; again referring to it in his annual statement, which was ordered to be printed "after revision by the Medical Officer of Health and the Clerk." The town quickly became divided in opinion concerning the health administration of the Board, and one section, led by the Rev. Dr. T. H. Gregg, a Bishop of the Reformed Church of England, who had founded Trinity Church, Southend, demanded more energetic supervision of sanitary matters. Dr. Gregg had the advantage of holding a medical degree of a Scotch University, and being a man of immovable purpose and controversial skill, he quickly joined issue with the Local Board. He first complained in June, 1887, of the state of certain drains, and in December criticized the sanitary condition of the whole district. The Board decided it was unwise to read his letter in public, as it might be prejudicial to the town's welfare. In January, 1888, the Bishop renewed the attack, and at a special meeting the Board decided to obtain a report from an expert and to take proceedings against Dr. Gregg. The Ratepayers' Association also urged enquiry into the state of the town's drainage. Dr. (now Sir) Shirley Murphy came down, at the request of the Board, and made a report, after consideration of which the health authority agreed that although Bishop Gregg had "rendered himself amenable to the law," they would not take further proceedings against him, "which might by some be considered vindictive." Should the Bishop, however, be so ill advised as to repeat the charges, it was recommended that prompt and decisive action be taken. But the Bishop's work was done, and the effect of his agitation was to introduce into local government circles a real and abiding concern for the sanitary condition of the town. In July, 1889, the surveyor was instructed to examine the drainage, and in October the medical officer was ordered to make a full report thereupon. In 1890 an isolation hospital was opened as a result of pressure by the Local Government Board, and Dr. Thresh (County Medical Officer of Health) was called in to report upon the recurrence of typhoid fever and the steps to be taken to deal therewith. Everybody's attention was concentrated upon drainage and sewerage problems. Gullies and sewers were copiously flushed and disinfected ; house drains were smoke tested and water tested ; attention was paid to the ventilation of drains and sewers. It is probable that during the next five years house owners were made to spend £30,000 upon improving the drainage of their properties.

The necessity for a better system of sewerage was illustrated in 1891.   Princes Street had been one of the centres of the recent epidemic of typhoid fever.   The Board ordered the sewer to be bared in two places, and it was then discovered that at each position the gradients ran at opposite levels. The Princes Street and Park Street sewers were at once relaid, with an immediate improvement in the health of the district. Notwithstanding the activity in health administration, a source of anxiety remained in the inability to detect the cause of the repeated outbreaks of typhoid fever, and it was not until 1895, when the Local Board had given place to the Town Council, that the medical officer (Dr. A. C. Waters) directed attention to shell-fish as an agent for the propagation of this fever.   His successor (Dr. Nash) confirmed the theory, and as a result of increased attention to the sanitary condition of shell-fish layings, epidemic typhoid fever has ceased, and the sporadic cases notified are few.   Dr. Bruce Lowe, a Local Government Board medical inspector, reporting in 1896, certified to the "abundant evidence of increased efficiency in the sanitary administration of Southend, and promise therefrom of discouragement of preventible disease in the future."

In the above remarks upon the general question of health reference has been made to sewers, and the inauguration of a drainage system is dealt with in more detail below.

The need of proper sewerage was a subject constantly brought to the notice of the Local Board.   Complaints about the lack of drainage for High Street and Marine Parade were frequent, and Mr. C. Woosnam essayed in February, 1867, to pass a resolution for the construction of "a sewer to convey the drainage from beyond the Middleton Hotel, including York Street and along the High Street to the foot of the Hill (Royal), and thence along the beach, or in the high road, gathering up all the outfalls from the houses as far as Hay's Corner, and conveying the outlet to such a distance on the foreshore as shall be found necessary for the

abatement of the nuisance arising from a number of outfalls."
Owing to opposition the resolution was withdrawn.   Outside
agitation grew, and shortly included residents in Royal
Terrace.   Towards the close of 1868 Mr. Woosnam tried
once more, but was beaten by the casting vote of the chairman,
in favour of " full enquiry into the dry earth system."   Early
in 1870 Mr. Woosnam made a third attempt with a short
motion, "That the providing of sewerage for the town be at
once considered by the Board," and this time succeeded.
Interest cannot survive a history of the discussion, agitation,
and opposition which went on or had to be surmounted, and
it will be sufficient to state that in 1870 the Marine Parade
(East) sewer was put down, with an outfall 125 yards from
the shore, and a sewer in High Street (instead of along the
valley lying immediately to the east, as the engineer proposed)
with an outlet into the Swatch, later known as the " Pier
outfall system," so called to distinguish it from other outfalls.
The High Street sewer was at once continued up Queen's
Road in order to drain the Park Estate, and in 1881 Porter's
Town and Prittlewell were connected with the " pier outfall
system," causing much subsequent flooding in High Street
cellars at periods of heavy storm.   In 1879 the Hamlet
Valley sewer outfall was constructed, also with an outlet into
the Swatch, at a point about 2,000 feet from the shore.   As
the town developed sewer troubles were constant, and after an
abortive attempt by Mr. P. Dodd, the surveyor, the late Mr.
J. Mansergh, C.E., was asked to suggest a sewerage scheme.
His report was submitted to a meeting of the Local Board
held in its last months, and ordered to stand adjourned for
Town Council decision.   His report was adopted by that
body, and the Eastern and Western Valley sewerage
systems came into work in 1896-7.   A development of the
scheme was carried out for Prittlewell in 1902-3.   Mr.
Mansergh's plan was to take the sewage to two tanks, either
by pumping or gravitation, and store it, for discharge on

the best of the ebb tide. It is shortly to be superseded by a system of treatment ; all the sewage being collected at a site on the north-eastern boundary of the Borough, there treated, and the effluent discharged by gravitation into the sea.

At the time the Cliff Town Estate was developed an esplanade was made, and the cliffs planted with trees. When, however, the properties had passed into other ownership, the original vendors took less interest in "the front," and it was neglected. In the autumn of 1881 a meeting of ratepayers resolved that the prevalent conditions were threatening to destroy an important feature of the town. The state of the cliffs was, indeed, very bad. The earth was tumbling down, the top layer slipping over the London clay. Frost and rain caused the removal of large sections, and as it fell the earth blocked the esplanade, which became a series of little hills and hollows, running north and south. Fear was expressed for the safety of Cliff Town Parade. At the close of 1878 the then owner, the late Mr. H. A. Brassey, intimated willingness to hand over the cliffs to the town, together with a cheque for £500. Cliff Town residents were unanimously in favour of accepting his offer; the Board were equally divided, and the project dropped. The agitation continued. One suggestion was for the cliffs to be put under a trust similar to that which controlled the Shrubbery. Nothing came of it, however, and in 1881 the Board resolved to accept the cliffs and the owner's cheque if the owners of Cliff Town properties undertook to indemnify that body against loss by reason of the slipping or cracking of their houses, and one-half or one-third of the cost of repair of the cliffs and esplanade were given by the adjacent owners and occupiers. The negociations were not completed until 1885, and then Mr. Brassey paid £750 and the other owners and occupiers £250, in consideration of the cliffs passing into the possession of the town and being suitably protected. The method to be employed in stopping the fall of the earth was the subject of much controversy. The difficulty was over-

come by the then surveyor (Mr. P. Dodd), who constructed
great trenches from the top to the bottom, and filled them
with brick burrs and chalk. This, of course, only concerned the heights in front of the Cliff Town Estate. The
owner of the undercliff lying to the west of Wilson Road
offered to sell it to the town in 1887, but the Cliffs Committee made no recommendation thereupon. At a later
date this portion of the cliffs was divided into plots and sold.
The Corporation adopted the policy of buying these plots
whenever they were offered at reasonable prices, and, as a
consequence, a large part of the land has now passed into the
Council's possession.

There were, of course, numberless other matters dealt
with by the Local Board, and among the more important the
following are selected. In 1867 the police force consisted of
one sergeant. This was increased by the addition of one
constable, and then in 1872 the Board memorialized for two
constables for a winter population of 3,000 and four for the
summer, with a "lock-up." As a result, Essex Quarter
Sessions ordered the provision of the present police station and
quarters in Alexandra Street. The first court house was
erected in 1883 and the second comparatively recently. The
opening of these premises resulted in the transference of the
sittings of the County Court to Southend from Rochford.
The Vicar of Prittlewell (Rev. S. R. Wigram) in 1867 asked
that the Board should provide a burial ground. The appeal
was fruitless. It was not until thirteen years later that a
Burial Board for Prittlewell was established, which resulted in
the laying out of the cemetery in North Road. A proposal
was made in 1868 to construct a Southend and Shoeburyness
railway ; the intention being to raise High Street eight feet and
cross upon the level. The project was not revived until 1881,
when the L.T. and S.R. Company promoted a Bill giving them
powers to carry out the extension ; the line being taken over
High Street by a bridge, and the roadway lowered. The

Local Board decided to oppose the Bill, but a town's meeting refused to sanction the cost of opposition being borne by the rates, largely at the instigation of Mr. A. L. Stride, the managing director of the Railway Company. The following year the Board approved the proposal of the G.E.R. Company to construct a branch line from Shenfield to Southend. In 1868 the Lower Town asked for a kerb to be laid along the path by the Hope Hotel, but the Board at that time "deemed it inadvisable to incur the expense," and six years elapsed before the kerb was placed from the foot of Royal Hill to Rayleigh House. At the close of 1871 the Board might have purchased the Water Works, for the undertakers were willing to sell. In 1873 the east side of High Street was kerbed and channelled, and the opposite of the road in the following year. Serious disturbances arose among the "trippers" on the last Saturday of August, 1874, and the services of the military had to be requisitioned from Shoeburyness.

In 1875 the late Mr. Thomas Dowsett (first Mayor of the Borough) entered public life, and in 1879 he led the movement in favour of a more direct route to Prittlewell. He offered, on behalf of a syndicate, to provide the land and £700 towards an estimated cost of £1,500. The offer was refused, yet five years later, under a special Act of Parliament, the Board obtained compulsory powers to acquire the necessary land for the purpose and constructed the road; having to pay Mr. Dowsett and his partners £15,848 17s. 6d. for the area taken from them, in addition to purchasing other land at the Prittlewell end.

The enclosure known as Southend Park, situated between Park Road and Avenue Road, the home of the first cricket and football clubs, could have been purchased for £800, but the offer was refused. Pawley's Green, on the Marine Parade, might have been acquired in 1885 for £300. The Board offered £150. Negociations fell through, and in 1901 the Town

Council paid £3,500 for the green ; that, too, only part of its purchase price ; the other portion being found, it was understood, by those associated with the Kursaal speculation. A resolution was passed by the Local Board in 1877 directing the attention of the Justices to the large number of houses in Lower Southend licensed for the sale of spirits and beer, and requesting "no more grants until the increase of population is such as to call for increased accommodation." A specification for the making up of Milton Street, in 1879, included : "Carriage way, twelve inches of hard core, covered with six inches of Kentish flints ; footways to be stubbed and levelled and covered with gravel three inches in thickness ; the kerbing to be twelve inches by six inches Kentish rag, laid on four inches of sand, with surface water gullies." This specification, except that the kerbing was altered to concrete blocks, was in force for several years, and it was not until 1887 that tar paving for the footpaths was generally adopted ; followed by artificial stone slabs by the Town Council after the development of the electric light undertaking. Darlow's Green, Lower Southend, was purchased in 1890 at a cost of £2,000, and this was followed at later intervals by the acquisition of Pawley's, Fairhead's and Britannia Greens. Some feeling was aroused in 1881 owing to the proposal of the L.T. and S.R. Company to construct a siding upon the Cliff Town approach to High Street. The Local Board were appealed to, but rendered no assistance, and outside help was sought. Messrs. Scott and Webster, two neighbouring landowners, gave the requisite land, £300 was subscribed towards the cost of making what is now known as Cliff Town Road, and the Board then took it over. In 1884 Mr. (now Sir) Lloyd Wise moved the first resolution in favour of tree planting in the streets of the town.

During the early part of 1888 there was some talk in Southend about incorporation, possibly owing to the establishment of a Town Council at Chelmsford, and in September of that year the Board ordered a committee "to consider the advisability of taking the necessary steps to procure the incorporation of the town." Three months later its members reported favourably. Outside the Board the movement was pushed by Mr. R. S. Fraser, and it was determined to proceed with the task. A guarantee fund of £150 was raised, and in March, 1891, the seal of the Board was attached to a petition for incorporation, on the motion of the chairman (Mr. J. H. Burrows), seconded by Mr. T. Dowsett. The consent of the Privy Council was obtained, and the final meeting of the Board was held on the 5th November, 1892. All the twelve members were present, and the last motions passed were of hearty thanks to chairman and clerk.

The chairmen of the Local Board were :—

1866—1873	- -	JAMES HEYGATE.
1873—1878	- -	GEORGE VANDERVORD.
1878—1879	- -	J. U. HEYGATE.
1879—1882	- -	F. THACKERAY (The Rev.).
1882—1889	- -	W. G. BRIGHTEN.
1889 (Dec.)—1890	-	F. WOOD.
1890—1891	- -	J. H. BURROWS.
1891 (April to August) -		C. PALMER.
1891—1892	- -	J. H. BURROWS.

Mr. William Gregson occupied the position of clerk throughout the period of the Board's existence.

Town Council Administration.

After an existence of twenty-six years the Local Board in 1892 gave place to a Municipal Corporation. Under the old authority there had been an increase of rateable value from about £11,000 to over £80,000, and in population from 3,000 to 13,500. During the seventeen years of corporate life the growth has been enormous. The rateable value has risen to nearly £400,000 and the inhabitants to about 60,000. Great changes have also occurred in the methods of

o

administration and in the provision of public facilities. The roadways are now made up with granite and the pathways with artificial stone slabs, instead of with flint and tar paving; the street lighting is now either by means of electricity or incandescent gas, in place of the old open flame system; two public parks have been opened—Southchurch Hall and Chalkwell Hall; a tramway service has been inaugurated; higher education has been fostered by the opening of the Secondary Day School; a separate Commission of the Peace for the Borough has been in operation since 1894; the system of seaside promenades has been greatly extended by new works, both east and west; and, finally, the power of appointment of overseers and assistant overseers has been transferred from the Vestry to the Town Council.

The Charter of Incorporation is dated August 15th, 1892. The successful appeal to the Privy Council was the work of a town's committee, which had been appointed as a result of a moderately well attended public meeting. A house-to-house petition secured 1,571 names in support, out of a voters' roll of 2,226. The Charter was received on September 19th with great rejoicing. The day, which was gloriously fine, was kept as a public holiday; the Lord Mayor of London (Sir David Evans) attended with the Sheriffs and all the Mayors of Essex, the Chairman of the County Council and the Member of Parliament for the Division. There was a procession through the town; the Lord Mayor's escort being formed by a party of the Loyal Suffolk Hussars. A luncheon was held in the Pier Pavilion, the school children were given a treat and a medal each, the latter having been specially struck for the occasion.

The new municipality was divided into three wards— North Ward (the town lying north of London Road), East and West Wards, the dividing line of the two last named running from London Road, through High Street, Cliff Town Road, Nelson Street and Devereux Terrace to the sea. There was a contested election for six Councillors in each Ward, and upon the appointment of six Aldermen from among the eighteen, further elections were held; the Council then being complete with a membership of twenty-four. The new body consisted of: Councillor T. Dowsett (Mayor); Aldermen W. H. Allen, J. H. Burrows, D. W. Gosset, J. R. Hemmann, J. C. Ingram, and F. Wood; Councillors G. Allen, J. R. Brightwell, E. J. Bowmaker, W. J. Chignell, W. T. Darke, H. Dennis, E. H. Draper, P. Forbes, H. Garon, R. Gooch, J. B. Howard, J. C. Hudson, W. T. Nichols, J. Pawley, A. Prevost, W. Trigg, J. C. Underwood; with the Town Clerk (Mr. W. Gregson).

On the 9th November the first meeting was held; Mr. C. A. Tabor, J.P., the Provisional Mayor, taking the chair. Mr. T. Dowsett, J.P., was unanimously elected first Mayor, with Mr. J. H. Burrows (the Chairman of the Incorporation Committee) as Deputy Mayor. At that gathering Major Rasch, M.P., presented a silver mace. Later in the year the Mayor gave the chain and robe of office, the treasurer contributed the seal, and Mr. E. Wright, a local architect, constructed a Mayoral chair out of oak timber from the old Pier.

The Borough was enlarged in 1897 by the inclusion of the parish of Southchurch. The extension was brought about owing to the necessity for a new sewerage and outfall system. At first fierce opposition to amalgamation was waged by Southchurch parishioners, but whilst the Local Government Board enquiry was being held the various interests were conciliated (mainly by the conclusion of a differential rating agreement in respect of certain areas) and the absorption of Southchurch within the Borough became an accomplished fact. From time to time there have been suggestions made for the incorporation of Leigh. That parish was granted an Urban District Council in 1897. Its members took up their task with zeal. Sewerage works were constructed; the local gas undertaking was bought ; the water undertaking was inherited from the Rural Council, and several streets were made up. The water and gas undertakings did not at first prove remunerative, and the charges in other directions increased the rates to such an extent, that partnership with Southend was seriously suggested. There was, however, no response from the Borough. When the tramway was laid, which connected Leigh more closely with Southend, and later, Borough support was given to an amalgamation movement, but by that time the steady growth of Leigh and its gradual emancipation from financial troubles led the majority there to a contrary way of thinking, and the movement has not since increased in favour.

A feature of the Town Council's administration has been its frequent promotion of Bills. No fewer than five have been presented to the legislature, of which only two have been passed. The purport and history of the five Bills, put briefly, are : 1898, successful, mainly Pier Extension ; 1900-1, unsuccessful, General Powers, the variety and complexity of which were chief causes influencing the town's meeting refusal to allow the cost of promotion to come out of the rates ; 1904-5, unsuccessful, General Powers, the scope and extent of which again alarmed burgesses ; 1906-7, unsuccessful, the late Mr. Strachan's Sewerage Scheme, the preamble being rejected by a House of Lords Committee ; and 1908-9, successful, for sanction of the Borough Engineer's Sewerage proposal and increase in the membership of the Town Council.

When the Local Board made Victoria Avenue, with a view to recuperate the cost of road-making the frontage on either side was purchased for re-sale, but the experiment was not a success. For years sales were only occasional, and restricted to a few plots, until in 1894 it was reported that a rate of $3\frac{1}{2}$d. must be levied in respect thereof, 2d. of which was for accumulated interest. The prospect of a $3\frac{1}{2}$d. rate for each year for a land speculation was serious ; but, happily, two years later the frontages sold, at reduced prices, with considerable rapidity, enabling the town to save some part of the contemplated loss.

The Fire Brigade was inaugurated in 1875, but it was not until 1901 that permanent quarters were secured ; a handsome fire station and hose tower being erected in Tyler's Avenue. A year previously the town had taken over the existing fire hydrants from the Water Company, and added considerably to their number. The Fire Brigade now possess two steamers and a fire escape, with a branch station at Westcliff. In 1908 they won the national shield for steamer drill at the annual meeting of the National Fire Brigade Union at Scarborough. The drill was carried out in the quick time of 29⅕th secs. Upon the arrival of the winning team at Southend they were accorded a public welcome and there was much rejoicing. The present captain is Mr. W. G. Harvey, and his predecessors were Mr. F. Woosnam, Mr. G. Lingwood, Mr. W. Baker and Mr. H. Garon.

The Mayoralty is an unsalaried office ; the only exception having been in Coronation year (1902), when the Mayor was voted £750 for special expenditure.

In 1897 the Borough, which originally had only one member upon the Essex County Council, was given a second representative ; the town being divided into two wards, known as Eastern and Western.

Consent was given in 1899 to a system for the pumping of sea water for road cleansing and moistening purposes ; the estimated cost being £9,300. The work was carried out in due course, but at the close of 1904 there came an adverse report upon the machinery, with the result that a further sum of £1,000 had to be spent. The loan service for this installation accumulated to £12,777, and the annual expenditure, apart from loan charges, ran to £450.

After years of agitation and enquiry, in the early part of 1902 it was decided to make a modified provision of forty houses (Ruskin Avenue) for the working classes, at an inclusive cost of about £10,000. The amount actually expended was £14,447, and a yearly deficit of £150 has to be defrayed out of the rates.

A great task awaited the Health Committee of the new authority upon its advent in 1892. Much had already been done by the Local Board, but a good deal still remained to be accomplished. In addition to the provision of an outfall system, street sewers remained to be cleansed and ventilated, house drains to be examined and tested, an infectious diseases hospital to be provided, and an over-filled churchyard (St. John Baptist) to be closed after the acquisition of a new cemetery site. Stricter byelaws for the building of houses were passed, and closer supervision ordered of residences in course of erection under powers obtained by the Council in 1895. These made up a great and onerous task, in the carrying out of which little popularity could be secured, but much criticism endured, and the Borough owes to no other body of workers a greater debt of gratitude than to those who have assisted in health administration during the past seventeen years. It was weary work obtaining assent to Mr. Mansergh's sewerage scheme (Eastern Valley). Almost every burgess was a sewerage engineer, and by public meeting and private agitation the Council was sought to be pulled hither and thither. It was not until August 9th, 1894, that the Local Government Board held its enquiry respecting loan sanction, and then thirteen further months passed before consent was given. At once the Town Council ordered that preparation should be made for placing the Western Valley scheme (also Mr. Mansergh's) before the Local Government Board, and tried to get forward with the sanctioned proposal. The question of sites for storage tank and pumping station brought about further delays, and it was not until December, 1895, that the Council were informed and agreed to accept an offer by Messrs. Baxter, Dowsett and Ingram of sites on the Southchurch Hall Estate. The temper of the moment may be judged by the fact that something akin to a fight took place at the close of the Council meeting on the evening of acceptance. Early in 1897 sites were secured for pumping station and storage tank at Westcliff, and during the following year both schemes were got to work. The provision was for the collection of the sewage into two tanks, there to be held until half-an-hour after the tide commenced to ebb, and then to be discharged for the space of four hours, by means of an outfall pipe, from an opening half-a-mile east of the pier and some-what to seaward of the line of the new pier head. In the middle of June, 1899, it was further resolved, owing to growth of population in the North Ward along the slopes of the Prittlewell Valley, to collect and pump the sewage of that area for discharge into the sea at the same outfall. This work was carried out in 1902, and subsequently, by great sewer extensions along the western front, Leigh Road, West Road, etc., the Borough has been efficiently sewered. Leigh, in 1901, at an expenditure of £18,072, constructed sewerage and treatment works, thereby helping towards the improvement of the foreshore. Thus matters stood until the disastrous Hobart action in 1907 ; the judgment in effect fining Southend £1,500 damages with about £8,000 costs, and holding that the byelaw of the Kent and Essex Sea Fisheries Committee, prohibiting the deposit or discharge of any solid or liquid substance detrimental to sea-fish or sea-fishing, applied to Southend's outfall works, although it had not been thought so to apply by the Board of Trade and the Sea Fisheries Committee when it was sanctioned in the year 1895. The Borough had once more to embark in the tedious, expensive business of sewage disposal. Mr. Strachan (who had acted locally for Mr. Mansergh) was called in and devised a scheme for collecting and conveying all the sewage to a distant part of Southchurch, there separating the grosser elements for burning, the remainder to be discharged into the estuary by a new outfall situate well to the east of the Borough. At once the Sea Fisheries Committee said that the balance of sewage would, unless treated, be detrimental to sea-fish and sea-fishing. Opposition was also urged by Metropolitan Authorities—in respect of the disposal of whose sewage, both in the neighbour- nood of the estuary and higher up the river, much has still to be done—and the House of Lords refused to pass the Bill through Committee stage. In the 1909 Session of Parlia- ment the Town Council promoted another Sewerage Bill. Its feature may be shortly explained. By deep sewers the sewage will be taken to land situated at the north-east of the parish of Prittlewell, there treated, and a purified effluent discharged into the estuary. This project by the Borough Engineer (Mr. Elford) is as generally supported as its immediate predecessor was opposed.

Early in the life of the Town Council an infectious diseases hospital, known as the Sanatorium, was erected in Balmoral Road, succeeding a temporary hospital in North Road. In later years both site and building have been extended ; the total cost amounting to nearly £18,000. In the northern part of the Borough separate provision was made for smallpox, and, happily, it has only been used on one occasion.

As a result of frequent representations and a visit of an Inspector of Home Office, a closing order was obtained in 1898 in respect of St. John Baptist churchyard. Three years after that the Town Council bought fifteen acres of land on either side of Sutton Road, at the northern extremity of the Borough, and there laid out a cemetery, which was opened in 1900. Controversy arose in respect of the conse- cration of the ground. Free Churchmen desired that Churchmen should unite with them in a dedication service.

The latter objected upon conscientious grounds, and urged that if a portion of the cemetery were consecrated they would themselves discharge the "legal consequences," so that the cost should not fall upon the general body of ratepayers—that is to say, build a chapel, provide a chaplain, and pay the consecration charges. Ultimately a compromise was arrived at upon those lines.

In respect of the Cliffs, in February, 1894, a decision in the High Court settled a point which had caused much contention, viz., whether or not the esplanade (Pier to Shorefields) and the inclined road thereto was useable by horses and carts. The Town Council's opinion was upheld, and such right of user denied. . The Local Board had already been held to be wrong in fencing off the esplanade from the Undercliff, as it used to be called, and the Town Council had to face a claim for damages as a result, but the Court held no injury was proved.

The Corporation decided in 1902 to employ a band to perform in an enclosure upon the Cliffs during the summer. The experiment proved a great success financially. The quality of the bands was subsequently improved; leading military combinations of the country now being engaged. Until 1909 the musicians were accommodated in a small bandstand, but in that year a more commodious structure was raised, and the original building transferred to the Happy Valley, in the Cliffs below. This spot had been used for variety entertainments for some years with much success, and in 1908-9 the Unemployed Committee, as part of their scheme of work for the winter, made arrangements with the Corporation whereby a considerable sum was spent in enlarging the Valley and making it more commodious.

In 1899 the Southchurch esplanade and roadway were constructed, and in 1903 the Western and Chalkwell esplanades were carried out at a cost of about £38,000;

the expenditure upon the extreme eastern and western
improvements together totalling at over £50,000. The
section of the esplanade from the Shrubbery to Westcliff
remains practically as taken over from the Local Board,
possibly owing to the fact that all the Undercliff (now
called Westcliff by the Town Council) is not in its possession. Southchurch Park of twenty acres came as a gift
from Messrs. Baxter, Dowsett, and Ingram at the close
of 1895. Since then it has been the home of cricket ;
several County matches having been played on its pitches.
Towards the close of the summer of 1901 the Council bought
the house called Chalkwell Hall with surrounding grounds
and 26½ acres of land. The total cost was, roughly, £20,000.
As part of the same transaction the Council obtained land for
the Chalkwell Esplanade and the whole of the Chalkwell
Estate foreshore ; also payment towards the cost from the
conveying Syndicate of £1,250 for the first two years, £1,000
per annum for the following three years, and £500 per annum
for the five years.

In 1891 the Local Board obtained an Order for Electric
Lighting, but it remained in abeyance—notwithstanding an
offer of the Gas Company to buy or lease it—until the autumn
of 1897, when the Town Council passed a resolution ordering
work under the Order to be proceeded with. The question
of a town tramway was associated with that project, and it was
decided in October, 1898, to proceed for a Light Railway
Order. The lines ultimately asked for were those now in
existence, save the portion going along the eastern front from
the Kursaal, which was opened in the summer of 1908.
The routes, in short, were from the Kursaal to Southchurch
Road ; from Southchurch Church to Leigh Church ; from
Victoria Corner round Prittlewell by North Road to the
Cricketers ; all these lines converging upon a terminus
opposite the Middleton Hotel, High Street. In June, 1899,
very favourable terms were negociated with a Mr. Gibbins,

of Bradford, for the working of the Electric Lighting Order and the supply of electrical energy, but a public meeting's condemnation stood in the road, and the project dropped. In August of 1900 a tender was accepted for the machinery room, car shed, etc., at the London Road depôt, and the laying of the track, all save the cars ; the contract figures being : Works, £87,500 ; cars, £3,370. On June 4th, 1901, the first trial run took place. Litigation occurred over the way in which the track had been constructed, which was not settled until December of 1903. A year later the Town Council sought and obtained an Order for the construction of further tramways, from the Kursaal to Shoeburyness, and from the eastern end of the existing tramway at Southchurch to Bournes Green. A small portion of the former only has been carried out, and the remainder of the Order expired by effluxion of time. The delay so fatal to the Order was caused by a strong divergence of view. The owners of Thorpe Hall Estate wished for a shore route to Shoeburyness, whereas the authorized route cut through their estate, in an effort to get a reasonably short journey and saving of time and mileage cost. The capital expenditure on electric lighting up to the end of March, 1908, totalled at £114,440, and on tramways to £86,725.

The list of Mayors to date is :—

Mr. THOMAS DOWSETT	- -	1892-3
,, DANIEL WRIGHT GOSSET	-	1893-4
,, JOHN RUMBELOW BRIGHTWELL		1894-5
,, ALFRED PREVOST	- -	1895-6
,, BERNARD WILSHIRE TOLHURST		1896-7
,, JOHN HENRY BURROWS	-	1897-8
,, FREDERIC FRANCIS RAMUZ	-	1898-9
,, ,, ,, (re-elected)		1899-1900
,, JOSEPH FRANCIS -	- -	1900-1
,, JAMES COLBERT INGRAM	-	1901-2
,, ALBERT MARTIN -	- -	1902-3

Mr. JAMES BERRY - - - 1903-4
„ ARTHUR CHARLES LOURY - 1904-5
„ JOHN RUMBELOW BRIGHTWELL 1905-6
„ WALTER ROBERT KING - - 1906-7
„ JAMES COLBERT INGRAM - 1907-8
„ „ „ (re-elected) 1908-9

Town Clerks :—

Mr. WILLIAM GREGSON - Resigned 1898
„ WILLIAM HENRY SNOW „ 1909
„ H. J. WORWOOD - - ———

Robert Buchanan's Association with Southend.

Robert Buchanan, a poet whose works are increasing in favour, and some of whose compositions appear destined to take high places in our national literature, had a close and intimate acquaintance with Southend. From Miss Harriett Jay's biography we gather that he first came to the town at the beginning of 1882. His wife, to whom he was devotedly attached, was gradually dying of cancer, and she longed for a sight of the sea. He brought her to Southend, and they stayed in Cliff Town Parade. At first the change of air seemed beneficial to the invalid, but later she had a relapse. The pain became incessant and unbearable, but throughout the patient bravely refused to have morphia administered. She gradually sank, and in November of that year died in her husband's arms, to Buchanan's intense grief. She was buried in St. John's churchyard, and in a volume of selected poems which he published in that year the dedication ran : "To Mary. Weeping and sorrowing, yet in a sure and certain hope of a heavenly resurrection, I place these poor flowers of verse on the grave of my beloved wife, who with eyes of truest love and tenderness watched these growing over more than twenty years. Robert Buchanan, Southend, 1882." After his wife's death Buchanan intended to reside permanently at Southend, but later altered his mind

and travelled for some months in France ; subsequently
residing in London and making frequent trips to this town,
often accompanied by Mr. G. R. Sims.   Mr. Sims wrote an
experience he had upon one of these occasions.   "On holiday
he lived every hour of the day.   The long walk never tired
him, the long drive never made him sleepy.   He would sit
far into the night and smoke cigarettes and talk, and be up in
the morning eager for work or play.   Once at Southend we
went to bed at three o'clock.   At half-past eight he was up
and ready for a stroll before breakfast.   We walked about
Southend for an hour.   Suddenly my companion left me,
saying, 'Go back to the hotel ; I will be with you directly.'
When he came in I noticed that the knees of his trousers
were covered with chalk.   He had gone to the graveyard to
see the grave of his wife.   He had found the gate locked and
had climbed over the wall."   In 1884 Buchanan resolved to
make Southend his home, and rented Hamlet Court, which
had formerly been occupied by Sir Richard Cunliffe Owen
and then by Sir Edwin Arnold.   It was whilst residing there
he wrote "The City of Dreams," a poetical work which
produced a eulogy from the late Mr. W. H. Lecky, at the
annual dinner of the Royal Academy.   After two or three
years, Buchanan moved to Byculla House, the Cliffs, and then,
finding his work in connection with the stage becoming much
heavier, he removed to South Hampstead.   In 1894 Buchanan
suffered another bereavement in the death of his mother, whom
he buried with his wife in the grave at Southend, and in
respect of whom he made the pitiful entry in his diary : "At
11 a.m. to-day, after several days of suffering, my beloved
mother died, leaving me heart broken.   Worn out with days
and nights of watching I was dazed and stupefied.   O, mother,
mother, if we are never to meet again, the whole universe
contains nothing to live for !   But we must, we shall !"
Later on he wrote : "I have laid her to rest at Southend, in
a beautiful graveyard by the sea, close to the place where she

used to be very happy." He dedicated to her memory one of his last volumes of poetry, which contained verses perhaps the most pathetic ever addressed by a son to his departed mother. In June, 1901, Buchanan himself passed away, and he, too, was buried in the churchyard with his wife and parent. A substantial memorial was placed over his grave as a result of subscriptions of friends and admirers.

The Parliamentary Elections.

For many years prior to 1885 Rochford Hundred for purposes of Parliamentary representation formed part of the South Essex Division, a two member constituency. In the year named a Re-distribution Act was passed, by which Essex was allotted eight members, in addition to three members for the Borough constituencies of Colchester and North-West and South-East Ham. A scheme was prepared by the Boundary Commissioners, and the eight divisions were named respectively Southend, Chelmsford, Epping, Romford, Walthamstow, Saffron Walden, Maldon, and Harwich. It was proposed that the Southend division should include Rochford, Orsett and Dengie Hundreds, with a small number of the parishes round about Pitsea added. On January 14th, 1885, Mr. Joseph J. Henley, the Boundary Commissioner appointed for the purpose, held an enquiry into the proposals at Chelmsford. Representations were made that the Dengie Hundred should be taken away from the Southend Division and added to Chelmsford, though, so far as can be gathered from meetings held at that time, feeling in Southend was in favour of the scheme of the Boundary Commission. Another suggestion was that Pitsea and adjoining parishes should be apportioned to Chelmsford, and Rainham and Wennington added to Southend. Grays also made representation that the name of the division should be altered to Grays, on the ground that in point of population Southend was no bigger than their own town, and that the promise was

that Grays would become a great manufacturing centre. In
the end, the Commissioner made very little alteration. The
official name given to the constituency was that of South-East
Essex or Southend, the Dengie Hundred was retained, Pitsea
and adjoining parishes were removed to the Chelmsford
Division, and Rainham and Wennington added to South-East
Essex. At that time the electorate was 9,367. In 1906,
at the last General Election, it was 20,591 and is still growing
rapidly. The first election was fought in the same year as re-
distribution took place. It was a very close and exciting
contest. The late Colonel (afterwards Sir) W. T. Makins,
one of the former representatives for South Essex, was the
Conservative candidate, and Mr. W. H. Wills (now Lord
Winterstoke) led the Liberal forces. There was a good deal
of feeling displayed, and some disgraceful scenes of rowdyism
took place in Southend streets. The poll resulted :

Col. W. T. MAKINS (C.)	-	3,707
Mr. W. H. WILLS (L.)	-	3,500
Con. majority -		207 .

The dissolution brought about by the defeat of Mr.
Gladstone's Home Rule Bill in 1886 saw another keen fight.
Upon this occasion Colonel Makins retired, and was succeeded by Major (now Sir) F. Carne Rasch, of Danbury,
who had unsuccessfully fought the Elland division of Yorkshire
the year before. Mr. W. H. Wills again represented the
Liberal interest. The result was :

Major F. C. RASCH (C.)	-	3,758
Mr. W. H. WILLS (L.)	-	2,916
Con. majority -		842

The next election was in 1892, by which time the
voters' list had increased to 11,960. Major Rasch again
contested the seat, and he was opposed by Mr. E. W. Brooks,
cement manufacturer, of Grays. The electioneering on both

sides was skilful and keen, and until the poll was declared there was doubt in the popular mind as to the successful candidate. The record was :

Major F. C. Rasch (C.)	-	4,901
Mr. E. W. Brooks (L.)	-	4,359
Con. majority	-	542

The term of office of the Liberal Government ended in 1895, and the polling in South-East Essex revealed the fact that Major Rasch had greatly increased his hold upon the electorate. His opponent (Mr. D. Milne Watson, a London barrister) was a stranger to the constituency when Parliament was dissolved. The result was :

Major F. C. Rasch (C.)	-	5,460
Mr. D. Milne Watson (L.)	-	3,520
Con. majority	-	1,940

Before the next election took place, Major Rasch had accepted an invitation to contest the Chelmsford Division in the Conservative interest, and his successor in the candidature in South-East Essex was Lieutenant-Colonel Edward Tufnell, a well-known Islington ground landlord. Mr. Rowland Whitehead, a barrister, second son of Sir James Whitehead, Bart., a former Lord Mayor of London, led the Liberal forces, and a keen and vigorous fight ended :

Colonel E. Tufnell (C.)	-	5,815
Mr. Rowland Whitehead (L.)		4,461
Con. majority	-	1,354

Although the vote against the Liberal candidate was heavy, he had made such a good impression upon the constituency, and become so popular with all parties, that successful efforts were put forth to induce him to stand again. Before the election came in 1906, Colonel Tufnell announced his retirement, and Captain J. R. B. Newman, an estate owner in the South of Ireland, was adopted in his stead. The contest was remarkable for the great revival of Liberalism, for the poll showed an increase of nearly 5,000 upon that of 1900, and ensured the first victory of the Liberal Party in the Division. The result was :

Mr. Rowland Whitehead (L.)   9,230

Captain J. R. B. Newman (C.)   7,170

Lib. majority - 2,060

Earthquake, Gales and Floods.

An exciting event of local history was that of the earthquake on the morning of April 22nd, 1884. The centre of disturbance lay to the north-east of the Hundred, in the district of Colchester, but the phenomenon was distinctly felt at Southend and surrounding places, although no damage was done. Southend and district also felt the full force of the blizzard of Tuesday, 18th January, 1881, when the down express train was snowed up in the neighbourhood of Barking, and vehicles were embedded in snowdrifts. The most disastrous rainfall of last century in this locality occurred on August 2nd, 1888. The rainfall of July had been unusual, and after three wet days, during Wednesday afternoon and evening nearly three inches (2.8in.) fell. The flooding of basements was considerable, but a more serious consequence was the stopping of the train service on the London, Tilbury and Southend line for the remainder of the week and over the Bank Holiday. The 5.5 down express got through the new route via Upminster, its passengers noting with anxiety the washing away of the ballast, but the 7.18 p.m. ex-Fenchurch Street did not arrive at Southend until 8 o'clock the following morning, after being detained at Stanford-le-Hope from 10.15 p.m. to 5 a.m. On Thursday morning a newspaper train got through, then all bookings below Plaistow were stopped, and a full train service was not restored for days. The flooding of the countryside was

P

general, large sections of sea walling were destroyed, and New England Island was under water. The last Monday of November, 1897, was the occasion of another tremendous flood at Southend, Leigh, and other places on the Thames side. Practically the whole of Marine and Southchurch parades and intervening roadways, etc., were covered with water to a depth of several feet ; the school children from the National School having to be rowed home. The cause of the flood was the prevalence of great gales during Sunday and Monday, combined with a high tide. Other parts of the Hundred suffered severely ; the railway line between Leigh and Benfleet being flooded, and the service temporarily suspended.

Gales bring to mind the means provided for saving of life. A lifeboat station was first established at Southend in 1879, when a boat was provided by means of a special fund collected by Mr. Edwin J. Brett, through the medium of a magazine called " The Boys of England," and manned by Southend watermen. The vessel was withdrawn from the station in 1891, after a useful career, in the course of which the crew were instrumental in saving twenty-three lives. In 1885 another lifeboat, the " Theodore and Herbert," was sent to Southend ; the cost having been defrayed by a legacy bequeathed to the National Lifeboat Institution by Mrs. F. S. Smith, of Lisheen, co. Cork. The lives saved by means of this boat totalled thirty-four. In 1899 the "Theodore and Herbert" was superseded by the "James Stevens, No. 9," and to February, 1909, this vessel possessed the fine record of fifty-two lives saved from eleven craft, all sailing vessels. It will thus be seen that in thirty years the local lifeboatmen saved 109 lives; beside being of considerable assistance to vessels in navigating them to places of safety.

Southend Victoria Hospital.

Southend Victoria Hospital is one of the best known of local institutions, providing medical and surgical aid not only for the inhabitants of the Borough, but for the Rochford Hundred as well. It has been twenty-one years in existence, and each year that has passed since its doors were opened has demonstrated its necessity. On September 28th, 1886, a meeting of local medical practitioners was held with a view to inaugurating a fund for the establishment of a hospital, as a suitable form of commemorating Queen Victoria's Golden Jubilee of her accession to the throne. Notwithstanding a good deal of criticism from those who were not convinced of the need of such an institution, the representative committee formed to forward the movement went steadily to work, with Mr. W. Gregson as hon. sec. (now chairman of the Committee). Dr. Warwick, as chairman, issued a statement, in which he urged that an object of local benevolence would appeal more closely to and accord more nearly with the sympathies of the loyal inhabitants. Such a local memorial should, nevertheless, be neither temporary nor restricted in its usefulness, and it should be for the direct and permanent advantage of all creeds and all classes—especially of the more needy class. Nothing appeared to more fully possess these characteristics than a hospital. It was estimated that a sum of £2,500 would be required to inaugurate the project. On January 12th, 1887, a public meeting pledged itself to support the committee in carrying out the scheme, and in May of the same year a site of half an acre at the eastern extremity of Warrior Square was purchased from Mr. Venables at a cost of £350. Two months later the land was conveyed to seven trustees—Messrs. W. G. Brighten, G. D. Deeping, T. Dowsett, W. Fairbairns, G. F. Jones, H. Luker, and F. Wood. A contract with Messrs. Baker and Wiseman for the construction of the building was accepted at £1,267 4s. 7d., and on August 13th Lady Brooke (now Countess of Warwick) laid the foundation stone. It was found, when all expenses had been paid, that the cost of building and equipping the hospital had been kept within the original estimate of £2,500. The institution was opened on May 30th, 1888, by Mrs. (now Lady) Rasch. The first annual report dealt with seven months' work. During that time forty-two cases had been treated, and the income more than sufficed to meet the expenditure. The next year's report, which covered the full period of twelve months, stated that fifty-five patients had been admitted, and that the receipts had more than counter-balanced the expenditure. The income was close upon £500, and the outgoings £348; £50 being placed on deposit. A sum of £66 was paid to cover the deficiency on building account, but this was met on the other side by the proceeds of a bazaar, which amounted to just over £66. Subsequent development is clearly shown by a contrast with 1908—twenty years later—when the ordinary income was £1,593, and the ordinary expenditure £1,608 17s. 8d., with treatment provided for 601 cases in twenty-two beds and a children's ward, and 8,565 visits paid by nurses to the sick poor in their own homes. In commemoration of the Queen's Diamond Jubilee (1897) it was decided to institute a system of visitation by district nurses. The public appeal resulted in a subscription list of £1,440, and this sum, with £745 taken from the accumulated reserve fund, gave a total of £2,185 in hand for building a nurses' home and an additional ward, raising the accommodation from eight to fourteen beds. The cost was expected to be £3,030, and next year the gratifying report was made that the whole amount had been secured. In 1900, at the time of the Boer War, two beds, and, if possible, a third, were placed at the disposal of the Mayor's Fund, which was inaugurated to aid reservists or volunteers invalided home. Fortunately, no necessity arose to take advantage of the offer. As the result of a gift of £1,200 by Mr. G. F. Frooms, an enlargement of the women's ward was carried out, as a memorial to the late Mrs. Frooms. Upon Mr. Frooms' death, a short time after, the hospital received another benefaction of £1,000. Several other sums of money were ob-

RUINS OF HADLEIGH CASTLE.

tained as legacies about this time. A contribution of £2,738 was handed over to the funds as a share of the estate of the late Mr. G. J. Lawrence, of Epping, the hospital being one of six institutions in the southern half of Essex selected as "being best managed and for the most benefit of the objects for which they were founded." Miss Baddams, the beneficiary under the will of the late Mr. Frooms, died in 1902, and left £2,000 towards the endowment fund. The committee also received £766, half share of the residuary estate of Miss Martha Burletson, of Southend. A freehold house of the yearly value of £70 was also conveyed to the hospital by Mrs. Ray, and Mr. Alfred Tolhurst gave a triangular piece of ground adjoining, which was needed for the purposes of enlargement. In 1903 a sum of £756 was paid into the funds as a share in the residue of the late Mr. Frooms' estate, and under the will of the late Mr. Philip Patmore, of Creeksea, £1,160 was received. A cot was endowed by public subscription and named after the Rev. T. Varney, in commemoration of his "devoted and self-sacrificing labours in this hospital, town, and neighbourhood, 1890-1902." In 1904, £600 fell to the funds under the will of the late Mr. J. Richmond, and a year later an additional piece of ground was bought. A children's ward was built in 1906 at a cost of over £1,000, provided by the family as a memorial of the late Mr. Thomas Dowsett. In the same year the operating theatre was enlarged and improved, and an anæsthetic room added; Sir Horace Brooks Marshall fitting up the theatre with a supply of instruments. The cots maintained in the children's ward include :

NAME OF DONOR.		NAME OF COT.
Coun. W. R. King, J.P.	-	"Irene King."
Mr. F. Agar - -	-	"Bruce-Agar."
Mr. H. A. Dowsett -	-	"Margaret."
Mr. A. J. Gibson -	-	"Gibson."
Technical School -	-	"Technical School."

The Story of a Crime.

In June, 1894, feeling in the countryside was deeply stirred by the discovery of the body of a young woman named Florence Dennis in the Prittle brook, running through Coleman's Estate, about a mile and three quarters westward from North Street, Prittlewell. The subsequent elucidation of the mystery created much excitement, and the tragedy became for a time a national sensation. Miss Dennis, who had been shot through the left temple by means of a pistol bullet, was a prepossessing young lady, somewhat advanced in pregnancy. She was the sister-in-law of a milk vendor named Ayriss, living in Wesley Road, with whom she had been staying for a short time. It was subsequently proved in evidence that upon the evening of Sunday, June 24th, she met a clerk employed at the Royal Albert Docks, London, named James Canham Read, by whom she was alleged to have been seduced. The couple were observed talking very earnestly as they walked up Sallendines Lane (now Hamlet Court Road North), and also in Prittlewell. From that time they were not seen together again, but late on the following Monday the body of the girl was discovered in the brook; appearances pointing to the probability that she had been shot as she walked along, and then thrown into the water. An inquest followed at the Blue Boar Hotel, Prittlewell, and the jury, after two sittings, returned a verdict of wilful murder against Read. The man was, however, not to be found. He had left his employment at the docks, taking away over £100 in money, with which he had been entrusted to pay wages. For a fortnight no sign of him was discovered, but on Saturday, July 7th, Inspector Baker, of the Criminal Investigation Department, Scotland Yard, and Detective Sergeant (now Superintendent) Marden, of the Essex Constabulary, effected Read's arrest at Mitcham, Surrey, where he and a young woman had been living as " Mr. and Mrs. Benson." He was brought to Southend the same evening, and on Monday appeared before a special sitting of the Borough Bench. At the commencement of the proceedings Mr. T. Lamb (of Messrs. Todd, Dennes and Lamb) prosecuted, but later on the services of Mr. Charles Gill (now K.C.) were retained. The defence throughout the local hearing was in the hands of Mr. H. Warburton, barrister-at-law. The prosecution conducted the case with skill and sagacity, and were met by a defence which fought tenaciously; Read assisting counsel by a cheerful demeanour and easy confidence. Sensation upon sensation followed the investigation before the local Justices. It was proved that, although married, Read had been carrying on an irregular intercourse with several women. Public feeling ran high. On one occasion Mr. Warburton bitterly complained of the unruly conduct of the crowd as Read was being driven from the Court-house to the G.E.R. station, en route for Chelmsford prison. The special editions of the "Southend Standard" were eagerly purchased, and some people offered one shilling per copy in their eagerness to read the latest information of the trial. At the tenth hearing, on September 7th, Read was committed to the Assizes, and on November 12th, at Chelmsford, he was brought before the late Chief Baron Pollock. The leading Counsel for the prosecution was the late Sir F. Lockwood, Q.C., Solicitor General; whilst the late Mr. Cock, Q.C., and Mr. Warburton were retained for the defence. For four days counsel made a great effort to save Read's life, but without avail. The jury returned a verdict of guilty, and in sentencing him to death the Chief Baron said he had been rightly convicted upon evidence which could leave no

doubt in the mind of any person who heard it. A petition
for a reprieve was forwarded to the Home Office, but the
sentence was confirmed.   Upon being informed that no
chance of life remained, Read wrote a remarkable letter to
his brother, in the course of which he said : " In spite of
truth and in defiance of evidence presented to him proving my
innocence, the Home Secretary has endorsed the murderous
conspiracy of his professional brethren.   Blood, I suppose, is
thicker than water, and cliqueism is stronger than justice."   The
new evidence alluded to was to the effect that he slept on the
night of the crime at a house in Southchurch Road, and that
he was in bed at the hour the murder was alleged to have been
committed.   The execution took place on Tuesday, December 4th.   Read all along protested that he had not seen
Florence Dennis for many months, and he left no statement
throwing light upon the tragedy.   He met his death with
the utmost composure, and his last words upon the scaffold
were, " Button my coat ! "

HADLEIGH CASTLE:

ITS FOUNDATION, RESTORATION, AND DEMOLITION.

Hadleigh Castle is the most interesting historic relic of this locality ; interesting not only because of its massive architecture and magnificent situation, but also because it figured prominently in the lives of several of the Plantagenet Kings, that oft-times glorious, oft-times tragic chapter in English history. The date of the foundation of the Castle is well known, and the royal licences which were issued from time to time in connection with its building are still extant. The estate was comprised in the Honour of Rayleigh, long in the possession of the Sweyn family, whose seat was situated at Rayleigh, some three miles from Hadleigh. Henry de Essex, grandson of the founder, was stripped of his property for cowardice whilst serving with the King in Wales, and the estate passed into the hands of Henry II. The year Hubert de Burgh became owner of this great fief is unknown. There is an entry in the Patent Rolls under date July 24th, 1217, which shows that the young king, Henry III, who had just ascended the throne at the age of nine, issued a mandate to the knights and freeholders of the Honour of Rayleigh that they should hold under Hubert de Burgh, Justiciar of England, "to whom the King has granted the same, to hold during pleasure, as John, the King's father, before had done," showing that Hubert first entered into the profits of the estate some time prior to 1216, the year when Henry III came to the throne. Hubert owned the property at the most influential period of his career. His rise to the high and honourable position of Justiciar, and subsequently to that

of one of the guardians of the young king, was achieved
by great administrative ability and a patriotic desire to serve
his country. It has been said of him that, "bred in the
school of Henry II, he had little sympathy with national
freedom ; his conception of good government, like that of his
master, lay in a wise personal administration, in the preservation of order and law. But he combined with this a
thoroughly English desire for national independence, a hatred
of foreigners, and a reluctance to waste English blood and
treasure in Continental struggles." It is probable that the
mandate of Henry III was issued in the ordinary course
of events upon his accession, and not as a special recompense
for services, for its date is just a month before the great sea
fight off Dover, when Hubert, at the head of the men of the
Cinque Ports, assisted to put an end to French designs upon
the English throne, making him for the time the most
popular and powerful statesman. For thirteen or fourteen years
following this fight he was the virtual ruler of the country,
and it was in those years that he erected the magnificent castle at Hadleigh, the scanty ruins of which afford
little idea of its extent, though the massive walls of the
two remaining towers give ample evidence of its supreme
strength. Its position was picturesque and peculiarly suitable.
Seated in the centre of the range of cliffs which stretches from
Leigh to Benfleet it commanded on the east and south fine
views of the Thames, whilst on the north there stretched from
its walls an almost illimitable forest, so that the recreation of
hunting could add to the charm of situation. In 1227
there was a confirmation by charter of the grant of the
property to de Burgh, but it was not until 1230—thirteen
years after he became Lord of the Honour—that licence was
obtained from Henry for the construction of the Castle. This
was two years before the Justiciar's fall from power. The
great structure could not have been reared in that time, and
this suggests that Hubert had for some years previously been

engaged in building his seat, and obtained the permission to erect when it was finished and ready for occupation. A licence to crenellate was granted at any time either before, during, or after construction. The terms of the King's grant were :—

"Know ye that we have granted for us and our heirs "to Hubert de Burgh, Earl of Kent, our Justiciary of "England, and Margaret, his wife, that they may by their "will construct for themselves and their heirs of the same "Hubert and Margaret descending or other heirs of the "same Hubert if it shall happen to the heirs descending "from the same Hubert and Margaret to die (without "issue) without contradiction and difficulty a certain "castle at Hadlee, which is of the Honour of Rayley, "which Honour we formerly gave and by our charter "confirmed to the same."

The Castle has been described as a "rare example of the military architecture of the early English period, which, though rich in ecclesiastical edifices, is poor in military structures." It is largely composed of blocks of Kentish ragstone and chalk, bound together by a strong, rock-like cement, in which pounded cockle-shells largely figure, probably obtained from the neighbouring flats of Leigh and Canvey. There is no stone deposit in this part of Essex, and it was a matter for speculation how Hubert procured his building material. During the laying of the railway track which runs almost at the foot of the Castle hill, however, those assisting in the construction of the culverts which span the numerous ditches and fleets of this marshy country, at a depth of about twelve feet, came upon planks of timber. These appeared to be the remains of sunken rafts or vessels by which ragstone had been floated over the river from Kent, together with considerable quantities of the material; showing, further, that one of the arms of the Thames in that day almost washed the foot of the hill upon which de Burgh had erected his stronghold. The Castle occupied the whole of the top of the height upon which it was situated. It was almost oblong in shape, rounded upon the south-western and northern sides to suit the contour of the small plateau. The principal entrance was from the north, access most likely being obtained along the present lane leading from the high road and the village of Hadleigh. Immediately before the gate was a platform of earth 210 feet long, ten feet high, and of an average width of seventy feet, whilst the door itself was defended by a great circular tower twenty feet high, and with walls eight feet thick. The two principal towers were on the eastern side, and the remains of these are to-day the principal feature of the ruins. They were of great height and strength, and the key of the system of the defence upon the seaward side. Before them spread a mound of earth, and on a lower level a long flat hill, now known as the Saddleback, which probably served for the purposes of exercise, and, it may be, as a tilting ground. The banqueting hall and other family apartments were on the southern and western portions of the interior ; domestic offices being mainly grouped about the entrance. Water was obtained by means of pipes from a spring upon Plumtree Hill, an elevation a short distance to the west of the Castle Hill. The skulls and bones which have been found in great quantities upon the western side show that the occupants had a rough-and-ready method of disposing of offal, and it has been suggested that the drainage found an outlet on the south and meandered at will down the hillside until it became absorbed in the waters of the Thames. The courtyard was over 110 yards long and ninety yards wide. Mr. H. W. King thinks there was no moat facing the Thames ; the defence relying upon the marshes at the foot and the steepness of the ascent, but on all the other sides there are traces of moats, which, combined with position and strength of masonry, made the place one of the most powerful in the country. Local gossip is very fond of asserting that the Castle had dungeons

REFERENCES TO GROUND PLAN of HADLEIGH CASTLE.

A—N.E. Tower. **B**—S.E. Tower; the sides of the hexagon in each measure 10ft. and walls are 9ft. thick at base. **C**—Semi-circular Tower, its base being 12ft. below the area of the ballium; walls 8ft. thick. **D**—Apartment 25ft. by 8ft. **E**—Apartment of unequal sides, 30ft. by 24ft. and 16ft. **F**—Apartment of unequal sides, 65ft. long by 19ft. 6in. and 18ft. in width. **G**—Basement of a square tower. **H**—Basement of a square tower. **I & J**—Probably the sites of apartments. **K**—Foundations of a circular tower, 20ft. in diameter, within the walls; walls 8ft. thick. **L**—Principal gateway. **M**—Semi-circular buttress, the curve measuring 21ft. **N**—Circular Tower, or perhaps semi-circular, like the opposite tower (**C**); Diameter within walls 16ft. **O**—Platform of earth, 210ft. long, 10ft. high, from the gateway to the extremity of the moat. **P**—Mound of earth in front of the east towers, defended by a deep ditch. **Q**—Ballium, or castle yard, 337ft. long and 180ft. wide.

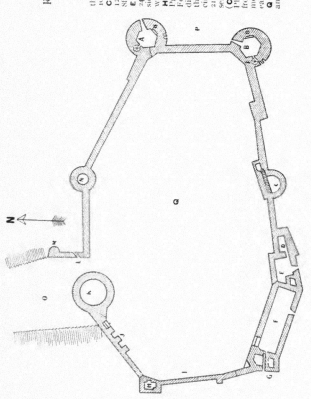

HADLEIGH CASTLE (GROUND PLAN).

and that there were also underground passages connecting it
with several places in the neighbourhood, notably Rochford
Hall. Antiquarians have been unable to find any trace of
subterranean apartments. It is forgotten that the foul air
which would accumulate in underground passages would
render them impassable. Dr. Laver, in a letter to the
writer of this book, trenchantly observed : " In the opinion
of many people there is always a subterranean passage
connected with old castles, ruined monasteries and earth
works, sometimes miles in length. But why they should
imagine that neighbouring lords, who as often as not were
generally quarrelling, should desire an underground means of
communication, is more than I can understand. I remember
at Hadleigh Castle an opening was pointed out as the entrance
to this passage from the inside of the Castle, whereas, in fact,
it was only the opening of the drain outside, and the wall
they supposed to be outside it was only a portion of the wall
over the opening, which had fallen outwards. Underground
dungeons were in castles, according to my experience, very
rare, and in monasteries still more so."

De Burgh's enjoyment of the estate was not of long
duration. In 1231 he obtained the right to hold a market
every Wednesday at Hadleigh, but the following year was,
through intrigue, deprived of his possessions. He was arrested
at Brentwood, where he claimed sanctuary. The Bishop of
London remonstrated on his account, and he was accorded
the privilege he sought until starvation compelled him to
surrender. His property, including Hadleigh Castle, passed
into the hands of the King. One effect of this locally was to
restore to William le Bigod and his wife, owners of the
Hundred of Barstaple, the right to require the men of the
Honour of Rayleigh to make suit of court to that Hundred,
of which it is alleged they had been unjustly deprived by
Hubert. We suspect that this refers not to the whole of the
Honour, but to two parishes which were anciently in the

Hundred of Barstaple, viz., Thundersley and South Benfleet, and which did not come within the civil jurisdiction of Rochford Hundred until the Poor Law Unions Act of 1834. The Royal occupancy of the Castle estates was this time of short duration, for in 1235 a mandate was issued restoring to the fallen Earl the Castle of Hadleigh and the manors of Hadleigh, Eastwood, Wakering and Foulness ; the escheators, Richard de la Lade and Adam Fitzwilliam, being ordered to give him possession. A charter was granted in 1239 showing that De Burgh had surrendered four castles at the time of his disgrace, and that pardon was given him for all offences up to the Feast of St. Luke, 1238. The Justiciar did not long survive his troubles. In 1243 John de Burgh succeeded to the estates, and shortly the property passed again to the King. He controlled it by appointing governors, who succeeded each other at rapid intervals ; four (Imbert Pugers, William Gifford, Stephen de Sabines, and Charles de Genevre) holding the office in the short space of eleven or twelve years. The Castle fell into disrepair, and in 1256 the Sheriff of Essex and four knights of the county were ordered to enquire into the condition in which Sabines had left it. They reported that it was "in a bad and weak state, the houses being unroofed, the walls broken down, and all utensils necessary for the Castle were wanting." In 1268 Richard de Thany or Tany had the grant of it for life. In 1273 it was assigned, with other manors, for the maintenance of Henry the Third's widow ; the King, Edward I, ordering that if their value should exceed £1,000 a year (i.e., about £25,000 nowadays), the surplus was to be paid to him, but guaranteeing to meet any deficiency up to that sum.

The reigns of the three Edwards were the great days in the Castle's history. They were all hunters, were frequently following the chase in the forest close by and spending the night either at the Castle or some manor house in the vicinity. When Edward I married as his second wife

Margaret of France, in 1299, her handsome dowry included
the Castle, Hadleigh Town, the Rayleigh manor and other
lands in Rochford Hundred. For several years Constables
were appointed by the Crown, including Richard Filiol,
Roger de Blakeshall, Alan of Clavering, and Roger of Woodham, and during this time they frequently entertained
Edward II. The influence of a great trouble was felt by
de Woodham. In his later years Edward II largely rested
upon the advice of a family known as the Despensers.
Upon the King's fall, the spirit of vengeance waxed fierce
against them, and father and son were executed for
treason. Queen Isabella and Mortimer ruled for a time until
Edward III, in 1330, as regent, assumed authority by force
of arms. The first matter in which de Woodham was
concerned was revealed in a petition by John Gifford, of
Bowers Gifford, to "My Lady the Queen and my Lord the
Duke." He complained that the Constable, accompanied by
Hugh le Despenser, with a force of fifty men, came to the
manor and seized two horses, and " upon the same horses
caused to mount two robbers and thieves of his company."
On the way back they entered the house of Gifford, and, not
finding him at home, they searched the warren and took all
the rabbits they could find. The petitioner concluded :
"Wherefore, most noble lady, may it please you to grant to
the said John a commission to arrest the said Roger and to
bring him before you and your Council, as he is your
contrarient and rebel, and to appoint another Constable in
his place, who may be Constable to you and the country."
He got little satisfaction, for he was told he could sue at
common law, if he felt so disposed. The second matter with
which de Woodham was concerned had relation to the seizure
by Edward II, at the instigation of Hugh Despenser, of
twelve acres of land in Hadleigh belonging to Roger de
Estwyck and his wife Alice ; this property being worth
six shillings a year, with certain privileges in Hadleigh Park.

Estwyck alleged that Despenser came to his house whilst exiled and asked to be concealed there. Estwyck refused, and, as a consequence, when fortunes changed for the better, Despenser procured possession of the land. This remained in the King's hands for some years, but as a result of the petition de Woodham was ordered to hand the property back to the Estwycks. Another Constable of Edward the Second's, de Blakeshall, had trouble with the "lieges and free tenants of the town of Hadleigh" concerning damage which he had done them, and the King ordered the keeper of the manor, Humphrey de Walden, to report as to the truth of the complaint. On receipt of his statement justice was ordered to be done.

Upon the death of Edward II, Queen Isabella was given the income for life of the manors of Eastwood and Rayleigh, the park and Hundred of Rochford, the castle and town of Hadleigh, and the manor of Thundersley. When Edward III obtained the reins of power he seized, among other items of his mother's estate, that of Hadleigh, allowing her the use of her dower manors for maintenance. He sent an order to Richard de London, described as keeper of the Castle for Isabella, to deliver to his successor, Richard de Retlyng, the growing crops, farm utensils, etc., after a valuation had been made; the latter having agreed to pay a rent of £16 10s. yearly. De Retlyng was not long in enjoyment of the property, which was let in 1335 to John de Sturmy, who had some remission of rent. William de Bohun, Earl of Northampton, in 1344, obtained the Constableship for his kinsman, Roger de Wadham. In 1359 Edward ordered certain of the houses in the Castle to be repaired by John de Tydelside; his wages to be 12d. per day. Walter White-horse, an esquire of the King, was appointed Constable in 1375, and he was probably the same gentleman who, twenty years before, was remitted the rent of five marks for the Castle farm on account of his good service. Whitehorse's tenure was very short, and two years after Walter Felbrigge occupied his place.

During the later years of Edward's life he ordered an extensive repair and refit of the Castle. This was carried out so thoroughly that it gave it that character of Edwardian architecture which puzzled antiquarians aware of its foundation by Hubert. The discovery of the various rolls of accounts which were rendered for the work gave the clue to the mystery. The renovation cost in present day values thousands of pounds, and it is suggested, although no documentary evidence supports it, that the celebrated William of Wykeham was the architect, as he received orders about this time to put others of the Royal Castles into habitable repair. In the Hadleigh accounts there is an entry of the cost of transhipping labourers from Essex to the Isle of Sheppey; the reparation of which castle he did, without doubt, superintend. Some of the names of the various towers and apartments are disclosed in the accounts. Thus we have the King's Chamber, Queen's Chamber, Old Chapel, New Chapel, High Tower, New Tower, Prince's Tower, Prison, etc., though the situation of these can only be the subject of conjecture. To those unaware of the ramifications of trade in those days, and thinking that localities were dependent upon themselves for means of living and habitation, the distances from which goods were brought will be astonishing. Reigate stone was carted to Battersea and there shipped; ragstone was brought by boat from Maidstone; chalk from Greenhithe; and tiles from Flanders; whilst sea sand was brought by the ton from Milton (Prittlewell), and timber in great quantities from Baddow, East Hanningfield, Maldon, and other localities. Some of the accounts, which were rendered in much detail, contain amusing items. The King's armour was the cause of considerable expenditure of pence. For instance, "Two bushels of bran for the cleaning of the King's armour, 3d."; "Carriage of one chest for putting the King's armour in from the mill to the

Castle, 2d." ; "One quart of olive oil bought for the armour, 12d." ; "One bottle to put the oil in, 12d." ; "One sack to put the bran in, 18d." Plaster of Paris for making the chandelier in the King's Chamber cost 22d. ; a hanging lock for the gate at the entrance to the Castle was procured for 12d. ; the mending of the windows of the King's and Queen's Chambers with glass required the expenditure of 4s. 2d. ; five iron vessels for the candles in the King's bedroom were entered at 12d. Pargetters for pargetting and whitewashing received 6s. 10d., whilst labourers for digging mud and daubing the walls were allowed 109s. 8½d. The restoration was of the most thorough description. It included the Castle itself, and the enclosure round it, together with the keeper's lodge and the mill. The foundations of the former have been traced to a spot about a quarter of a mile to the north of the Castle, upon a gentle slope. Though the keepership of the Park was an important office, and its holder usually a man of some substance, the building itself was not pretentious, and comprised two rooms on one floor, about 14ft. square. The mill of the manor, in those days an important means of raising money in corn growing lands, is conjectured to have been situated upon Mill Fleet, at a spot where means of transit by water were easily procurable.

Edward III did not long enjoy the comfort of his new seat, and on his death in 1377 it passed into the hands of Richard II. He gave the custody of it for life to Aubrey de Vere, one of his favourite ministers, and when the Peasants' revolt broke out in 1381 the Castle was garrisoned and held for the King ; being used by the gentry hereabouts as a refuge, for the spirit of discontent in this Hundred was widespread and destructive. De Vere, one of the men who profited much by the popularity of his kinsman, Robert de Vere, Earl of Oxford, with the King, was active in suppressing the rebellion in the Hundred and county ; he and his colleagues being armed with the most stringent powers.

He was not allowed to enter into possession of the Castle estates without a bitter legal struggle with Walter White-horse, whom he ousted from the custodianship. De Vere was given the life custody of Hadleigh Castle, the profits appertaining to the King from the town and market of Rayleigh, and also of .the Manor of Thundersley, upon payment of the same rent as Whitehorse, viz., ten marks per year for the Castle, but nothing for the other property, save the usual ancient services attaching thereto. He had, in addition, to bear the expense of suitably enclosing the park, paying the parker threepence a day for his wages, also the parson of Thundersley twenty shillings a year for the tithe of land acquired and enclosed within the park, and to bear all outgoings. To obtain this grant De Vere surrendered the annual rent of fifty marks payable out of the revenues of Chester. As compensation for disturbance, White-horse was given a life grant of forty marks from Kingston-on-Thames. He was dissatisfied with this, and a month later obtained from the Great Council a confirmation of his right to his Hadleigh possessions and the bailiwick of Rochford. This latter office was an important one in those days, constituting its holder the chief legal functionary in the Hundred, and it illustrates the local importance attaching to the person of the occupant of the Castle, that in many cases he was both custodian and bailiff. There was also a good deal of uneasiness among officials at this time, and, among others, the keeper of the King's wardrobe in Hadleigh obtained confirmation of a pension of one hundred shillings yearly, which had been bestowed upon him by Edward III. There were two minor tenants with whom De Vere quarrelled, but he eventually compromised with them. Whitehorse's opposition was, how-ever, not easily to be overcome, and in 1380 De Vere was given the reversion of the bailiwick of Rochford on the death of Whitehorse, and the grant for life of the Manor of Eastwood, rights of herbage in Rayleigh Park, and the profits

of the Honour of Rayleigh.   In 1381 he was given the office
of life keeper of Hadleigh Castle, "to stay there with his
household."   He had evidently by this time got rid of his
trouble with the former custodian, and in 1385, perhaps as a
reward for services during the Revolt, he was granted for
life the fishery in Hadleigh Ray, and also the right to take
undergrowth for fuel in the royal parks of Rayleigh, Hadleigh,
and Thundersley, "without felling large trees."   His kinsman,
the Earl of Oxford, rapidly fell into disfavour with powerful
peers, and was forced to fly to France.   An official of the King's
household, who was prominently concerned in the repair of the
Castle in the last reign, named John Blake, was in 1388
hanged on a fictitious charge of high treason, at the imperious
will of the Duke of Gloucester.   Whether Aubrey enjoyed the
amenities of residence at the Castle for long we do not know,
but it was not until 1391 that the reversion of the whole
of the property passed to the King's uncle, Edmund, Duke
of York.

In 1394 the King paid a visit to the Castle, and five years
later Richard granted his mother, Anne, the right to dwell in
his lodges in Hadleigh, Rayleigh, and Thundersley, with the
privilege of cutting what timber she required for fuel.   The
same year he confirmed his gift of the Castle to his uncle, the
Duke of York, and there were also appointments of porter and
keeper of the wardrobe, offices of some importance apparently.
The estate passed into the hands of the Earl of Rutland, son of
the Duke of York, who in 1400 played some part in warning
Henry IV of a plot against his throne by certain of the nobles.
Professor Oman says of this dramatic episode: "Treachery
intervened to frustrate the 'coup-de-main,' yet it was betrayed
so late that King Henry was saved only by a few hours of
warning.   Who was the traitor?   The best chroniclers take
refuge in generalities ; one source says that the matter was
divulged by a woman, but the most detailed and probably the
most correct version is that the miserable Rutland, always

a broken reed to the party he was serving, frustrated the scheme. On January 4th, 1400, as the tale runs, his accomplices sent him word to be at Kingston with his retinue that same night. Struck with qualms at the eleventh hour, and well aware that failure meant inevitable death, he revealed the plot to his father and asked his advice. York, remembering what an evil account of his stewardship he would have to give to a restored Richard, forced his son to turn informer. The fateful message from York which revealed the conspiracy reached Windsor that afternoon. Henry, appalled at the sudden danger, bade his sons mount in haste, though night was coming on, and galloped away with them to London. He did not think himself safe till the Mayor had closed the gates and called out the City militia in his name. Orders were simultaneously despatched to the sheriffs of the home counties to raise their levies." The conspiracy was quickly frustrated by the capture of the leaders, although Rutland is said to have given them warning that the King was on the march against them with his troops. It was in connection with this same trouble that the Earl of Huntingdon fled to Prittlewell, was captured at the mill there, and was subsequently tortured to death at Pleshey, at the instigation of the Dowager Duchess of Gloucester, for the part he had taken in the murder of the Duke of Gloucester. The incident is referred to in an earlier page of this volume.

In 1402 Henry the Fourth's "very dear son," Humphrey, Duke of Gloucester, was granted the reversion of Hadleigh upon the death of his "very dear kinsman," Arundel, who was killed in 1415, dying without issue. Duke Humphrey played a prominent and perilous part in the troublous reign of his nephew, Henry VI, and in 1447 his lordship, who has been described as "one who had long been discredited, and who throughout his career had shown himself incapable of managing a party or conducting a policy with common capacity," was arrested on a charge of high treason. He died some days later

either through illness or the agency of the assassin, more probably the latter, the same fate which had befallen the previous
holder of the title. The succession to the property was obtained
the same year by Richard, still another Duke of York, a general
and administrator of great ability, subsequently leader of the
Yorkist armies in the Wars of the Roses until he was slain at
Wakefield in 1460; his successor in command, Edward of
York, subsequently becoming King, under the title of
Edward IV. Years before that time, however, in 1452,
the property passed to Edmund of Hadham, Earl of Richmond, the King's "very dear uterine brother"; the patent
being in the terms of an absolute gift, "to the aforesaid
Edmund, his heirs and assigns, for ever." In 1461
there were several appointments to offices in the Castle;
Sir Thomas Montgomery holding that of steward. The
Constableship was evidently a separate office, for a month
later John Skelton was granted that post; both men having
similarly served under Richard III and transferring their
allegiance to Edward IV. In the grant to Skelton there
is an inkling to a previous holder, not mentioned speci-
fically elsewhere, for the document stated that he was
to render £14 yearly to the King, as did Henry, Earl of
Exeter, and forty shillings beside. Skelton obtained no
pecuniary advantage from his charge, for four years later he
was given £17 11s. 7d. out of the revenue of the property,
because he had received no wages during his years of service.
It was further directed that in future he should receive threepence a day.

An interesting sidelight into the system of granting
pensions is afforded by a patent, dated 1463, in which
Henry Abingdon, clerk of the Chapel Royal, was awarded
a pension of £8 from the revenues of the estate in lieu
of an annuity of the same amount given by Humphrey,
Duke of Gloucester, out of the issues of Hadleigh and Leigh
Rays. On March 19th, 1465, Edward IV gave the manor to

his sister Anne, but on July 5th his Queen, Elizabeth
Woodville, entered into possession of Castle and manor.
There was evidently some re-arrangement of property,
for in 1465 the sister obtained lands in other parts of the
Hundred. After this date the Duke of York, brother
of Edward V, enjoyed the profits, and in the reign
of Henry VII the King resumed ownership. During
the next fifty years it remained in Royal hands, when
it ceased to belong to English sovereigns, and passed
into private keeping. In 1504 Leo Craiforde was appointed the custodian, his position being defined as:
"Constable and door ward of the Castle, Bailiff of the
Lordship and Parker of the Park." On the marriage of
Henry VIII to Katharine of Aragon, the Hadleigh estate
formed part of her dower, and Sir John Raynesforde was
mentioned in 1511 as the Constable. When the ill-starred
Anne of Cleves came to marry the fickle King she was also
granted the property for her maintenance, which was described
as the "Castle, lordship or manor of Hadleigh, a sholpa called
Hadleigh Ray, and the draggings for mussels in Tilbury
Hope." The estate settled on her on Henry's prompt divorce
included lands at Hockley, Paglesham, and Canewdon.
The King's last wife, Catherine Parr, also received the revenues
of the Castle and manor as part of her allowance, and she was
the final Royal owner. In 1551, in the reign of Edward VI,
Lord Rich brought the property for £700, and his entry
sealed the fate of what had already become a dilapidated
edifice. He had country houses at Great Leighs, Mid-Essex,
and Rochford Hall; which places he maintained in stately
magnificence, and there is little doubt he allowed the Castle
to become the quarry by means of which Leigh and other
churches were erected. At any rate, not many years after
Camden wrote of the Castle as being in ruins. From the Rich
family the property passed into other hands, until now it is
part of the farm colony of the Salvation Army.

In 1863 Mr. H. W. King gave the Essex Archæological Society a resume of his excavation of the remains, which had been undertaken with a view of obtaining an accurate idea of the extent of the building, and also of tracing the position of the various apartments inside the walls. One of the results of his work was to make it clear that there were no vaults or under crofts in any part of the building. A few Roman tiles were used in the construction of an arch, but none were to be seen in any other part of the structure; tiles, however, of the same shape and thickness as modern roof tiles occurred frequently among the masonry of the outer walls. He went on : "The soil has not been very prolific of antiquities, still many objects not entirely devoid of interest have been exhumed. These include a few encaustic tiles ; a small example, bearing the fleur-de-lys, being of the Edwardian period, and the others are clearly of the Fifteenth Century. They were found with the other plain glazed tiles in close proximity to the fireplace. Then a few fragments of painted glass, deeply opalized, are relics which attest the rich decorations of the chief apartments, tenanted often, no doubt, by some of the highest nobles of the land, as well as by the powerful baron who laid the deep and massive foundations, and who reared so vast and magnificent a pile. Here, too, beneath the fireplace lay the antlered skull of a noble stag, which centuries ago had ranged the adjacent park, and many tusks of boars, which roamed and fed in the surrounding forest. One, which must have belonged to a huge beast, measured six inches in length. Shreds of mediæval pottery were strewed upon the ground floors of the various rooms and elsewhere along the walls. Most of it is red. Some is coated with green glaze. Other fragments are glazed with a yellow stripe. The lip of a large pitcher, fashioned into a grotesque face five inches long, is a curious and interesting specimen of manufacture. The forehead is encircled by a wreath or band of head-dress embroidered in lozenge pattern, and long braids

of hair depend from the temples to the neck; the chin is
beardless, but the upper lip is graced with a long, curled and
drooping moustache. Rude and grotesque in the extreme, it
might not improbably be intended as a caricature of an
exquisite of the time. The clay is red and yellow. Among
the remains of culinary utensils is the bottom of a large
mortar, one foot in its outer and $8\frac{1}{2}$ inches in its inner
diameter, wrought in hard gritstone and used in bruising corn
or triturating other vegetable substances. The implements of
iron comprise a large key, the point of a sword blade, a pair of
scissors, a candle casket with spike, which was fixed in the wall,
a horse shoe, several large nails; the head of one, the stud for
a heavy oaken door, measures $3\frac{1}{2}$ inches by two inches square.
Only one small silver coin of the reign of Edward I was
discovered, and three Nuremberg or Abbey tokens of the
common types found so frequently all over England; one of
these bears the legend 'Ave Maria Gratiae.' A fourth piece,
which belongs equally to the not very interesting series of
jettons and counters, bears on one side an obvious resemblance
to the coins of the time. The obverse exhibits a King
enthroned; the reverse a moneta. There was also found a
very hard piece of plaster among the debris upon which
some tenant of the apartment to which it belonged had
scratched his name in old English characters—Gray. The
Christian name is lost. The writing is evidently that of a
person much above common rank. But it is in vain to
conjecture who he was or what was his position. Upon
a fragment of stone moulding in my possession is scratched a
coat of arms."

The Castle and estate were acquired as a land
and industrial colony in 1890, in connection with the
General Booth's "Darkest England" Scheme. The Salvation
Army makes use of this Colony to receive various classes of
destitute men. The majority of these men in the first
instance have been found homeless and destitute in the streets

of London and other large cities, and been received into the Workhouses or into the Army's shelters and homes. They are then—after a period of test and probation—drafted to Hadleigh Colony, where they receive training in the initial stages of farm work, in order that they may eventually be able to earn their livelihood upon the land. Large numbers of these men are afterwards emigrated to Canada and other Dominions beyond the seas. The total area of the estate is about 3,000 acres, but this includes a portion of the foreshore and saltings covered by tidal waters at certain periods, and also farms let out to old tenants on long leases. The area actually occupied for Colony purposes is a little over 1,000 acres. A considerable portion of this acreage is laid out as fruit farms and market gardens ; a ready market for the produce being found at Southend. The orchards contain over 14,000 fruit trees, besides large acreages of bush fruits and strawberries. The farm carries 700 sheep, 150 cattle, and 60 horses. The poultry bred on the poultry farm have won over 1,000 prizes at the leading shows throughout the country. There are usually about 2,000 pure bred birds in this department. The Colony is managed by a governor, who is responsible directly to General Booth for the good government of the institution. The names of previous governors are : Colonel Wright, Colonel Stitt, Commissioner Cadman, Colonel Lamb. The present governor is Lieutenant-Colonel Laurie. The Colony has been visited by many of the leading statesmen and philanthropists, and has been inspected by the Royal Commission on Poor Law and the Royal Commission on Coast Erosion. Distinguished visitors have included the late Right Honourable Cecil Rhodes, Earl Grey, Earl Aberdeen, the late Lord Overtoun, Lady Warwick, Lord Newton, Sir Walter Besant, and Mr. Rider Haggard.

Hadleigh Castle is our chief historical ruin ; interesting to us not only as representing an iron age which has

passed, but because it links the locality with some of the
greatest names of our nation's story. The growth of
Southend and district is year by year encroaching upon the
ample acres of the Castle domain. Before long the pressure
may be such that facilities will have to be offered thereon to
the builder. Such a precious relic should be in the custody o
a public authority, charged with its preservation ; thus placing
a safe barrier between it and the maker of the modern villa.

PRITTLEWELL PRIORY.

In earlier portions of this volume references have been
made to the foundation of Prittlewell Priory in the Eleventh
Century, the riot between ecclesiastics which took place there
early in the Fourteenth Century, and its dissolution in the
reign of Henry VIII. Prittlewell was a subordinate cell to the
monastery of Lewes, the headquarters in England of the
Cluniac monks. This order sprang from the Benedictines
at the close of the Tenth Century. Several priories were established in this country, but it remained for several centuries
a foreign institution. The English houses were often seized
by the Plantagenet monarchs when at war with France and
their revenues expended upon military preparations. The
Cluniacs celebrated service with much liturgical splendour,
though having severe regulations respecting fasting and silence.
No description has been handed down to us of the monastic
buildings at Prittlewell. When the Priory passed into private
ownership, in the reign of Henry VIII, the greater part of the
structure was destroyed in an endeavour to adapt it for the
purposes of a Tudor residence. The roof of the chapter
house still exists, and the refectory, considerably curtailed, is
situated at the south-east corner of the present building. In
the inventory which was prepared at the order of Henry VIII
there was a detailed description given of the contents of
the rooms. There were six bedchambers, with a hall,
pantry, kitchen, butler's and porter's room, with a small
chapel beside the prior's room, and a church with a choir
(in which there were altars to St. John and St. Thomas),
a lady chapel, a rood chapel, and a vestry, with a burying
place near by the church. Prittlewell was never a monastery
of first rank ; the number of monks was, so far as documentary

evidence shows, never more than eighteen, and the office of prior was oftentimes treated merely as an honorary position, for several priors were sent abroad on diplomatic missions upon appointment, and some died whilst so engaged. Its revenues were derived from a grant by Robert de Essex of the manor of Priors (a large part of the parish of Prittlewell), the tithes of the hamlet of Milton, the church of Prittlewell, with the chapels of Sutton and Eastwood ; the prior being ordered to pay a silver mark yearly on the feast of St. Pancras to the prior of Lewes as an acknowledgment of subjection. There was another condition revealed in a subsequent petition, to the effect that no contribution should be sent abroad to the mother house of Cluny, but that all revenues should be spent upon this particular monastery. Thomas à Becket placed eight churches under the control of Prittlewell, and its estate in this respect grew to comprise no fewer than thirteen churches and an interest in four others. Its temporalities were not great in value, but included varying amounts from properties in London and seventeen other parishes.

The precise date of the establishment of the monastery and the installation of the first prior are not known, but as early as 1203 a William is mentioned as prior. In that year, in return for an interest in the advowson of the church of North Shoebury, Richard de Cornhill and his heirs were granted the right of presentation for ever of one clerk to be a monk in the house. In 1227 Hubert de Burgh was given the advowson of the Priory. Henry III appointed Simon de Waltham prior of Prittlewell in 1241. He was a monk of Lewes, and received the appointment on the recommendation of the prior there. The post was in the gift of the King as owner of the Honour of Rayleigh, and William FitzRichard, the keeper, was commanded to let him have free admission. In 1258 Peter was prior, and William de Verge was appointed in 1261. In 1273 the holder of the post went abroad ; the King granting him protection on October 15th until Mid Lent. The name William occurred as prior in 1275. Five years later, in July, 1280, the prior was sent abroad and obtained protection until Whit Sunday. He probably died abroad or obtained another post, for in May, 1281, Nicholas de Cokefield, prior of Cliffe, was promoted to similar office at Prittlewell. Cokefield died in 1290, and Peter de Montellier, a monk of Lewes, reigned in his stead. Upon the outbreak of war with France in 1294, Edward I sought financial aid by taxing ecclesiastical property. There was considerable opposition offered by the clergy ; the Pope in 1296 assisting their cause by publishing a Bull forbidding the payment of the taxes. The King replied in 1297 by practically outlawing the clergy, and then the resistance soon collapsed. Many had yielded long before, including the prior of Prittlewell. In cases of the foreign orders of monks and friars the King adopted the plan of granting the head of the institution protection for a limited time, and then treating the property as forfeited, re-granting it to the head as tenant-at-will at a rent, and thus assuring himself of their submission to taxation. On December 15th, 1295, Prior Peter obtained a grant to permit him to "remain in the Priory, notwithstanding the King's order to remove alien men of religion from the realm ; security being given that damage to the King or realm shall not arise from him or any of his men, or of his procuration, as it has been testified to the King that the prior was not born of the power of the King of France." The protection was renewed on June 26th, 1297. In the same year the Royal manors of Eastwood and Rayleigh and other lands were also farmed out to Peter by the King. When he died he left behind arrears of rent due to the monarch amounting to £128 6s. 10d., and these Edward granted to Queen Margaret. Shortly after this the new prior superintended, on behalf of the King, the construction of a prison at Rayleigh, the repair of houses at Eastwood and Mayland, and a mill at Rayleigh.

In 1276 John, the Prior of Wenlock, and Arnulph, Constable of the Abbot of Cluni, visited Prittlewell and reported that they found there fifteen monks, and that the house owed £100 sterling. An earlier return stated that eighteen monks were in residence. Three and a half years later the Priors of Mont Didier and Lenton inspected the institution, which then had "fourteen monks leading good lives." The prior was re-building his church; the other premises were in good condition. The house had no other debt than 100 marks, for which it was responsible through Miles, the then Abbot of Vezelay, when he was Prior of Lewes; and the provisions were sufficient to last until the new harvest. The prior was a person of good life and fame. In 1305 the visitors found four monks lacking, and the Prior of Lewes was ordered to make up the deficiency unless prevented by some reasonable cause. In case of negligence the number was to be made up by the Lord Abbot. Montellier was succeeded by John de Monte Martini, who went abroad, in Queen Margaret's service, in 1304 and 1305. The headship of the priory became vacant in 1308, and a monk of Lewes (Henry de Frautariis) was appointed. He had been promoted ten days when he, too, left England. He never returned, and Giles de Seduno succeeded to the position, only to go away upon similar service in 1310. In the same year Thomas de Shelvestrode became prior, but his occupancy of the office was also short, and a year later William de Auvergnat was appointed.

The Priory, in common with other ecclesiastical foundations, was ordered by the Pope to pay a tenth of the revenues for three years to the King. It got into arrears, and it was not until the close of 1311 that the Abbot of Colchester, the sub-collector for the diocese, could account for the balance due of £9 11s. 10½d. Auvergnat was accused of incontinency in London in 1314, and the Cluniac visitors, unable to obtain full information, ordered the Prior of Lewes to enquire into the matter. This official deprived Auvergnat of his office, and in 1315 presented Guichard de Cara Loco or Cherlieu to the Priory. The King rejected this nomination, as Auvergnat was in possession. This prior went abroad in the same year, and his grant of protection included the clause : " Nothing to be taken against his will of his corn, carts, carriages, victuals, or other goods for the use of the King or any other persons." The prior was granted protection again in 1316, and upon this occasion the King took custody of the institution on account of its poverty, miserable condition, and indebtedness. On February 10th he appointed Adam de Osgodeby, a Royal chaplain, to be its keeper, and ordered that after reasonable provision had been made for the maintenance of the prior, monks, and the poor, all rents and profits were to be used at Adam's discretion to discharge the debts and make good the state of the Priory. So long as Osgodeby was in charge no sheriff or other Royal officer was to lodge in the Priory or in its granges without his permission. The struggle to oust Auvergnat continued. The Prior of Lewes appointed James de Cusancia, and he was admitted by the King. The story of Prior William's subsequent career is told in another chapter, under the heading " Priestly Faction Fight at Prittlewell." The matter was finally settled by the death of William in 1321, and Cusancia occupied the office until 1334. An example of a class of land transactions in which the Priory became involved may be taken from the year 1320. On January 11th Royal confirmation was received of a grant between the Prior of Prittlewell and the convent there and William de Cusancia, canon of Ripon, and John de Cotown, a London citizen, whereby the latter had conveyed to them the Manor of Shoebury (except thirty-two shillings of rent) and all the tithes out of the Manor of Sir Hugh Neville, in Great and Little Wakering, for their joint lives and the life of the survivor, upon condition that they kept the buildings in repair, and paid the Prior and Convent of Prittlewell 100 marks annually. The deed was dated St. Andrew's Day, 1319, and the witnesses included Sir

PRITTLEWELL PRIORY.

Robert of Rochford, Adam Fitzsimon, and John Bryanzon, local landowners.

Upon the renewal of the war with France in 1324 by Edward II the Priory was again accorded protection, and in 1331 Cusancia acknowledged, on behalf of the convent, that he owed fifty marks to the parson of West Tilbury, named John de Marton, "to be levied in default upon his land and chattels in Essex." In 1332 Prittlewell and the other Essex convents received a request for a subsidy for Edward the Third's expenses in marrying his sister Eleanor with Reginald, Count of Guelders; the promise being that, if complied with, it would not be used as a precedent. We do not know the result. An order issued "to the bailiffs of Queen Philippa of the Hundred of Rochford" upon the resignation of Cusancia in 1334 shows that, upon a vacancy occurring, it was usual for the escheator to take possession in the name of the King, and to depute a janitor to take account at the gate. Both escheator and janitor departed immediately the new prior brought to them his letter of admission from the monarch. War broke out between Edward III and France in 1337, and the Priory was again held to ransom. The prior was ordered to pay, as promised, £16 to the King and one hundred shillings for the custody of the foundation. In March, 1338, the collectors of triennial tenths were told not to exact any from Prittlewell; the prior being already bound to pay £40 yearly to the King. In May of the same year Edward directed that £20 of the rent should be paid to Robert of Artois for his maintenance whilst in the King's service. A year later Robert's maintenance allowance, which included sums from several Priories, was exchanged for a charge upon the Exchequer. On March 12th, 1341, the prior was ordered to appear before the King's Council "to hear certain things which will be expounded by the Council, and to do what should be enjoined upon him, bringing with him all tallies and memoranda relating to the payment of

R

'ferm,' or rent, which he is bound to pay to the King for the custody of his Priory." The Sheriff of Essex was instructed to warn the prior to appear. The King's watchman, William Harding, was sent to the convent to receive the maintenance which a predecessor named Messager had, and in 1343 a man named Sweeting was sent to the Prior for the same purpose, in place of Peter Burgulon, the King's Sergeant-at-Arms, deceased. As war was still waged with France, it is probable these grants of maintenance were either made as rewards for distinguished service in the field or utilized as a means of providing retreats for wounded soldiers. In 1345 John de Chalons was summoned to the King's Council as Prior of Prittlewell. Crecy was fought in 1346, and men from this district served in that memorable engagement. A year after, the Prior of Prittlewell was again ordered to attend the King's Council. In the same year the Abbot of Cluny agreed to pay the King a sum of £200, to be levied upon the Priories of that Order in England, and as a consequence Prittlewell had to pay twenty-five marks at Michaelmas. The institution got into debt again in 1351, and acknowledged owing £20 to Thomas of Steeple. This was only a temporary convenience, for the entry was marked "Vacated on payment." The Prior in 1361 was Francis de Baugiaco, who resigned a year later to become Prior of Montacute, Somersetshire. Upon this vacancy Peter de Tenoleo, Prior of Monks Horton, Kent, applied to be made Prior of Prittlewell, and Denys de Hopton, Sub-prior and Almoner of Prittlewell, to be made Prior of Monks Horton. Both petitions were granted by the Pope, but it is uncertain whether they took effect. Following upon the peace which was patched up between Edward III and France, the Priory and lands were naturalized, and a charter, dated 1361, ordered : "Whereas we have lately taken into our hands, by reason of the late war between us and the French, the Priory of Pritewell, in the County of Essex, and all lands, tenements, fees, advowsons thereunto belonging (among other houses and Priories of foreign orders under the French power, together with the goods and chattels in the same Priories and houses then being), and had committed the custody of the aforesaid places to the Priors and others for a certain rent, to be paid therefor by divers letters patent. Whereas peace has now been made and declared between us and that great Prince the King of France, our most dear brother. We, therefore, for the honour of God and His Holy Church will and grant to our beloved in Christ the Prior of Pritewell all lands, tenements, fees, and advowsons belonging to the Priory aforesaid, with all goods and chattels now being therein, to have and to hold henceforth freely and entirely as he held before the aforesaid taking." In 1385 there was risk of invasion by the French, and the Prior of Prittlewell was among those appointed upon a commission to make preparations for resistance. In matters of this kind the services of the Prior were constantly requisitioned, and he was often employed in this district upon work on behalf of the Government. There was a rapid succession of priors about this time. John Saver was appointed in 1363 ; Ralph Miouns followed in 1368 ; Richard Ysewode in 1376 ; James Wygepole in 1385 ; the latter being freed for a time from purveyance. The name of James as Prior next occurred for some years. The Priory owned the Manor of South Shoe-bury, and in 1386 litigation occurred in respect of the stranding of a vessel upon the sand there. Sir John Fitz-Simond, John Osborn and others were appointed to enquire into the complaint of Peter Mark, merchant, of Florence, and Gerard Lomelyn, merchant, of Genoa, that men of the district had looted a ship of twenty-two bales of pepper and other goods after the crew had sought safety ashore. Orders were issued that men found with the goods were to be arrested until they gave security to appear before the Council. In 1399 John Pyrtwell, nobleman, and his wife, described as a noblewoman, were granted plenary remission in the article of death, being penitent. Boniface IX, in 1400, gave indulgences for ten years to all penitents visiting the church on Mid-Lent Sunday, on the Feast of the Nativity of the Blessed Virgin Mary, and the two days following each, and giving alms for its repair. He also licensed the Prior and five other confessors chosen by him to hear confessions and grant absolution, except in cases reserved to the Apostolic See. Thomas Boyle, a Prittlewell monk, was appointed a papal chaplain in 1410. Richard Lachemere was nominated Prior in 1428. He had a long reign, and 1454 came before the name of Lawrence Bristowe occurred, probably successor to Richard. An enumeration of the Cluniac houses in England was made about 1450; the Priory then being reported to be subject to Lewes and in the jurisdiction of the Diocese of London. There should have been fourteen monks. The only alms distributed were the fragments from the refectory and the Prior's chamber. Four masses were celebrated; three with chant and one without. In 1468 Hugh Suker, or Sugur, became Prior. He died in 1476, and was followed by John. He in turn gave place to John de Eston, and then the last Prior, Thomas of Norwich, succeeded to the office. He was deprived of his position by the Act of 1536 (the Priory then being of the yearly value of £155 11s. 2½d.). He was granted a pension of £20 per year. The property passed by sale to Sir Thomas Audley, and subsequently into the Rich family.

ST. MARY'S, PRITTLEWELL,
AND OTHER CHURCHES OF THE HUNDRED.

The parish church of Prittlewell, dedicated to the Virgin Mary, the advowson of which was formerly in the possession of the Priory, is situated at the northern boundary of the Borough. It possesses many features of interest to students of ecclesiastical architecture. Experts have declared it to be without question one of the finest churches in Essex; the tower in particular receiving unstinted admiration. The date of construction of the first building is unknown. A very early arch in the north wall is built of Roman bricks, and Dr. Laver is of opinion that traces of a former Saxon church are visible in the north side of the structure. It is further suggested that this early building formed the chancel, and that somewhere about 1100 a nave of Norman design was added, probably by a member of the Sweyn family, the local landowners of that day. Traces of Norman work are visible in the nave and, moreover, a sepulchral slab in the north-west corner, of Thirteenth Century origin, points definitely to the existence of an earlier building. The Rev. S. R. Wigram suggested that at about the Thirteenth Century an enlargement was made on the south side, of which not a vestige is left save in the three western arches of the arcade, which were evidently pierced through the Norman south wall. For two centuries little or nothing was added to the church, and then, catching some of the inspiration of the great movement for church building and organization which swept the country in the Fifteenth Century, the parishioners, probably led by the Prior and monks of the monastery, embarked upon a scheme of re-construction and enlargement which almost

completely obliterated the old building and established
in its place the stately pile we now see. Mr. Chancellor, in a paper read to the Essex Archæological Society,
said it was somewhat of a puzzle to know what was
really done. Starting with the nave and proceeding from
west to east, three of the columns of the original arcade on the
south side were left, the bases of which were undoubtedly
early, but the capitals were then renewed and pointed arches
replaced the original ones. That led to a most curious state
of things. Instead of continuing the arcade up to the chancel,
an entirely different design was introduced and the arcade
was continued with two very slender columns carrying three
arches, and these three bays were continued considerably
higher than the rest of the nave, possessing two tiers of windows. The work of alteration and enlargement extended over
a period of eighty years, during which time the Jesus Chapel
in the south aisle was constructed, at the expense of members
of the Jesus Guild; the history of the foundation of which is
given in an earlier chapter. The tower was evidently the first
portion enlarged or rebuilt, and in 1550, the rest of the
church having been re-constructed, the repair of the north
portion of the nave was proceeded with. In 1469 John Quyk,
of Berlonds (Barlands), Prittlewell, bequeathed forty shillings
towards making the pinnacles of the new tower, and in the
same year Thomas Warde left 6s. 7d. for the same purpose.
Mr. King, from whose researches the greater portion of the
knowledge of this restoration comes, thought these facts
pointed to the work in connection with the tower having been
well advanced at that time, perhaps approaching completion.
Thirty years later Richard Frende (or Friend), of Prittlewell,
desired to be buried in the "Chapel of Jesus by the lower
steppe in Pritwell aforesaid." He bequeathed £5 5s. 7d.
towards the making of the new south side of the church, if
the parishioners were disposed to carry it out within the space
of ten years after his decease. The money was to be paid by

his executors after the beginning of the work and prior to its completion. Frende also bequeathed ten shillings to the maintenance of the Jesus Mass in the church. In 1505 John Hoke expressed a wish to be buried in the new Jesus aisle (this may be intended to refer to the Jesus Chapel), towards which he bequeathed ten shillings. Another benefaction was made by John Harreis, of Prittlewell, in 1508, when he gave forty shillings "to the building of the new gild of Pritwell" and twenty shillings which he had promised towards the fabric. In 1524 William Fuller, of Temple Sutton, ordered that a stone should be bought and laid for him in the church, impressed and graved with the names of himself, his wife and daughter. To the building fund he gave ten shillings, to be paid when the work was proceeding towards completion ; the testator also providing for the gilding of the tabernacle of Our Lady in the Jesus aisle. It is evident at this date that the re-building of the church was still in progress, and that the Jesus Chapel contained a statue of Our Lady. John Patche, of Milton, by will proved in 1531 left his estate, failing issue, to the repair of the church and to the poor, and there was also a bequest in aid of the constructional work then undertaken at Prittlewell. Two years later, William Porte, of Prittlewell, also left a sum for the same purpose, and as late as 1544 Thomas Cocke, a yeoman of the King's Guard, bequeathed £40 towards building the northern part of the church. Mr. King believed this was the last portion of the fabric to be finished, but he did not think the design of the architect was carried out in its completeness, for a check was suddenly put by the Reformation to all Church restoration. It is, perhaps, useless to enquire upon whom the cost of a work of such magnitude chiefly fell. It is more than once spoken of as the work of the parishioners, whose testamentary benefactions were considerable, but it is most probable material aid was afforded by the Priory, who were the patrons of the church as well as the chief land owners. Prittlewell, like most of the other parishes of the Hundred, was affected by the change brought about by Henry VIII's quarrel with Rome. They raised a considerable sum in 1548 by the sale of church plate (silver-gilt monstance, three cruets, a censer and two paxes) for £37 16s., and a further sale at a later date realized £56 5s. 7d. The proceeds were spent in providing a new roof for the western portion of the nave. The commissioners who made an inventory of the property in the church on behalf of the King assigned a cope and vestment for the use of the clergy. In the reign of Queen Elizabeth the windows were enriched with painted glass, and twenty-four escutcheons and arms were noted, including France and England, Somers, Surrey, Boteler, Pantolfe, Marmion, Peltot, D'Albany, Gobyon, Riche, Tyrell, Beknappe, Drury and others. By what means they disappeared is not known. This kind of destruction is usually credited to Anti-Papist fanatics and Cromwell's soldiery, but whilst some damage was probably done to church property in that day, considerable havoc was wrought at a much later time. At the beginning of the Nineteenth Century, or thereabouts, monumental brasses were removed and several of the gravestones torn up and used to pave the yard and offices of a house in Milton Hamlet. They were found when the latter was pulled down by the contractors engaged in laying the railroad. There is no record of other changes or restorations until 1738. In that year the roof of the little chancel fell in. There was considerable controversy as to who was responsible for the repair, and it was unsuccessfully sought to cast the onus upon the incumbent, the Rev. Edward Underhill, who was at that time in the Fleet Prison. The roof of the nave had formerly been of copper; which was sold in 1796 and lead substituted, a still later change being to green Westmoreland slates, with which the roof is at present completed. In 1810 another attempt was made to make the Vicar liable for the repair of the south-east chapel, and again it was determined the onus was upon the parishioners.

Except for minor repairs, many years elapsed before the church
was thoroughly renovated. The Rev. S. R. Wigram in 1871
removed the high, square pews, destroyed the ugly flat plaster
ceiling and revealed the beautiful timber work of the roof. The
decorative effect was handsomely enriched some years later by
the erection of a fine stained glass window in the eastern end
of the Jesus Chapel, in memory of Sir Arundell Neave, the
owner of the great tithe of the parish, who died in 1877. It
is a fine specimen of Sixteenth Century glass, and was brought,
towards the close of the Eighteenth Century, from the Church
of St. Ouen, Rouen. It remained in the keeping of the
Neave family, stored away in a cellar, until it was utilized to
serve as the beautiful memorial of Sir Arundell. The present
Vicar (Rev. T. O. Reay, R.D.) has thoroughly restored the
pinnacles of the tower during his vicariate, for which work a
fund was raised and subscribed to by parishioners.

   For several centuries the church has possessed a peal of
bells. In 1853 there were seven bells, three of which were
cast in 1603, and have the following inscriptions : " Love God
and man " ; " God save His Church " ; " Jhesus be our spede."
The tenor bell, which was then cracked, was made by John
Darby in 1683. A bell fell down in 1772, and was re-cast
by Pack at a cost of £30 18s. ; the expense of hanging
being £2 18s. 6d. The sixth was the treble bell, and it was
re-moulded in 1805 by Thomas Mears and Son at a cost of
£26 4s. 3d. The seventh was a small one, weighing
one cwt. three quarters, and utilized to strike the
hours upon. The peal of six bells, with the exception of
the treble, was re-cast in 1872 by Mears and Stainbank. It
was re-hung in an oak frame capable of holding eight. As a
memorial of the Coronation of King Edward VII a fund was
inaugurated to increase the peal to nine and to carry out
some alterations and improvements. On March 20th, 1902,
the Mayor of Southend, accompanied by the Vicar and
Wardens of the Parish Church, paid a visit to the foundry of

Messrs. J. Warner and Sons, Cripplegate, to watch the process of re-casting the large tenor bell. The old bell was broken up, melted and more metal added to bring the new mould to the weight of half-a-ton. By permission of his Majesty it was named the King Edward the Seventh. The new and enlarged peal was re-hung in time for the Coronation. The bells were originally rung upon all public holidays and occasions for public rejoicings. In 1788 the ringers were allowed to attend upon the 29th May, 4th June, 5th November, and 25th December, receiving from ten shillings to twelve shillings for each day. If a great victory was celebrated the ringers were allowed refreshment at the public houses. The cost of bell ropes was very heavy, and the constant ringing brought about an unpleasant encounter between the Vicar and his parishioners, which is recorded on page 191. Prittlewell church has also possessed a clock for many years. In 1663 the sexton was appointed upon condition that he kept the clock in order and rang the bell at four in the morning and at eight in the evening, beginning at Hallomas and continuing until Candlemas. The old chiming barrels of this clock were lying about as lumber at the beginning of the Eighteenth Century. The present clock was bought in 1800 of Thwaites, of Clerkenwell, for the sum of £77 10s. The font is of octagonal shape, 2ft. 6in. across, upon a shaft 13½in. square, and standing upon an octagon step. Six of the sides have a mutilated representation of the Crucifixion, whilst another contains the rose and the pomegranate entwined, emblematical of the marriage of Prince Arthur with Catherine of Arragon, or subsequently of Henry VIII with the same princess. At the demolition of an old house ("Reynolds") in West Street, Prittlewell, in 1906, a fine Jacobean fireplace was discovered bearing the same emblems. It was carefully taken to pieces and rebuilt at South Kensington Museum. The pulpit, a beautiful structure of Caen stone, dates from 1873, and the organ from 1876.

The list of Vicars is complete from 1323. The registers of marriages and deaths date from 1645, and that of baptisms from 1649.

The church, with the churchyard, occupies an area of one acre, two roods, four poles. At one time the burial place was used as a receptacle for rubbish, for the purpose of drying linen, and for grazing horses and other animals. At fair time it was a common resort for debauchery, but other days brought other ways, and the churchyard and the tombs are now preserved with care.

Prittlewell church is enclosed by small shops, completely hiding its noble proportions from the street. Often the hope has been expressed that a fund could be raised to purchase the adjoining property, pull it down and throw the land into the churchyard ; thus revealing the church to the street and making a fine architectural view, looking east from Victoria Avenue corner.

Southend was separated from Prittlewell ecclesiastically in 1842 ; the Church of St. John Baptist being built in 1842, at a cost of £1,500. North and south aisles and raised roof were added in 1869, a new chancel in 1873. An extensive restoration and enlargement took place in 1907. The Vicars up to the present have been : Revs. G. Lillington, A. Tarbutt, R. Aldridge, W. G. Macdonald, T. W. Herbert, E. R. Monck-Mason, and F. D. Pierce (1908). All Saints' Church was built in 1877, then followed in succession St. Alban's, St. Mark's, St. Erkenwald's, and St. Saviour's, and a Mission Church of the Good Shepherd on Southchurch Beach. The Wesleyan, Congregationalist, Baptist, Primitive Methodist, and Peculiar denominations are dealt with in other chapters. The remaining churches in the Borough include: Reformed Episcopal Church (1878), the first rector being the Rev. T. Huband Gregg, D.D., who was also the first Bishop of the Church in England ; Roman Catholic Church (1869), opened by the Archbishop of Westminster, the Mission having been founded

by the Rev. John Moore in 1862 ; St. George's Presby-
terian (1897), one of the foundation stones of which was
laid by the well-known railway engineer, the late Sir George
Bruce ; the opening sermon being preached by the late
Rev. Dr. Watson ("Ian Maclaren"). Other religious bodies
which at present exist or have been in existence are : United
Methodist Free Church, Salvation Army, Plymouth Brethren,
Church of England (unattached), Quakers, Christadelphians,
Spiritualists, Zion Church, etc.

Below are given architectural details and historical
incidents connected with other of the churches of the
Hundred.

Ashingdon.—Dedicated to St. Andrew ; a small building of stone and brick, tower, nave, and chancel, with traces
of Saxon, Norman and Thirteenth Century work ; restored in
the Perpendicular style. There has been some controversy as
to whether or not any part of the Saxon building exists at the
present day. A church was built there by Canute to celebrate
the victory over Edmund Ironsides at Ashingdon, and Stigand,
afterwards Archbishop of Canterbury, was its first priest.
Some antiquarians have asserted that an arch over the
doorway on the north side and a portion of the tower
are undoubtedly Saxon. This opinion is not upheld by Mr.
Chancellor, who says : "If ever there was an earlier church in
Saxon or Danish times, it was swept away, and the present
nave and chancel erected late in the Twelfth or early in the
Thirteenth Century. The east end of the chancel was,
however, rebuilt late in the Fifteenth Century, and alterations
made in some of the windows at the same period." The
Rev. W. H. Barnes, the present rector, has also written upon
this point : "Discoveries lately made of foundations to the
south-east of the church would appear to show that there was
at one time an extension of the building in that direction, but
recent expert examination reveals that the present tiny
tructure of tower, nave, and chancel, fifty feet in length over

all, does not differ greatly in dimensions from when it was originally dedicated nine centuries ago by the Royal Dane. The rubble walls, containing Roman tiles, may well be those hallowed with such pomp in 1020 ; the doors, the fine old king-post roof, and some of the windows speak of a restoration A.D. 1150 to 1180. Though since then repairs and minor alterations have been necessary from time to time, there has been no material change in the building since that date, except that the tower, by many regarded as undoubtedly of Anglo-Saxon workmanship, is by an expert assigned to a period subsequent to that of the nave and chancel." In the Fourteenth Century the church attained considerable notoriety, due to the possession of an image with alleged miraculous properties, particularly in the cases of barren women, and the Bishop of London was moved to investigate the truth of the story. The parish was united with Hawkwell in 1429, but separated again in 1457. In the reign of Edward VI the bells were seized by Sir William Stafford and sold, whilst the church was also broken open and robbed. The Rector was deprived of his living by Queen Mary. At a visitation of Archdeacon Layfield, nephew of Laud, in 1638-9, the reading desk was ordered to be taken down from defacing the entrance to the chancel. In an inquisition as to the various livings, made in 1650, the incumbent, John Nogoose, was described as a "hopeful young man and well approved of by the parishioners." The residents signed the Solemn League and Covenant in the troublous times of the Civil War. In 1717 a man did penance for marrying his deceased wife's sister, and in 1763 service was restricted to once a fortnight. The church was re-seated and generally repaired in 1879. The register of baptisms commenced in 1566 ; marriages in 1568 ; and burials in 1564. The font is a simple octagon, of Fourteenth Century carving, and the chalice bears the hall mark of 1564. It is a little over five inches in height, simple in design, but with delicate orna-

mentation.   From the parish registers the rector (Rev. W. H.
Barnes) has gleaned some interesting details respecting the
method of exacting the tithe in 1568.   The entry runs:
"Tithes of geese.   If there be above five and under ten, one is
due for tithe, paying so many halfpennies back as there wants
of ten.   The same of ducks, turkeys, pigeons, etc.   Of pigs
the like ; of calves a penny back.   For the fall of a foal
or colt, 2s. 6d.   For lambs, one due for tithe out of six, and
one penny due for each that wants of ten.   For wooll, either
by the tenth pound or the tenth fleece.   Hay by tenth haycock.
Corn by the tenth shock, or the tenth sheaf, as the parson
chooseth.   For cows the tenth day's milk or four shillings a
cow as parties can agree with the minister."   The Rev. John
Imrie, late Rector of Ashingdon, who lies buried there,
wrote of his church :

> " 'Neath the shade of the old church tower,
>   Where celandine and daisies peep,
> Where nestling violets sweetly flower—
>   I'll lay me down in peace, and sleep.
> Where waves the grass so green and lush,
>   And gentle zephyrs spread their breath,
> Where over all there falls a hush—
>   There let me sleep the sleep of death."

Barling.—Dedicated to All Saints.   Nave, north aisle,
tower and porch ; probably erected in the Norman period,
but practically entirely rebuilt in the Perpendicular style.
The advowson was given by Edward the Confessor to
the Dean and Chapter of St. Paul's.   In 1297 a visitation was made and the church and its furniture described
in detail.   The chancel was reported to be well covered
in ;   one glass window there being broken.   A covering
was lacking behind the altar, and the lower parts of
the chancel required whitewashing.   There were seats of
"seemly shapes," and a lectern, but several of the service books
were missing.   In the vestments and drapery of the church
much was lacking.   A cloth chasuble and a cloth choir cope

were much mouse eaten and required mending; there were
worn-out surplices; the frontal tablet to the altar required
painting; the silver chalice (16oz.) had the foot broken; the
roof of the nave was very much decayed and the walls of the
cemetery were ruinous. There were images to the Virgin
Mary and Mary Magdalene. At a visitation in 1458
certain repairs to the nave, tower and windows had been
executed. ˉThe chancel was defective in the roof, and the
responsible officials had arranged with a carpenter to make a new
roof; having paid him twenty shillings as earnest money.
The church was extensively restored in 1863-4, and at that time
a sepulchral slab of late Fifteenth Century work was found
in the north aisle. In removing the brickwork from the west
window in the same aisle two figures without heads were
discovered—the Virgin and child and S. Dominic holding
a book, with a rosary, composed of ten beads, attached
to the girdle. The will of a former vicar, named William
Creyke, dated 1393, affords a very good illustration of the
wealth of a clergyman of those days. His estate included two
pots, a Sunday rosary of amber, with a brooch of silver,
inscribed "Jhu Nazarenus," two brass pots, five spoons of silver,
one salt, a table with trestle, to be kept in the hall of Barling
Vicarage; for stock in the vicarage, one great red cock, with a
yellow hen; an ornamental dagger, a white rosary, blue and
red cloaks, a fur garment, a folding table, a book called
"Manual de Peeches," a blue gown furred with calabre (cloth
of Calabria), a russet gown furred with "buyches" (probably
lambskin with the wool dressed outwards), a red girdle
furnished with silver, a silver spoon decorated with garnets, a
gold ring with one diamond, a surplice and a signet ring; the
will concluding: "Whatever the residue may be of my goods
not bequeathed, I give and leave to William Winchestre and
Katherine his wife, to pay my debts and keep my obit
honestly, and also to dispose for my soul as they would
dispose for their own souls." Robert Timperley, a member

of the FitzSimond family, who formerly held the manor of
North Shoebury, by his will, dated 1494, left to the high altar
of the church 2s. 3d. and the maintenance of the light of the
Blessed Virgin Mary 20d. In the reign of Edward VI the
church was broken open and robbed, and in Queen Mary's
time Francis Clopton, of Barling, was bound over in the sum
of £100 to cause decent altar cloths to be set up. In
1792 an arrangement was come to with Little Wakering,
whereby a bass viol and subsequently a clarionet were
purchased, to be the joint property of the two parishes.
Seven years later, owing to dissatisfaction with the singing,
a blind man from Prittlewell was called in to assist. A beautiful set of communion plate was presented by the late Vicar
(Rev. S. B. Smyth) in memory of his wife. In addition the
church possesses a silver communion chalice, with paten, of the
date of 1683. There are no brasses, but one of the slabs in
the aisle suggests that a brass cross has been removed.
Memorials exist to the Asser family. There is a Jacobean
sounding board over the pulpit. The spire on the tower was
at one time used as a landmark by the captains of barges
coming up the creek. Registers are defective up to 1695,
when a new book was commenced for christenings, marriages,
and burials.

South Benfleet.—Dedicated to St. Mary the Virgin ;
nave, north and south aisles, chancel, south porch of timber,
and a west tower ; dating from 1100 to 1140, the west doorway opening from the tower into the nave. There are also
traces of the Decorated, English and Perpendicular periods.
The chancel is of the Fifteenth Century ; the tower was added
about 1390 ; the north aisle, with existing credence, etc.,
of Lady Chapel, 1435 ; the south aisle, with existing
credence, etc., of Lady Chapel, 1450. The existing Norman corbels upon the nave walls inside include the
four cherubic symbols—lion, man, ox, and eagle, as well
as grotesque faces. Holman, in 1727, reported he saw

Photo by]   St. Mary's Church, Prittlewell.   [Mr. J. Archer.

in the chancel a fine example of a "bracket brass." When
the church was visited in 1748 it had disappeared, and
Mr. King surmised that it was either broken up or
covered by a marble pavement. This latter work was
undertaken by the Rev. Dr. Clarke, Ll.D.; to whom
there is a mural monument. The Doctor left a benefaction of £30 a year to the parish church organist.
Extensive floor and seating restoration work was carried
out in 1860 by the late Rev. J. T. Henderson, and
after some thirty years it was continued by the present
Vicar (Rev. C. F. Box). So far, the belfry has been
repaired at a cost of £110 and the north aisle roof restored
for £210. The next important work will be the stripping
and re-tiling of the nave roof. There is one brass (illegible)
and a very ancient tomb, with crosier and cross upon it,
supposed to be Norman. The porch is a magnificent
specimen of carved oak, pronounced to be one of the
finest outside Nuremberg. Its date is 1435. There are
five bells of Seventeenth Century origin; the tenor weighing
19 cwt. A new organ was erected by subscription about
eight years ago. It is a chancel instrument, designed by
Sir C. A. Nicholson, Bart., who also designed the reredos,
which was painted by his mother. The list of incumbents
dates from 1309. The registers of baptisms, marriages, and
deaths commenced in 1583, and there are many interesting
entries concerning the former Dutch inhabitants of Canvey
Island. In the churchyard is the following curious epitaph to
the memory of a mariner :

> " Sixty-three years our hoyman sailed merrily round,
> Fourty-four lived parishioner where he's aground;
> Four wife's bear him thirty-three children, Enough,
> Land another as honest before he gets off."

The church, with its lands, was the gift of William the
Conqueror to the Abbot of Westminster, and (with the
exception of a short lapse in the reign of Henry VIII) the

s

patronage of the benefice has remained in the gift of Westminster Abbey ever since.

Canewdon.—Dedicated to St. Nicholas.   Chancel, nave,
and north aisle, south porch and massive embattled tower of
Perpendicular period, with Roman tiles worked in.   The
ordination of the vicarage took place in 1231.   The tower
bears upon it the Royal Shield, quartered with the arms of
France in the manner peculiar to Henry V, and so the date of
its erection may be determined with some certainty.
Henry the Fifth's mother, Mary Bohun, either had property
in the parish or connection with it through her ancestors,
the Mowbrays, De Warrens, etc.   Respecting the age of the
church, Mr. Chancellor says: "I am always unwilling to
interfere with old traditions, but to assign this church to the
time of Canute, which has been gravely stated, and I understand is believed in the neighbourhood, is really a pious fraud.
I cannot find even a fragment of any older work than the
Decorated period, although hidden up in the walls themselves may be some fragments."   He is, however, of
opinion that a church has existed on the spot from Saxon
times.   There were formerly many monuments to the memory
of the various lords of the manor, but these have been
destroyed.   The present Vicar (Rev. C. R. Hardy) has in the
past three years received £290 towards the restoration fund,
through a small charge of threepence made to visitors
inspecting the church.   Since 1900 Mr. Hardy has worked
continuously towards the improvement of the building.   One
of his first efforts was to cleanse the pulpit of many coats of
paint, revealing a fine specimen of carved oak work, probably
by a pupil of Grinling Gibbons.   In 1908 the ceiling to
the roof of the nave was removed, opening to view the
original oak timbering of a date previous to the erection of the
tower.   The roof generally was also completely restored.   In
the north aisle there are evidences that an altar once existed,
dedicated to the Virgin Mary.   This is probably associated

with the memory of William Totham, who died about 1250, and by his will left a charge upon New Hall of 14d. yearly for a service to be held on the anniversary of his death, the rest of the rent with profits to be given to the poor. At the Reformation Henry VIII claimed the 14d., and on his death Edward VI seized the whole property. The Vicar (the Rev. J. Howseman) and the churchwarden (Mr. H. Baker) resisted, and, after a lawsuit of eight years' duration, the man who bought it of the King was allowed to keep it, subject to a charge of 52s. 2d. for the benefit of the poor. At this church goods were sold to the value of £26 15s. 8d. In 1552 the Commissioners who took the inventory of church goods on behalf of the King left a cope and vestment for use. It is said that seven Hundred churches may be seen from the tower; the explanation being that seven churches in Rochford Hundred may be observed. A former Vicar was reported to be very fond of port. Feeling that his health would be better without so much of it, a relative slipped when going to the cellar and apparently by accident smashed the jug, which was replaced by a smaller vessel. The Vicar said nothing, but took an early opportunity of slipping in his turn and breaking the new jug, obtaining a fresh one of more capacious dimensions. The registers commenced in 1636, and there are notes relating to the year 1598. The parish records show that men and women were whipped there for vagrancy. There is a peal of five bells and some curious epitaphs may be found in the churchyard.

Canvey Island.—Dedicated to St. Katherine. A structure of wood, with chancel, nave, and transept. The present church replaced an earlier and smaller building, dating from 1712. The porch and some of the windows of the old church are incorporated in the new structure. The first independent incumbent was the Rev. H. Hayes, who became perpetual curate in 1872. When the Island was made a separate civil and ecclesiastical parish in 1881, he became first

vicar. The incumbents of the various parishes into which the
Island was carved prior to the last given date still draw
the tithe, except in two instances ; where a part has been
given up to the Island incumbency. In the south transept
there is a picture on the wall representing our Lord, the
models for which were inhabitants of Canvey Island, except
the central figure. Registers of baptisms date from 1819,
of marriages from 1861, and of burials from 1813. On
this subject the late vicar (Rev. W. Hagger) writes : "Previous
to 1846 there were but few burials, generally those of bodies
washed ashore, so it would seem from the register of burials.
Baptisms used to be entered in the South Benfleet register,
though, I suppose, they were solemnized at Canvey. Marriages,
I think, took place in one or other of the various parishes into
which the Island was carved, and to which the contracting
parties or one of them, belonged ; e.g., a man might belong, for
the purpose, to the parish of Bowers Gifford, the woman to
Hadleigh ; and the marriage would have to be solemnized at
one or other of these places."

Eastwood.—Dedicated to St. Lawrence and All Saints.
Nave, chancel, south aisle, tower, with a priest's chamber in
the north-west corner ; early or late Norman. There were considerable alterations in the Fourteenth and Fifteenth Centuries.
There is an original Henry III window. There are specially
fine examples of ironwork of the Transitional period on two
of the doors. Of the tower Godman has written : "It is surmounted by a later belfry and spire of timber, which are often
supported by a heavy timber framing from the floor inside and
do not rest on the walls. The reason for this might be
twofold—either the tower was left unfinished at first, or
the tower being built complete, the upper portion soon
became unsafe, because of the poor quality of the materials
used and the unskilful methods of building, and had to
be taken down. To avoid the expense of re-building in
stone, timber was used." The church possesses one of

the finest "tub-shaped" fonts in the country. It is of circular shape on a wooden base. The bowl slopes inwards from the top and has a pretty arcade of intersecting arches running round it, standing on flat pilasters, with moulded caps and bases. The stem is of circular shape, a few inches only in height, and stands on a well-moulded plinth. The first incumbent was instituted in 1393. A Vicar was deprived of his living by Queen Mary. In 1612 the church was in a dilapidated state. The roof was defective, the seats were in a ruinous condition, and there was no vessel in which to put the wine for the communion service. Poverty was pleaded as an excuse, a commission was ordered to make a survey, and as a result a rate was levied on the parish for repairs. There are three bells; two ancient, each with Latin inscriptions, and the third dated 1693. The register or baptisms dates from 1685; of marriages, 1686; of deaths, 1685. There is a fine brass to the memory of Thomas Burrow, who died in 1600.

South Fambridge.—Dedicated to All Saints. A small building, standing on the site of another more interesting structure, which was demolished in 1846, on account of the insecurity of the foundations. In 1552 the Commissioners making an inventory of church goods on behalf of the King left there a cope and vestment. It was near South Fambridge that the daughter of the Earl of Warwick was supposed to have eloped with a Captain Cammock. The Earl was proceeding with his daughter from Leighs Priory, in Mid Essex, to Rochford Hall, when the girl fled with her lover. They made for South Fambridge, pursued by the irate Earl. The ferry boat was on the other side and the water rough. The chase was so hot that the captain had to take to the water with his horse and swim across; the lady refusing to be parted from him and riding with him. When they were half over the pursuers arrived at the riverside, a horse neighed and Cammock's animal turned towards it. With much difficulty the other shore was reached, and they rode to Maldon, where they were wedded; the Earl's benediction coming later. Over one hundred years ago a man and woman had to undergo trial by water for witchcraft at South Fambridge. After being nearly drowned the husband was adjudged innocent, but the wife floated and her guilt was thereafter firmly believed by the ignorant public. The church registers date from 1765.

Foulness Island. — Dedicated to St. Mary the Virgin. Chancel, aisles and tower; a modern structure, erected in 1850-3 on a foundation of concrete at a cost of £2,000. The organ was built in 1908, the steeple restored in the same year, and minor improvements effected. A mural tablet was also erected by the parishioners to the memory of the late patron and lord of the manor, the Right Hon. G. H. Finch, M.P., P.C. A church was founded in 1386, the presentation being in the hands of Lady Joan de Bohun. It was slenderly provided for, and the curate was rarely resident. A chantry was established in 1408 and endowed by Lady Joan. It was dissolved in 1554, and the Island constituted a parish; the first incumbent being instituted on the 8th July of that year. The former church was of wood, with a spire, and a vestry underneath. In the reign of Edward VI, Sir William Stafford seized all the bells, except one, and sold them; the proceeds being expended on the repair of the sea wall. The remaining bell was sold in 1779, and a new one substituted at a cost of £10 19s. 11d. The rector was deprived of his living in the reign of Queen Mary, and in 1645 the then rector, Roboshobery Dove, was dispossessed because of his Royalist sympathies. The registers commenced in 1695. Early in the Nineteenth Century the churchyard was a favourite resort for pugilistic encounters.

Hadleigh. — Dedicated to St. James-the-Less; wholly Norman, with an apsidal chancel; nave, south porch and west

tower ; windows of the Early English, Decorated and Perpendicular periods. During the restoration in 1855, by Sir George
Street, the removal of the whitewash revealed the walls as
covered with paintings. They were described in considerable
detail by the Rev. W. E. Heygate in the Transactions of the
Essex Archæological Society. The first was a huge entablature
containing texts ; the colour originally being yellow. They
were of Jacobean character, and generally executed with
considerable care. Of the same date was a border pattern,
some twelve inches wide, on the north wall, about six feet
from the chancel arch, and running perpendicularly from the
ground to the roof. Next to the texts, on the west face of the
chancel arch, appeared the Lord's Prayer and Commandments,
in a dark red framework of greater freedom in design and
earlier date. On the south side of the church was an elaborate
picture landscape, representing the legend of St. George and
the Dragon, evidently executed during the Fifteenth Century.
The picture was seen to be brilliantly coloured on exposure,
but quickly faded. The faces of the figures had been
purposely slashed with a chisel before the Jacobean work was
executed, and the painting, not being on the original plaster,
came off with the coats of whitewash above it. In the midst
of the painting coats of arms were emblazoned in several
places, only one of which was sufficiently perfect to be
deciphered. A border appeared to have run round the
church at a level of 8ft. from the ground. On the north wall,
to the west of the door, was the figure of a Virgin crowned,
standing behind a throne on which the Lord was seated in the
act of blessing, apparently executed in the early part of
the Fourteenth Century. The splay of the Norman window
was nearly filled with angels vested in copes ; one was blowing
a trumpet, from which a banner was hung. To the west
of the first painting was a figure of a saint, very indistinct,
supposed by some to be St. James the Less, bearing a club, the
instrument of his martyrdom. On the south side of the west

wall was an almost obliterated figure, which might have been intended to represent St. Michael. On the western splay of the lancet window, 7ft. by 18in., was the figure of St. Thomas à Becket, of Canterbury, in full pontificals. Among the arms formerly in the church were those of the Strangman family, who owned for many years a considerable quantity of land in Hadleigh district; residing in a mansion called Strangman Place, since destroyed. James Strangman, who lived in the time of Queen Elizabeth and James I, was the first person to collect materials for a history of Essex, which were subsequently utilized by Dr. Salmon. He was an original member of the Harleian Society, founded by Archbishop Parker in 1575, and which included Camden, Cotton, Spelman, and Stow in its membership. The rector was deprived of his living in the reign of Queen Mary. The commissioners who took an inventory of church goods in the reign of Edward VI reported that a silver chalice and certain of the church furniture had been sold. For instance, Mistress Strangman the younger bought a red and white satin altar frontal cloth and a coverlet for three shillings. A custom formerly existed for cows, sheep, etc., to be bought with the offertory money and hired out, the proceeds being devoted to the relief of the poor. The register of baptisms commenced in 1653, and marriages and deaths in 1568.

Hawkwell.—Dedicated to the Virgin Mary. Decorated period; nave, chancel, tower and porch. The church bells were among those seized by Sir William Stafford at the time of the Reformation. Alterations and improvements were made in 1885. There is one memorial brass of the Seventeenth Century. The first incumbency dates from 1300. The carved oak pulpit was erected in 1870 by the Rev. J. Montagu, succeeding one dated about 1650. The font is of Caen stone, and was installed in 1870. The register of baptisms commenced in 1693, of marriages in 1696, and of burials in 1695.

𝕳𝕠𝕔𝕜𝕝𝕖𝕪.—Dedicated to St. Peter; Transitional Norman and Early English periods with later additions and alteration about 1350; nave, aisle, chancel, and low, massive west tower. The last named was originally started on a square foundation and finished octagonally; Godman supposing this to be done to obviate the necessity of procuring worked stones for corner quoins. Originally the walls were painted, but the colouring was destroyed by whitewashing about 1800. The commissioners who took an inventory of church goods on behalf of the King in 1552 allowed the cope and vestment and also a case for holding the holy oils. A curate, William Tyms, was one of the martyrs in the Marian persecution. In 1842 an east window was inserted and the church re-pewed. A plain Norman window, glazed with tinted quarries, was revealed in 1849. There are three bells. The Norman font (restored in 1896) is the largest of the kind in the county, and is a frequent subject for illustration in books devoted to ecclesiastical architecture. It has an octagonal bowl with remains of arched panels, two on each side. Part of the stem remains, of similar shape, each external angle bearing a small circular shaft, having now neither capital nor base. The whole stands on a modern stone slab. The font was discovered in 1896 buried beneath the tower, and a modern font was turned out to make room for it on re-erection. Remains of a former church have been discovered, which it is claimed was the one erected by Canute to celebrate his victory over Ironsides. In the chancel is the tombstone of William de Cadewell, the last rector before the alienation of the great tithe, who died in 1326. The portion of register left commenced in 1728-9.

𝕷𝕖𝕚𝕘𝕙.—Dedicated to St. Clement; later Perpendicular; nave, chancel, north aisle, and chapel of corresponding length, with fine tower on the west, and spacious brick porch of the Tudor style. The church was restored in 1837-8, and re-pewed. A building existed upon the site from earliest

years, and in Elizabeth's reign it contained the arms of
Neville, Bohun, Ormond, le Marney, Boleyn, etc. There
were also many memorials to seafaring Leighmen of the day ;
the removal and destruction of several of the tablets about the
time of the restoration being noted by Mr. King. The
church still contains many memorial inscriptions, and the
churchyard is filled with tombs of Leighmen, some of whom
achieved national reputations in maritime affairs. There are
also several brasses, including those to Richard and John
Haddock, 1453 ; Christina and Margarita Haddock, 1453 ;
Richard Chester, 1632 ; one of a civilian and a lady,
unknown, 1640 ; and Elizabeth Chester, 1632. The font is
a copy of the one in Prittlewell Church. At the time of
the Reformation a sale of church property realized £8 6s. 8d.
The music provided in 1837 consisted of a violoncello, violin,
flute and clarinet. In 1838 a small organ was placed in the
gallery at the west end of the church. There is a peal of six
bells. The Rev. R. Eden, rector, was, in 1851, consecrated
Bishop of Moray and Ross, and Primus of Scotland in 1862.
He was succeeded by the Rev. Walker King, grandson of the
Bishop of Rochester and brother of the present Bishop of
Lincoln. A clock was placed in the tower by the late
Mr. Millar, Q.C. Some years ago the tower was struck by
lightning and considerably damaged. The register of
baptisms commenced in 1684, of burials in 1685, and
of marriages in 1691.

Paglesham.—Dedicated to St. Peter ; of Norman
foundation ; nave, chancel, south porch and west tower. The
nave was greatly altered in the Fifteenth Century. There
are three old doors and some antique ironwork. The church
was restored in 1883 at a cost of £1,482, mainly provided
through the munificence of Mr. Z. Pettitt, of " Loftmans,"
and Mr. J. Wiseman, of " The Chase." The first recorded
notice of the church tells of the gift of the benefice, together
with the manor of Church Hall, by Ingulph to the Abbey of

Westminster on December 29th, 1066. The earliest known rector was John de Pretwella, who was presented by Edward II about 1307, during a vacancy in the abbacy of Westminster. The interior, no doubt, was once illuminated, but it was spoilt by whitewashing. The Rector was deprived of his living in the reign of Queen Mary. There is a peal of three bells. South Hall, in this parish, was registered as a place of worship for Quakers in 1704. The registers date from 1716; the earlier records having been lost.

Rawreth.—Dedicated to St. Nicholas; Perpendicular; nave, north aisle, Zion chapel, and chancel, with a low ragstone tower of the Fifteenth Century. All the church, except the tower, was re-built 1882. In 1552 the commissioners taking an inventory of church goods left a cope and vestment for use. In the reign of Queen Elizabeth there were probably a number of armorial bearings in the windows. There is a small brass of Edmund Tyrrell (1579), a well-known supporter of the Catholic cause. The font is of the Fifteenth Century. The church records show that in 1661 a collection of 11s. 6d. was made for the benefit of the Duke of Lithuania; in 1664, of 9s. for the church of Strasburg; and in 1669, 5s. 10d. for the redemption of the captives under the Turks. Zion Hospital trustees own Beaches' farm and have proprietary rights over Zion Chapel, in which was originally a second altar. The registers commenced in 1539.

Rayleigh.—Dedicated to Holy Trinity; Perpendicular, with traces of work of greater antiquity; chancel with side chapel, nave with north and south aisles, north vestry, south porch and west tower. Of this building Mr. King wrote: "No church within the Hundred was more splendidly adorned; none were so richly furnished with plate, vestments and other accessories for the celebration of the divine service; none were so rich in painted glass, or, perhaps, in sepulchral memorials; none have been more mercilessly despoiled. At the survey of church goods, in 1552, it possessed fifteen chasubles, with apparels, seven copes and as many altar cloths, mostly of the precious stuffs, surplices, rochets, and about 155 ounces of altar plate, beside various other sacred utensils and appliances ; numerous heraldic devices of benefactors sparkled in glowing colours in the windows or otherwise adorned the interior of the structure. One of the benefactors ordered by will that a window should be glazed with the life of that popular English saint, St. Thomas the Martyr ; not impro- bably others were painted with sacred and legendary story : and as it was not the custom of the mediæval artists and architects to offend eye and taste by exhibiting broad spaces of blank whitewashed wall, no doubt the whole interior was delicately polychromed. The defacement of the structure, the destruction of much of the painted glass, the demolition of tombs, and the spoliation of monumental brasses occurred at a time long subsequent to the Reformation. One of the Lansdowne MSS., supposed to be written by William Shower, Norroy King of Arms, temp. Elizabeth and partly in the reigns of Edward VI and Mary, contains a record of between sixty and seventy coats of arms, single and quartered, formerly in Rayleigh church. In 1876 I found only five escocheons of arms in the east window, and these, I was told, had been collected from other windows and placed there, as was obviously the case ; a practice that cannot be too strongly deprecated, as much of the historical evidence is thus destroyed. In the present instance, too, the glass having been replaced by an ignorant person, some of it is inverted or transposed. For- tunately in the Harl. MS., 5195, we have a record of the particular windows to which some of it belonged. With the exception of the five escocheons referred to, all the inscriptions and arms noted by the antiquaries of the Sixteenth, Seven- teenth and Eighteenth Centuries have been destroyed." The Rector of Rayleigh (Rev. A. Girdlestone Fryer), in "Rayleigh in Past Days," tells a humorous story of the early Nineteenth Century concerning the removal

of one of the coats of arms, which contained a grotesque-look-
ing figure : " It might have remained to this day only a lady
of the congregation, who occupied a seat where the organ now
is, so frequently complained that whenever she turned her gaze
eastward this diabolical face looked with such distracting
grimace at her, and so filled her with fear, that at length the
churchwardens, to quiet her fears, had the remaining coats
of arms removed from the window." The north chapel is
presumed to have been built about the Fifteenth Century and
to have been named after St. John the Baptist. The south
(or Alen) chapel was erected about 1517. It is named after
a Rayleigh resident named Alen, who left a bequest for that
purpose. His tomb has disappeared, but that of his son is
still intact, although the figures have been mutilated and the
coats of arms have gone. A fraternity of the Holy Trinity
was founded at the church in 1369 and a chantry priest was subsequently appointed, who acted as schoolmaster for Rayleigh
and Rawreth. At the establishment of the chantry there were
300 " houseling " people in the parish. A chapel, dedicated
to the Blessed Virgin, formerly existed in Chapel Field, below
the hill on the north side of the town. Its endowment, of an
annual value of £10 12s. 2d., was confiscated in the reign of
Edward VI. In 1549 he bestowed the site upon Edward
Remy, who had been a gentleman of the bedchamber to
Henry VIII. In 1549 and 1551 the churchwardens and
parishioners sold a considerable quantity of plate and church
furniture ; upon the first occasion the money was devoted to
repairing the church and mending the clock, whilst in
1551 the 40s. received was used partly for paying stage
players, who appeared at Rayleigh on Trinity Sunday, and
partly for the repair of the corn market. which no longer
exists. The King's commissioners who made inventory in
1552 ordered the use of two chalices, because the parish was
great, a red velvet cope, a green cope, the altar cloths, all the
surplices, the care cloth (a bridal pall of fine linen held over

the bride and bridegroom during the marriage mass), the pulpit cloth, the canvas cloth, the hearse (parish pall) and towels ; the residue being placed in the safe keeping of John Coke and William Rawleyn, to be used at the King's pleasure. There have been several restorations of the church, 1711, 1794-1803, and 1842-2, whilst the present rector has initiated a fund in order to carry out extensive repairs to the roof. A chalice, flagon and paten of considerable age are still possessed by the church, and there is also preserved a curious old money chest, made out of solid oak. There is a peal of eight bells. The Rev. S. T. Caley, presented to the living by the Earl of Manchester, was, in 1662, ejected for refusing to make the required declaration on the restoration of the episcopacy. On the passing of the Reform Bill in 1832, the rector, Sir John Head, presided at a dinner given to 700 poor people in a booth erected in the street. A dinner to the gentry followed ; 200 partaking. One of the speakers was Dr. Rolfe, of Rochford, who, in after years, was conspicuous as one of the leaders of the rebellion in Canada. The registers date from 1549.

Rochford.—Dedicated to St. Andrew ; chiefly of the Perpendicular period, with some remains of very beautiful Decorated work ; nave with north and south aisles, chancel with sacristy on the north side, fine west tower of brick and embattled stone porch on the south. The builders of the church are purely conjectural. The Fourteenth Century structure is usually assigned to Humphrey de Bohun, Earl of Essex and Lord High Constable from 1335 to 1361, or Humphrey, his nephew and successor ; the Bohun arms having originally appeared in one of the windows. It was probably re-built by Thomas Boteler, Earl of Ormonde, who recovered the Rochford Hall estate upon the accession of Henry VII and died in 1515. A considerable quantity of coloured glass was in the church in the reign of James I, including forty coats of arms, but none are left. The church was restored in

1862 at a cost of £2,000. There is a brass to Maria Dilcot, dated 1514. Rochford church figured prominently in connection with the Puritan movement ; Earls of Warwick, owners of the estate, being pronounced adherents. In 1552 the commissioners taking an inventory of church goods left a cope and vestment for the use of the church. In the same century William Stafford seized three of the church bells and sold them ; leaving only one. At the time of the Marian persecution a martyr was burnt at Rochford. The most famous rector was Calamy, one of the greatest figures in Free Church history. He entered the living in 1639, but did not hold it many months, owing to ill-health. He was promoted to the perpetual curacy of Aldermanbury. He was one of the assembly of divines who took part in organizing the Solemn League and Covenant. He was a member of the deputation sent to persuade Charles II to come back to England. The Bishoprics of Coventry and Lichfield were offered him, but he refused. He would not conform, and upon the passing of the Act of Uniformity he was imprisoned ; his release being ordered by Charles II. He died of a broken heart in 1666, after witnessing the horrors of the plague. The registers commenced in 1678.

North Shoebury.—Dedicated to the Virgin Mary ; Early English ; chancel, nave and tower. Advowson belonged to Prittlewell Priory until the Dissolution. The rector was deprived of his living in the reign of Queen Mary, and James Baker was one of the local gentlemen bound over in £100 to cause decent altar cloths to be set up. The building was re-seated in 1881, and the inside of the roof boarded in 1902. There is an ancient square font. A fine marble slab, dated 1799, forms the top of the Communion table, "given by John Ibbetson, Esq., cost £50," according to an extract from the old register. Ibbetson was buried in the chancel in 1804, and there is a monumental tablet to his memory. There are other interesting memorials, including one to Mrs. Olive

Kelly, who died in 1746, and in respect of whom the following lines were written :—

> " Weep not, dear Friends,
> But for your sins,
> In peace I do remaine.
> Weep not for me,
> Christ sett me free
> From Sorrow, Grief and Pain."

South Shoebury.—Dedicated to St. Andrew ; chancel, nave and tower. Advowson belonged to Prittlewell Priory until the Dissolution. The church bells were among those seized and sold by Sir W. Stafford at the time of the Reformation. An anecdote is recorded by Plume, a Maldon diarist of the Seventeenth Century, concerning a rector named Dent, who had a scholar from Cambridge to preach at the church upon fair day. Plume says : " He preached a starched Cambridge sermon, a St. Mary's sermon full of learning. Dent carried him out into the street at its conclusion and showed him the hoes and flails and pitchforks for sale. Then he asked him what he would think if London jewellers or goldsmiths should come thither thinking to utter their diamonds or rubies or silver ewers. The scholar said, ''Twould be absurd.' ' Just so,' Dent replied, ' with your Cambridge ware. The next time you come to my parish bring shovels and spades and plain truths.' "

Shopland.—Dedicated to St. Mary the Virgin ; Early English and Decorated periods ; chancel, nave and tower ; was in the possession of St. Osyth Priory until the Dissolution. There is a brass to Sir Thomas Stapel, Sergeant-at-Arms to Edward III (1371), with his effigy in armour, seriously mutilated. The Rev. F. Thackeray, a former vicar of Shopland, was "the long-armed, bareheaded, slashing-looking" cricketer described in "Tom Browne's Schooldays." The scene in which he appeared was on the occasion of the school match with the M.C.C., when the reverend

gentleman's prowess with the bat materially assisted the
Marylebone club. The reverend gentleman was a cousin
of the celebrated William Makepeace Thackeray. The living
is now united with that of Sutton. The first incumbent
took office in 1390. There is only one bell, with the
following inscription : "Peter Hawks made me, 1608." In
1900 a stained glass window was placed in the chancel to the
late Philip Benton and his wife ; subject, "The Virgin Child."
In the same parish is a house called " Beauchamps," possessing
some beautiful examples of pargetting work. The registers
date from 1620.

Sutton.—Dedicated to All Saints ; Norman and Early
English ; chancel, nave and tower. The edifice was thoroughly
restored and re-seated in 1869, and a stained glass east window
erected. There is one bell with the inscription "J. C. Giles
Aylett, Churchwarden, 1638." In the chancel is a large mural
tablet, to the memory of Chester Moor Hall, said to be
the inventor of the achromatic lens. The rector was deprived
of his living in the reign of Queen Mary. The incumbency
commenced in 1366, the register for marriages in 1757 and
for deaths in 1741.

Great Stambridge.—Dedicated to St. Mary the
Virgin and All Saints ; Norman, with extensive re-model-
ling in the Decorated period ; nave with south aisle, chancel
and west tower (base Saxon and upper portion Norman).
The church is unique in having a priest's room over
the only mediæval west porch in the country. In 1548
the parishioners sold their silver chalices and used a cup
of wood. The church was restored in 1881. The first
incumbent was John de Cumb, who was presented by
Edward I in 1300. There are several memorial windows. At
the visitation of Archdeacon Harsnett, in the Seventeenth Century, the minister refused to wear a surplice or to make the
sign of the cross at baptism. There was formerly a parish of
Little Stambridge, with church, but this was united with

T

Great Stambridge in 1891 and the church then demolished. The silver chalice of Little Stambridge church was sold in March, 1904, at Christie's, for £96, being at the rate of £10 per ounce. It was described in the sale catalogue as : " Elizabethan chalice, engraved with two bands of running arabesque foliage, the stem and foot decorated with bands of dotted ornament—6½ins. high—1562—maker's mark, a covered cup ; and a paten, with engraved band of foliage and seal top, with the date 1570—London hall mark 1569—maker's mark I.F., 9ozs. 12dwt." The money received from this sale was utilized to purchase an organ for Great Stambridge church. The registers date from 1559.

Southchurch.—Dedicated to Holy Trinity ; Norman and Early English, with Decorated windows ; originally nave with turrets, chancel and porch. The building was restored in 1856-7, but an extension on the north side in 1906 has reduced the old church almost to the condition of a side chapel. It had a fine Norman doorway on the north side, which was removed to the west at the time the recent alterations were carried out. The gallery in the west end was erected in 1756. The registers date from 1689.

Thundersley.—Dedicated to St. Peter ; Early English ; chancel, nave with two aisles and spire ; the capitals of the church are worth noting. The date of building is generally assigned to the reign of King John ; there being in existence a complete list of rectors from the advent of the second in 1328. About the year 1871 the chancel was restored and the flat ceiling removed, bringing once more into view the carving and the open wood work of the roof, and in 1906 the wooden steeple was restored. Included in the church property is a chalice bearing date 1539. The windows are mainly filled with memorials to members of the Talfourd family, including Sir T. N. Talfourd, the celebrated judge, dramatist, and poet, who so suddenly died at Stafford in March, 1854, whilst performing his duty as judge of assize, and to the late

rector, the Rev. W. Wordsworth Talfourd. A list of curates
is also displayed in the church, an examination of which
suggests the conclusion that during long periods the rectors were
not in residence. A rector (Drake) was deprived of his
living by Queen Mary and burnt for heresy at Smithfield in
1554, after holding the living for four years. The church is
well situate on an eminence, in the heart of what was once a
Plantagenet hunting forest ; the view from the hill, looking
over the Benfleets, is very fine. The registers are irregular
in date, also few in number and disjointed, and consist mostly
of marriages, the earliest date being 3rd July, 1569.

Great Wakering.—Dedicated to St. Nicholas ; Norman
and Perpendicular; nave and chancel with tower ; the
windows are of the Decorated period. There are indications
that the western porch and the parvise over were erected some
time after the tower, leading to the presumption that provision
was made for the priest's residence in the church itself and
not over the porch, as was general. The church was broken
into and robbed in the reign of Edward VI, and the rector
was deprived of his benefice by Bonner upon the accession
of Queen Mary. Restorations were carried out in 1892 and
1903, and some repair work has recently been done to
the windows. The registers date from 1685.

Little Wakering.—Dedicated to St. Mary ; Norman,
with details which suggest the transition period from
Norman to Early English ; traces also of Perpendicular
and Decorated work. There are two shields on either side of
the west door. The arms on the north side are those of John
Wakering, Bishop of Norwich from 1416 to 1425 ; those on
the south side of Ann, Countess of Stafford, daughter and
ultimately heiress of her father, Thomas of Woodstock, Duke of
Gloucester, youngest son of Edward III, who married the
Earl of Stafford and had, as second husband, Sir William
Bourchier. This indicates that the tower was built about
1416. Chancellor says : "It seems tolerably clear there were

two periods which materially affected the history of this church ; the one late in the Twelfth Century, when it was erected ; the other early in the Fifteenth Century, when the Norman windows were replaced by much larger ones, and the tower erected, probably at the combined cost of Bishop Wakering and the Countess of Stafford." A list of vicars is given by Newcourt from 1464 to 1667. In 1606 the minister was presented at Archdeacon Harsnett's visitation for refusing to wear a surplice, to name the holy days and to read the prayers on those days. The registers date as follows : Baptisms, 1784 ; marriages, 1785 ; deaths, 1797.

VISIT OF THE
HOME AND ATLANTIC FLEETS
TO SOUTHEND, JULY, 1909.

In May, 1909, reports were current that after the summer manœuvres the Home and Atlantic Fleets would pay a visit to the Estuary; making Southend their headquarters. Shortly afterwards the Admiralty officially confirmed the statement, adding that the Lord Mayor (Sir G. W. Truscott) desired to entertain the officers and men of the Fleets and to give the citizens of London an opportunity of viewing the ships which constituted the first line of Great Britain's defence. Under the re-organization scheme initiated by Sir John Fisher, First Sea Lord at the Admiralty, there had taken place a greater concentration of naval fighting strength in home waters. Squadrons serving in distant seas, were either abolished or reduced in strength, and gradually a Home Fleet was created, consisting of the latest and most powerful ships, whilst the Atlantic Fleet, also of considerable strength, had its base transferred from Gibraltar to Dover. These Fleets totalled 150 vessels—battleships, cruisers, scouts, torpedo boat destroyers and submarines. They did not include a single ship of the reserve, and represented the Navy which Great Britain keeps constantly at war strength and trained as nearly as possible under conditions resembling those of war time. The visit of the Fleets to the Estuary also possessed some political importance. The "Dreadnought"—the flagship—was the first vessel launched of a type of giant battleship designed upon what is known as the all big gun principle, and able to steam at high speed. Her construction revolutionized prevalent ideas of naval architecture, and she was quickly followed by other ships of similar design. Great Britain was not left long without competitors, and soon Germany, America, France, Austria, Japan and Italy entered the race; the first-named country embarking upon an ambitious programme, which caused some amount of concern in this country. In introducing the naval estimates in 1909, the First Lord of the Admiralty, Mr. Reginald McKenna, announced that four "Dreadnoughts" would be constructed during the current financial year, and that if the naval activity of other countries rendered it necessary, a further four ships would be placed on order. The public responded with enthusiasm to the invitation to visit the Fleets; Londoners realizing as they had never been able to do before the immense organization which protected British commerce and the necessity for efficiently maintaining it. Within a day or two of the departure of the Fleets from the Estuary the Government announced that they intended to construct the four extra ships foreshadowed, and the step was hailed as wise and prudent policy.

The visit lasted from Saturday, July 17th, until Saturday, July 25th. The depth of water in the river prevented the larger craft from passing beyond Southend, but a score of small cruisers, scouts, destroyers and submarines were moored at intervals from Gravesend to Westminster. The remaining 130 were anchored off Southend shore; the First Division of the Home Fleet in single line ahead and the remaining battle and cruiser squadrons in parallel lines— stretching away past the Nore. The destroyer and submarine flotillas arrived just before sunset on Friday night and anchored off the Pier head, proceeding next day to their stations up the river or immediately to the west of the Pier, ahead of the "Dreadnought." The battle and cruiser squadrons, which had been exercising off the West Coast of Ireland, steamed to the anchorage between one and two

Rood Stair in St. Mary's Church, Prittlewell.

o'clock on Saturday afternoon, the "Dreadnought" leading. A thick haze hung over the Estuary and spoilt the impressiveness of the scene; spectators at the Pier head just being able to discern the huge battleships adjacent the Pier as they loomed out of the mist. By three o'clock every vessel was at its appointed station, the Fleets being as below:

Home Fleet.

Commander-in-Chief, Admiral Sir W. H. May, K.C.B., K.C.V.O.

First Division.—First Battle Squadron : "Dreadnought," 17,900 tons (flagship) ; "Bellerophon," 18,600 tons ; "Temeraire," 18,600 tons; "Superb," 18,600 tons ; "Lord Nelson," 16,500 tons (flagship to Rear Admiral C. J. Briggs) ; "Agamemnon," 16,500 tons; "Bulwark," 15,000 tons; and "Irresistible," 15,000 tons. Four first named were battleships of the "Dreadnought" type, steaming over twenty knots an hour.

Second Division.—Second Battle Squadron : "King Edward VII," 16,350 tons (flagship of Vice Admiral Sir Archibald Berkeley Milne, Bt., K.C.V.O.) ; "Africa," 16,350 tons; "Commonwealth," 16,350 tons; "Hibernia," 16,350 tons (flagship of Rear Admiral J. Startin) ; "Britannia," 16,350 tons; "Dominion," 16,350 tons ; "Hindustan," 16,350 tons; and "New Zealand," 16,350 tons.

First Cruiser Squadron : "Drake," 14,100 tons (flagship of Rear Admiral the Hon. C. J. Colville, C.V.O., C.B.) ; "Indomitable," 17,250 tons; "Inflexible," 17,250 tons ; "Invincible," 17,250 tons; and "Minotaur," 14,600 tons. Second, third and fourth of these vessels were known as "Dreadnought" cruisers, accounted almost equal in fighting strength to a battleship, and able to steam at nearly thirty knots an hour.

Second Cruiser Squadron : "Shannon," 14,600 tons (flagship of Rear Admiral Robert S. Lowry) ; "Cochrane,"

13,550 tons; "Natal," 13,550 tons; "Warrior," 13,550 tons; and "Defence," 14,600 tons.

Fourth Cruiser Squadron : "Leviathan," 14,100 tons (flagship of Rear Admiral Arthur M. Farquhar); "Berwick," 9,800 tons; and "Donegal," 9,800 tons.

Atlantic Fleet.

Battle Squadron : "Prince of Wales," 15,000 tons (flagship of H.S.H. Prince Louis of Battenberg, G.C.B., G.C.V.O., K.C.M.G., Commander-in-Chief); "Albion," 12,950 tons; "Formidable," 15,000 tons; "Implacable," 15,000 tons; "Cornwallis," 14,000 tons (flagship of Rear Admiral W. B. Fisher, C.B.) ; "Albemarle," 14,000 tons ; "Queen," 15,000 tons; and "Russell," 14,000 tons.

Fifth Cruiser Squadron : "Good Hope," 14,100 tons (flagship of Rear Admiral F. T. Hamilton, C.V.O.) ; "Black Prince," 13,550 tons; and "Duke of Edinburgh," 13,550 tons.

To these were attached flotillas of destroyers, under the command of Commodore Charlton, flying his broad pennant on the "Topaze," together with submarines, repair ships and other craft.

Imposing in numbers and fighting strength as the Home and Atlantic Fleets were, they were not less imposing in the illustrious names which the ships bore—names which brought to mind vessels of other days foremost in fight; their crews keen for the honour of the Navy and Old England. They recalled many of the most glorious episodes of British naval history, from the critical days of the Armada, when England was struggling with desperate determination against the maritime domination of Spain ; on through the Seventeenth Century, when Englishman and Dutchman met in the Channel and the North Sea in bitter, obstinate fight for commercial supremacy ; then to the spacious times of Louis XIV and the alliance of France and

Spain for the destruction of our fleets; and, finally, to the last great war with France, which left Napoleon a fugitive and the Gallic people exhausted with their superhuman struggle against Europe. The ships conjured up memories, too, of the naval heroes of the past—Drake, the terror of the Spanish Main; Blake, the scourge of the Royalist, the doughty antagonist of Van Tromp; Rodney; Rooke and the capture of Gibraltar; Howe and the "Glorious First of June"; Jervis and the victory off Cape St. Vincent; Nelson in his trio of memorable achievements—the Nile, Copenhagen and Trafalgar; Broke, in the "Shannon," and his duel with the "Chesapeake," and Beresford and the "Condor" at the bombardment of Alexandria. From the dark, grey waters of the North Sea to the blue of the Mediterranean; from the perils of winter blockade in the Channel to the steaming heat of battle in the East Indies; from gale to calm; from cold to heat—the story of the ships fascinated by its heroism and thrilled by its memories of ardent combat against uncounted odds. Their mighty successors lay in an estuary more famous than any other in the world. From the time when Londinium first received the commerce of the Romans until the present day, the broad bosom of the Thames has borne a noble part in the making of our nation, whilst in 1909 the Port of London maintained the proud position of being the greatest in the two hemispheres. In war and commerce; national weal and woe; adventure and industry, old Father Thames has left his impress large upon the page of history. When he welcomed the Home and Atlantic Fleets—"Bellerophon," "Dreadnought," "Bonaventure," and the rest—he welcomed them as old friends, bearing with pride and dignity the burden of England's safety, which their predecessors had gloriously preserved.

The first official visit was paid on Saturday afternoon, by the heads of the Port of London Authority, who boarded the "Dreadnought" from the "Conservator."

They were followed by the Mayor of Southend, who warmly welcomed Admiral May and the Fleets to the Borough. The townspeople had generously responded to the appeal of the head of the municipality. Over £1,000 were raised by voluntary subscriptions, and expended in decorating the streets, in firework displays and illuminations, whilst most tradesmen and many of the private residents liberally adorned their premises. On several days during the week the ships were open to inspection, and thousands of people availed themselves of the privilege. On Sunday over 2,000 men landed and attended service at the Wesleyan, Presbyterian and Catholic Churches. Tuesday was known as Lord Mayor's day. His Lordship arrived at the G.E. station at noon and was driven to the Pier gates, where he and his party boarded trams. At the Pier head they were welcomed on behalf of the Admiral, lunched on the Admiralty yacht "Enchantress" with the First Lord of the Admiralty (Mr. McKenna) and Sir John Fisher, were then taken round the ships in tugs, subsequently proceeding on board the "Dreadnought," where tea was served. Two other parties of members of the Corporation of the City of London, together with representatives of the Turkish Parliament, reached Southend by later trains and were taken on board the "Bellerophon" and "Temeraire"; the whole company, numbering one thousand, witnessing an attack on the "Dreadnought" by destroyers. On Wednesday 1,200 seamen and marines entrained for London and marched through the streets of the City to the Guildhall with their guns, where they were entertained to lunch by the Lord Mayor. Captain Beatty was in command, and, in thanking his Lordship for his hospitality, said that the men were always ready, quoting as a warning the first verse of the hymn, "Watch and Pray." The same day 550 men lunched with the Mayor of Southend, and in the evening his Worship dined 130 of the officers. Admiral May, in

HOME AND ATLANTIC FLEETS OFF SOUTHEND, JULY, 1909 (LEIGH IN THE FOREGROUND).

a short speech during the proceedings, expressed his grateful appreciation of the hospitable way in which Southend had received the Fleets. On Thursday 400 officers had luncheon with the Lord Mayor at the Guildhall. Over 200 members of the London County Council and the Fleet Reception Committee were accorded special facilities for inspecting the ships. Distinguished visitors included Prince and Princess Kuni, of Japan, Mr. Kato, the Japanese Ambassador, and his Excellency the Chinese Minister. In the evening the Fleets were illuminated; the day's rejoicings being marred by three fatalities—a sailor falling overboard from the "Indomitable," and two Leighmen being drowned by the capsizing of a boat. On Friday members of the Southend Town Council and other local organizations had tea with the Admiral on board the "Dreadnought." During Saturday afternoon the great combination dispersed to various parts of the South Coast—Deal, Dover, Bournemouth, Portland and Torbay, to re-assemble a week later at Cowes, for review by the King and the Tzar of Russia. The weather had been gloriously fine during the stay off Southend, but on Saturday it changed for the worse, and the ships ran out of the estuary in a rainstorm of unusual violence.

This great naval pageant—to give it the name by which it was generally known—was of undoubted service in widely advertizing Southend's charms and unique position. It is estimated that a quarter-of-a-million visitors were received during the eight days. On Sunday the town was more congested than had ever been known; no fewer than 10,000 cyclists making Southend their rendezvous. The visit was also popular with the seamen, for it enabled thousands of liberty men to take a trip to London. Good order was maintained throughout. At times the Pier had to be closed against the enormous crowds which blocked the entrance. The visit was a great success, and the Admiral signalled his hearty thanks to Southend as he steamed out to sea.

THE LOCAL JUSTICIARY.

Up to the year 1894 the whole of the Petty Sessional business of Rochford Hundred was transacted by Justices of the Peace for the County of Essex, sitting first at Rochford and then at Southend.   Justices of the Peace are appointed either by Act of Parliament, or by Charter under the Great Seal, or by Commission.   The Commission was issued about the year 1327 ;   the earliest statute on record being I Edward 3, cap. 2, whereby the conservation of the peace was finally taken from the people and vested in the Crown.   The title of Justice was not, however, then conferred, and probably it arose about the time of Henry VIII ;   at any rate, it was clearly recognised by the statute 27, Henry VJII, c. 24. The Crown may grant Commissions for any particular district, and   such Commissions are from time to time granted. Legislation during the last fifty years has tended to regularize judicial procedure and to strictly safeguard the interests of the accused.   One of the principal statutes, namely, the Summary Jurisdiction Act, 1879, was the offspring mainly of one of our own Chairman of Quarter Sessions, Mr. A. Johnston.   Prior to that, the meetings of the local Bench, which were held once a fortnight, on Rochford market day, very largely took the form of a friendly gathering of half-a-dozen of the resident gentry.   In the Sixties, the Chairman would call in at the Clerk's office, enquire what was to be done, arrange the business, then walk upstairs to the Court, when, as a rule, an hour sufficed for dealing with the charges.   About this time the County Court was built in South Street, and this was a great convenience to the Justices, who at once removed to that building.   Previously

the Bench had sat at the King's Head Inn, and its official
documents were dated from that hostelry. The great day
of the year was known as the "Jolly Victuallers' Day," when,
in accordance with legal requirement, all the licensed
victuallers appeared in September to apply for a renewal
of their permits. The provision of licensing facilities
was not looked upon with the same concern as in the
present day, and the grant of the fresh facilities was made
the occasion of a social meeting. The growth of Southend
brought with it an increase of work, and also a demand for
the transaction of judicial business at Southend. At first an
office was opened for the issue of process, then in the
Eighties of last century the sittings were held once a week at
Southend. The grant of a Commission of the Peace for the
Borough in 1894 deprived the County Bench of a large
portion of its business, and it was not long after that the
Justices decided to hold sittings at Southend and Rochford in
alternate weeks.

There are no local official records of the Petty
Sessions which render it possible to make a complete
list of the Chairmen of the County Bench, but those
of recent years have been Mr. D. R. Scratton, of
Prittlewell Priory ; the Rev. Thomas Scott Scratton,
of Southend ; Mr. Holt White, of Clement's Hall, Hawkwell ; Mr. James Tabor, of Earl's Hall, Prittlewell ; and
Mr. C. A. Tabor, Earl's Hall, Prittlewell. Other
well-known gentlemen of the countryside who served as
Justices included Mr. Jno. Baker, of Hockley ; Dr. Mudge,
of Shoebury Cottage ; Rev. W. Twyne, Rector of Rayleigh ;
Rev. T. E. Heygate and Sir Charles Nicholson, of Hadleigh ;
Major Arthur Tawke, of Rochford, who took a great interest
in the Volunteer movement ; Mr. J. Page, of Southend ;
Dr. G. D. Deeping, Southend ; Lieut.-Col. Huntley Bacon,
Canewdon ; Mr. T. Dowsett, Southend ; Mr. A. Harvey
Moore, Leigh. The constitution of the Bench at present

is : Mr. E. A. Wedd, C.C., of Great Wakering (Chairman) ; Major-General Bally, Shoeburyness ; Messrs. J. R. Brightwell, Southend ; E. J. Beal, C.A., Southend ; J. H. Burrows, C.A., Hadleigh ; S. S. Baker, Hockley ; A. J. Dean, Little Wakering ; J. Millbank, Shoeburyness ; J. Osborne, Leigh ; H. Rankin, Rochford ; F. W. Senier, Leigh ; J. Tabor, Rochford ; and Sir Lloyd Wise, Southend ; with the Mayor of Southend and Chairmen of Rochford Rural District Council and Leigh and Shoebury Urban District Councils for the time being. Since 1860 there have only been three Clerks to the Justices—Mr. Swaine ; then Mr. W. A. Arthy, his partner, who was succeeded by his son, Mr. A. J. Arthy, the present holder of the office, in 1881.

Borough Petty Sessions.

List of Gentlemen placed upon the Commission of the Peace for the Borough of Southend-on-Sea since its grant in 1894 :—

April, 1894 : D. W. Gosset (deceased), G. D. Deeping (deceased), T. Dowsett (deceased), C. A. Tabor (deceased), W. Lloyd Wise, P. Bentall (deceased), J. R. Brightwell, J. H. Burrows, E. H. Draper, J. B. Howard (resigned), J. C. Hudson (deceased), D. Symington (deceased), H. Wood (deceased), C. Woosnam (deceased), and the Judge of the County Court for the time being.

Dec., 1896 : G. F. Jones, A. Prevost and R. H. Wright.

March, 1899 : E. J. Bowmaker (deceased) and A. Clough Waters.

April, 1901 : H. Cleveland Smith, C. Campbell, F. F. Ramuz and T. Whur.

Feb., 1904 :   J. Francis, J. C. Ingram, E. Van and A. T. Jay (resigned).

Dec., 1906 :   T. Crawley, A. G. Hinks, H. J. Osborn (resigned) and A. Steel.

Feb., 1909 :   J. W. Burrows, T. Dowsett, J. H. Heywood, C. Hubbard, and W. R. King.

Population Statistics.

(Taken from the Census Returns).

	1801	1811	1821	1831	1841
Rochford Hundred...	9,270	10,497	12,335	13,604	14,617
	1851	1861	1871	1881	1891
	14,776	17,178	19,411	22,979	28,874
	1901				
	49,094.				

	1801	1811	1821	1831	1841
Prittlewell	1,213	1,541	1,922	2,266	2,339
	1851	1861	1871	1881	1891
	2,462	3,427	4,589	8,009	12,380
	1901				
	27,299.				

	1801	1811	1821	1831	1841
Southchurch	291	355	353	401	432
	1851	1861	1871	1881	1891
	455	494	712	786	932
	1901				
	1,622.				

INDEX.

John H. Burrows & Sons, Ltd., Printers, Southend-on-Sea.

Lightning Source UK Ltd.
Milton Keynes UK
UKHW040353030919
349042UK00001B/283/P

9 789353 605933